Riches, Rivals & Radicals

100 Years of Museums in America

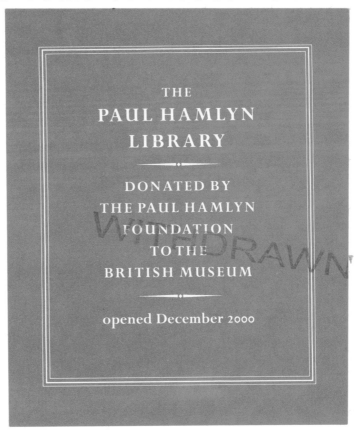

Riches, Rivals & Radicals

100 Years of Museums in America

MARJORIE **SCHWARZER**

AMERICAN ASSOCIATION OF MUSEUMS | AAM**100**

Riches, Rivals and Radicals: 100 Years of Museums in America

Copyright © 2006, American Association of Museums.

Design: Susan v. Levine and Christiane Riederer
Printed and bound by GraphTec, Jessup, Maryland

On the front cover:
John Singer Sargent (1856-1925), *Madame X* (Madame Pierre Gautreau), 1883-84. Arthur Hoppock Hearn
Fund, 1916 (16.53). Image © The Metropolitan Museum of Art. *Mixtec-Aztec shield*, 15th century. © National
Museum of the American Indian, Smithsonian Institution. *J. P. Morgan.* Image © The Metropolitan Museum of
Art. The Frederick R. Weisman Art Museum, University of Minnesota. Charles-Henri-Joseph Cordier (French,
1827-1905), *African Venus,* 1851. Museum of Art, Rhode Island School of Design. 1995.013.

On the back cover:
Coffinette from exhibition "Tutankhamun and the Golden Age of the Pharaohs." Padgett and Company, Jamie
Padgett, Chicago. Young visitors outside the Brooklyn Children's Museum, 1936. Xul Solar (Argentinian, 1887-
1963), *Jefa/Patroness,* 1923. The Museum of Fine Arts, Houston; museum purchase with funds provided by the
Latin American Experience Gala and Auction. Visitors outside the Smithsonian's Arts and Industries Building,
c. 1900. Smithsonian Institution Archives, Record Unit 95, box 32, f. 8, image #2002-10677. Butterflies ©
JupiterImages

Library of Congress Cataloging-in-Publication Data
Schwarzer, Marjorie, 1957-
  Riches, rivals, and radicals : 100 years of museums in America / Marjorie Schwarzer.
      p. cm.
  Includes bibliographical references and index.
  ISBN-13: 978-1-933253-05-3
  ISBN-10: 1-933253-05-3
  1. Museums–United States–History–20th century. I. American Association of Museums. II. Title.

AM11.S35 2006
069.09730904–dc22

                        2006006126

The publication of this book is dedicated to the memory of

STEPHEN E. **WEIL** (1928-2005)

TABLE OF CONTENTS

vii

ACKNOWLEDGEMENTS

In May 1906, 69 men and two women posed on the steps of the American Museum of Natural History in New York City for a group shot. No doubt they knew it was a historic moment. The photograph would document the birth of the American Association of Museums (AAM), the culmination of more than a quarter century of industrious museum growth. It was also a beginning. Over the next 100 years, American society would change in ways that these men and women, visionary though they were, could not have imagined. So too would American museums change, as they took on the daunting responsibility of presenting art, culture, history and science to a diverse and growing populace. *Riches, Rivals and Radicals* tells that story.

This book was the vision of John Strand and Jane Lusaka and I am profoundly grateful to them for providing me with this opportunity as well as for their editing and feedback. I also want to acknowledge the contributions of current and former members of the AAM Publications Department, including Julia Beizer, Lana Gendlin, Eva Heinzen, Amanda Litvinov, Susan Breitkopf, Leah Arroyo and especially Susan v. Levine and Christiane Riederer, who designed a beautiful book.

The generosity, advice and feedback of my colleagues form the backbone of this book. Bruce Altschuler, Robert Archibald, Leslie Bedford, Lonnie G. Bunch, Lou Casagrande, Raylene Decatur, Chesney and Marc Doyle, Tom L. Freudenheim, Elaine Heumann Gurian, Michael Hammond, Jeff Hayward, George Hein, Paulette Hennum, Carlo LaMagna, Kathleen McLean, Ann Mintz, Kris Morrissey, Mary Naquin Sharp, William Penniston, Bonnie Pitman, Wendy Pollock, Melissa Rosengard, Jay Rounds, Michael Sand, Fred Setterberg, Harold and Susan Skramstad, Susan Spero, Dan Spock, Michael Spock, Peter Tirrell, Dawn Thomae, George Tressel, Stephanie Weaver, Stephen E. Weil, Mabel Wilson and Elida Zelaya generously lent their time and expertise. I also want to thank Cliff Abrams, Jeffrey Abt, Jane Bedno, Timothy Chester, Maria Lieby, Frank Madsen, Julie Stiever and David Wattis for their correspondence.

The John F. Kennedy University community has been an inspiration to me. Special thanks go to Adrienne McGraw, Wendy Norris, Vanessa Van Orden, Jennifer Collins Daly, Lisa Granger, Glen Meyers, Salwa Mikdadi Nashashibi, Jessica Strick and Anna Marie Tutera for their research support and advice. JFKU's librarians Claudia Chester, Melinda Simms and John Taylor were supportive and responded quickly to my often-obscure library requests. Melinda Adams, Molly Matchett and Colette Walker managed the Museum Studies office. JFKU's Diversity Committee, chaired by Cyd Jenefsky, provided a grant for research support.

In addition to consulting scholarly studies, museum journals, newspapers, and oral histories, as well as conducting interviews and site visits, I did archival research at the University of California campuses in Berkeley and Los Angeles, Newark Museum, American Museum of Natural History, American Association of Museums and the Smithsonian Institution.

Most of all I want to thank my family. My mother, Barbara, an artist and poet, has been a devoted museum companion. My father, Allan, has offered sound advice and a willing ear, as has my brother Eric. My husband Mitchell contributed the intellectual heart and soul of this work, going through every word with an eye for big ideas, clarity and integrity. Throughout this project, he was both forthright and compassionate. I dedicate this book to him.

My purpose in writing *Riches, Rivals and Radicals* is to communicate not only salient historic trends and deeds, but the passion that underlies America's museums. This volume only offers a glimpse into a vast and complex history. My hope is that readers will be inspired to dig more deeply. Better yet, may this information enrich the reader's next museum visit and all the visits that are yet to come.

MARJORIE **SCHWARZER**
John F. Kennedy University
Berkeley, California

INTRODUCTION

It was positively civilisation condensed, concrete, consummate, set down by his hands as a house on a rock—a house from whose open doors and windows, open to grateful, to thirsty millions, the higher, the highest knowledge would shine out to bless the land . . . this museum of museums . . . a receptacle of treasures sifted to positive sanctity.

—HENRY **JAMES**, THE GOLDEN BOWL, 1904

The American museum is a prism of American society. Its buildings reflect civic pride, often serving as examples of outstanding architectural accomplishment. Its collections are evidence of the nation's boundless curiosity, our desire to know the achievements of other people, other lands, other times. Its exhibitions tell us stories, adding to the ever changing, sometimes contentious meanings we Americans give to history, to culture, to identity. The way the museum is managed and funded speaks to its position in the community, its many publics and political importance. The American museum today, more than at any time over the past century, is a place of exchange, encounter and education. As a chorus of different voices, an arena of differing, sometimes warring interpretations, the museum has grown to become a reflection of American democracy itself.

Above: Sisters Dorothy and Francine Berman admire Native American objects at the Brooklyn Children's Museum, late 1930s.

Left: Hydria, black-figure, 520-500 B.C., terracotta, by Antimenes painter, Greek Attica. John R. Van Derlip Fund. The Minneapolis Institute of Arts.

Long ago the museum in America ceased to be a repository for priceless and not-so-priceless objects, many of them the gifts of wealthy donors. The exclusive private collection that was once open only to those of the owner's race and social class has itself become a relic, largely banished after decades of struggle inside and outside the museum. Today's museum aspires to be much more. It is, at its most ambitious, a complex mix of town square, classroom, playground, forum, sanctuary, community center, temple, laboratory and probably much more. Even the word "museum" has a wide variety of definitions, not unlike the term "American." Once the authoritative interpreter of priceless objects, it now also acknowledges the many interpretations of its visitors. In the process it has become priceless in new and perhaps surprising ways.

Museums do matter. They are the only institutions that collect, preserve, display, interpret, and educate for the public good. They are stewards of who and what we are today, and have been in the past: our shared heritage, good and bad, accomplishments and failures as humans, the treasures of a natural world that we ourselves endanger. Museums offer us an opportunity to be informed and inspired, to be enriched culturally, intellectually, emotionally. Without them we would be infinitely poorer as individuals and as a nation.

There is a story here. How the American museum got from where it began to where it is today has required a long journey, sometimes arduous, often fascinating, filled with many notable and even a few notorious characters. It is a journey that continues today. The story of the American museum tells us as much about ourselves as it does about the institution and the objects in its collection.

■　■　■　■　■

Change, it has often been noted, is the one great constant of history. In the past 100 years the United States has experienced tumultuous change. Museums, some of them collecting and exhibiting artifacts of social and cultural transformation even as it occurred, were slower to change. But change they did.

Left: The Hall of Archaeology of North America in the East Court of the Field Museum, Chicago, c. 1896, featured tipis, Utah pottery and paintings by George Catlin in the alcoves. © The Field Museum, #CSA8193.

Right: Schoolchildren were the target audience for an exhibition on tuberculosis organized by the American Museum of Natural History, New York, as a public health service in 1907. Courtesy of AMNH.

In the late 19th century the typical museum was a collecting institution, organized in strictly hierarchical fashion. It was a place for the elite and privileged to teach the nation's working men and women what it meant to be cultured, civic-minded Americans. It was typically a paternalistic, somewhat moralizing institution. Its mission was, at least in part, the improvement of society through the display and explanation of art or historical artifact or scientific specimen or technological marvel. Its goals were, at one and the same time, idealistic and practical—not unlike the nation itself, then and now.

At the turn of the 20th century America was busily engaged in becoming an industrial power. Cities grew dramatically, immigration expanded, the population diversified. Science, scholarship and the arts began to flourish. A small class of the super wealthy established itself at the same time that a sizeable population of the working poor emerged. Museums of the day, managed and governed by a socially prominent patrician class, reflected the national struggle to redefine the values of public education, citizenship and American identity.

They did so in very different ways. Some were progressive and allied themselves with movements for social reform. Others were concerned with upholding and preserving tradition. Still others were pragmatic, hoping to prove their worth by being useful and efficient. Most had in common the ideal of being a beacon for their towns or cities, or even for the country.

With each ensuing decade of what came to be called "the American century," museums recrafted their visions of themselves, some more overtly and more publicly than others, striving to change as the nation changed. During World War I some museums displayed letters from soldiers fighting in the trenches, others the flags of America's allies. In the Roaring '20s the number of museums expanded suddenly as American society rose on a tide of prosperity. In the decade of the Great Depression, museums allied themselves with progressive social movements of the day, offering services to cash-strapped public schools and sharing in the largess of the Works Progress Administration. In the 1940s museums again reflected the patriotism of the war years, with some institutions serving as hospital wards and military research and training centers in support of the war effort and a few others displaying anti-Japanese propaganda.

A return to tradition and an interest in collections conservation marked the 1950s, along with increased prosperity and further expansion. The 1960s and 1970s were decades of radical change for some museums, especially those that embraced a more socially responsive role in light of the sweeping changes brought by the great movements in civil rights. An anti-hierarchical hands-on approach to learning took root in new models of children's museums and science centers. During the 1980s and 1990s museums found themselves in the crossfire of the culture wars as traditionalists and multiculturalists

Facing page, above: Anthropologist Franz Boas organized the American Museum of Natural History's North Pacific Coast Hall in 1899. The display included a 64.5-foot Haida canoe, later immortalized by J. D. Salinger in **CATCHER IN THE RYE**.

Facing page, below: Main exhibition hall, c. 1880, in Randolph Hall, a building that is now part of the College of Charleston. *Courtesy of the Charleston Museum, Charleston, S.C.*

This page, right: The Corning Museum of Glass is home to one of the world's greatest collections of glass objects. *Courtesy of the Corning Museum of Glass, Corning, N.Y.*

This page, below: Arlene and Harold Schnitzer Center for Northwestern Art, Portland Art Museum, 2002. *Courtesy of the Portland Art Museum, Portland, Oreg.*

battled over the interpretation of collections and exhibitions. Native Americans joined a movement of disenfranchised groups that challenged assumptions about the ownership of artifacts and the right to display them.

The early years of the 21st century saw museums grow again in number and size, expanding their missions and scope, emphasizing more strongly than ever education and community engagement. Like the rest of the nation, museums struggled to respond to the growing diversity of American society, the swelling chorus of different voices. All the while they were facing the same questions: What must we be, and for whom, and to what purpose? These, of course, are the questions that museums began with.

It says a great deal about how seriously museums take their missions and the respect they have for their publics when we note that the questions have remained the same for more than 100 years. It is the answers that continue to change. And it is no small thing to remark that the same can be said of the nation itself.

If we follow the story of the American museum it becomes evident that these institutions large and small do not merely collect and display the elements of our past, our heritage, our achievements. They are themselves evidence of these things, a sometimes surprising articulation of who we are as Americans, and for whom, and to what purpose.

■　■　■　■　■

In 1928 the American Association of Museums (AAM) estimated that the country's 1,400 museums received 32 million visits annually, a figure equal to about 25 percent of the population of the time. Seventy years later more than 10,000 museums were in business. The annual number of visits had skyrocketed to an estimated 865 million in 1998, more than three times the country's population. Museum visitorship has grown at a much faster pace than the U.S. population. Visits now far surpass attendance at all professional sports events combined.

Whatever else may be said of the changes over the past century, museums have made themselves more popular than ever.

As their numbers multiplied, museums have become more complex institutions. The very word "museum," once comfortably static and easily defined, now is used for institutions that would never have called themselves museums a few generations ago. Today museum buildings are often larger and host a greater array of activities, from large-format film to fine dining to feng shui classes and singles' evenings. Their collections overall are more extensive, better documented and researched. Exhibition techniques have become more sophisticated, incorporating the latest advances in technology. The people who visit are

more diverse in age, ethnicity, levels of education and income and far more international than ever before. The funding of museums, once almost exclusively dependent on the generosity of a few wealthy philanthropists, has become broader, increasingly reliant on earned income from admissions fees and sales at museum shops and restaurants.

The increase in scale and complexity has meant that the older identity of the museum, forged in Europe during the 19th century, has been refashioned. In Europe the public museum developed out of an aristocratic society uncomfortable with commerce. By contrast, business has long been a readily accepted aspect of life in America, this nation of immigrants striving to get ahead financially. The American museum, much more than its European predecessor, has been continually preoccupied with justifying its usefulness and value to society. Thus the repeated attempts, even in the present day, at bridging the gap between elite and popular cultures.

The American museum in its new complexity finds itself accountable to many more constituencies than in the past. It often is expected to be as cost-effective as a business while serving as an educational resource, a civic institution and a community partner—usually all on the same day. Inevitably the contemporary museum has had to embrace some apparent contradictions as it attempts to define itself for its many publics: being a charitable nonprofit organization in a marketplace culture, being a place of memory, reflection and learning in a nation that stresses action and immediacy, being a champion of tradition in a land of ceaseless innovation.

Nor are these changes without controversy within the museum itself. There are many proud traditionalists, those who sometimes also self-identify as "essentialists," who decry the steady drift away from scholarship, connoisseurship, the primary tasks of collecting, preserving and exhibiting. To these museum professionals, the diversity of functions within the institution serves not to strengthen it but to weaken it by fragmenting its focus and encouraging it to be too many things to too many people at the expense of the few things it has always done best.

These opposing visions, of course, are part of America's larger, endless battle over the meaning of its own past. And museums are a battleground.

■　■　■　■　■

A Brief History of Evolution—The Museum's

Even before there was a country, there was the country's first museum. In 1773, in the midst of the war for American independence, the Charleston Library Society gathered samples of animals, plants and minerals from the South Carolina low country. This collection formed the first American museum. In 1786 artist Charles Willson Peale opened his Philadelphia home as an American cabinet of curiosities. This display is regarded as the nation's first museum open to the public. Part of the Peale family's collection later was purchased and displayed by none other than P. T. Barnum, who included a "genuine" mermaid skeleton among the artifacts in his American Museum in New York. The tension between popular entertainment and authenticity began very early in the museum world.

During the next 100 years most public exhibits, often no more than a case of arrowheads or medical instruments, took place largely in the basements of libraries and colleges. Most early 19th-century American museums did not call themselves museums at all. They operated as antiquarian societies, open only to their members, many admitted by secret vote. These were private collections or esoteric amusements rather than public places of education.

The radical changes brought by the Civil War and its aftermath had their effect on museums no less than on American society as a whole. The issues of the day in the 1870s will sound familiar to the 21st -century reader: industrialization and sprawl, periodic stock market collapse, business scandal, urban poverty, the influx of non-English speaking immigrants, corruption of the clergy, political graft. In part to cope with this daunting list of woes, civic leaders in different cities relied upon public schools and museums to help promote a cohesive set of moral values in their communities.

"It is difficult to overemphasize the stress [museums] placed upon their pedagogical functions some 100 years ago, and the benefits they promised for industrial production, scientific curiosity and historical consciousness," writes Neil Harris, professor of history at the University of Chicago. Founders used the same arguments as proponents of public schools: museums could help to shape an informed citizenry, ultimately resulting in a more productive economy. Thus began such pioneering institutions as New York's American Museum of Natural History (1869) and Metropolitan Museum of Art (1870), Boston's Museum of Fine Arts (1870) and the Detroit Institute of Art (1885). In the South, emerging black colleges also recognized that museums could help form an educated class in post-Civil War society. In 1868 the Hampton Institute in Virginia founded the nation's the first African-American museum.

Henry Ossawa Tanner, **THE BANJO LESSON**, *1893. Oil on canvas. This masterpiece is in the collection of Hampton University Museum in Hampton, Va., the nation's first African-American museum.*

Museums quickly made good on their promise to educate. They offered free public lectures on a wide array of topics, from "the effects of water on the surface of the Earth" at the Public Museum of Grand Rapids to the arctic expeditions of Admiral Peary, a topic that captivated American imaginations in the early years of the 20th century as much as space exploration fascinates us a century later. Many of these lectures were geared to public school teachers to encourage them to use museums as new sources of knowledge for their pupils. In the 1880s librarian Henry Watson Kent began the tradition of bringing schoolchildren to public exhibitions when he invited classes to visit the Norwich Museum and Library in Connecticut. In 1899, concerned that almost one-third of the children living in Brooklyn received no formal school instruction, a curator named William H. Goodyear founded the world's first museum dedicated to youth education, the Brooklyn Children's Museum.

Librarian Henry Watson Kent introduced scores of children to museums in the 1880s. Courtesy of the Grolier Club of New York.

More than anyone else, educational reformer and philosopher John Dewey helped to make education central to the museum's mission and greatly influenced the children's museum movement. In 1896 at the University of Chicago he and his wife founded an experimental school, appropriately named the Lab School. Students spent one and a half hours per week at a museum, engaging in a variety of experiments and adventures. It is a model that is still used today. Dewey's work extended well beyond Chicago. He lectured widely on the failures of public schooling. Dubbing desks, blackboards and textbooks "dull drudgery," he called on teachers to look beyond the schoolyard and create real-life experiences for students who could "learn by doing." Dewey firmly believed that children learned a great deal by experiencing a museum's stately building and collection.

John Singer Sargent,
PORTRAIT OF ISABELLA STEWART
GARDNER, *1888. Oil on*
canvas. Courtesy of the
Isabella Stewart Gardner
Museum, Boston.

While educating the populace was always one of the stated goals of the museums founded during the late 19th century, there was also the less altruistic goal of pride. Some of the wealthy industrialists who emerged from this era of rapid growth amassed impressive collections of art and scientific specimens, later building museums to house the objects. At a time when there was no government money or foundation support for such efforts, these museums were financed entirely by their founders and namesakes, men and women such as Massachusetts industrialist Steven Salisbury, founder of the Worcester Art Museum, and Boston socialite and collector Isabella Stewart Gardner, who named her museum after herself. Such a move was philanthropic but also had its practical side. For the founder it represented a great increase in social stature.

For the visitor, too, the intended rewards were also practical. Displays of art were supposed to raise the level of Americans' aesthetic tastes. In the words of novelist Henry James, museums would display "not only beauty and art and supreme design, but history, fame and power." Collections of science and anthropology demonstrated the evolution of life and the belief that, as Harvard University president Charles Eliot Norton put it, Americans could "advance civilization from good to better." To be fair, many of these new museums were not entirely lecturing in tone, nor were they mere tombs of curiosities and relics. The best of them were at the forefront of a young nation's efforts to demonstrate its material and intellectual progress.

Yet despite their emphasis on education and public service, in reality these early museums sent mixed messages. Their doors were open every day of the week, even Sunday, and often at night, but to whom? Even with no admissions charge, museums asked a lot of the middle- and working-class visitor. The architecture was often grand and imposing, implying who might belong and who not. So too the location of choice for many museums: public parks, most of which were off-limits to people of color. Other museums opened their doors to "colored" visitors one day a week, but limited access to basic amenities, like restrooms. Even in northern museums that did not overtly abide by segregation laws, some museum guards refused entrance to black visitors.

Museums of this era promised to uplift humanity, but there was ambivalence about the practical details of reaching that goal. Directors frequently complained not only of visitors touching the objects, but of whistling, singing, nose-blowing, the spitting of tobacco juice on gallery floors and disruptions by unruly children. Many museum staff held definite attitudes about how visitors should look and behave. As if in church, visitors should be properly attired and reverent. As if in a stranger's house, they should be exceedingly polite and not handle anything that didn't belong to them. "We do not want," stated a director of the Metropolitan Museum of Art in the 1890s, "nor will we permit a person who has been digging in a filthy sewer or working among grease and oil to come in here, and by offensive odors emitted from the dirt on their apparel, make the surroundings uncomfortable for others."

Reaching and Teaching the Masses

Compared to their European prototypes, American museums at the turn of the 20th century lacked depth and quality in their collections. Instead they distinguished themselves by their educational programs. It was common practice to work closely with local boards of education, lending specimens to public schools as teaching aids. It was also common to teach free on-site classes in topics ranging from drawing to music appreciation. Around 1907 Boston's Museum of Fine Arts introduced the term "docent" (from the Latin *docere*), a person who explained artwork to visitors in the galleries. In 1908-09, when the country was gripped

The Smithsonian Institution's United States National Museum Building (now the Arts and Industries Building), c. 1900. The building opened in 1881 and exhibited everything from from Mammals and Geology to Engineering and Art. Smithsonian Institution Archives, Record Unit 95, box 32, f. 8, image #2002-10677.

Children from the South Street School learn about weaving at the Newark Museum, 1927. Unlike most museums of the day, the Newark Museum featured exhibitions designed to appeal to a working-class audience. Collections of the Newark Museum Archives.

with fear about a tuberculosis epidemic, the Smithsonian and the American Museum of Natural History focused on public health education, hosting exhibitions about the disease. Public health workers recognized that museums were more enticing places for instruction than the hospitals and medical clinics distrusted by most immigrants. The exhibitions— supported by pamphlets in different languages, including Yiddish, Italian and Chinese— illustrated TB's dreadful consequences and instructed visitors how to minimize their risks. A sign admonished visitors: "Do not spit."

In 1915 the Cleveland Museum of Art inaugurated one of the nation's first internal departments devoted to instructional programs, eventually hiring one of John Dewey's disciples, Thomas Munro, to run it. Within a few years nearly every major museum in the country offered a variety of free-of-charge educational services. They lent objects and specimens to schools, factories and army bases. There were children's story hours, "lantern-slide" lectures for the deaf, and how-to classes in topics like sketching or taxidermy. Museums organized "hobby" clubs and nature outings, sponsored concerts and music recitals and gave college extension courses for credit.

But the idea of public education was not without its skeptics, in museums and in American society. It was an expensive undertaking, opponents pointed out. Worse, it was potentially counterproductive. What was to be gained by developing a nation filled with overeducated citizens? Museum educators began to ask related questions. Was it right to bring uneducated people to museums? Did the lower classes have the ability to understand high culture? Perhaps museums weren't for everyone after all. As Benjamin Ives Gilman, secretary of Boston's Museum of Fine Arts, mused, "We are misled into thinking educational effort is the panacea for all the ills of society." He believed that "a museum of art is primarily an institution of culture and only secondarily a seat of learning." Its true role, according to Gilman and others like him, was to raise the bar of American taste through displaying the finest paintings and sculptures from abroad to an upper-class, educated audience.

Around this time there was a notable shift in emphasis as major art museums began to concentrate less on education and more on acquiring objects that would strengthen their collections. World War I had ended and the leading European nations were struggling to recover from the human and economic devastation. The new Soviet government and members of the former Russian aristocracy were among those who offered great masterworks for sale. Americans and American museums were active buyers of the formerly priceless paintings now suddenly not so priceless. By 1923, the American Art Dealers' Association estimated that Americans spent $250 million on art purchases. One third was spent on European old masters: Titian, Bellini, Rubens.

Populists like the Newark Museum Director John Cotton Dana bristled at the sudden dash to snap up European art. Museums would do better to create activities that catered to everybody, he declared, especially the factory workers who were building America. During the 1920s Dana created displays he believed would appeal more to a working-class audience, incorporating items such as merchandise from five & dime stores and scale-models of New Jersey river systems built by schoolchildren.

Among American museums at this time, Gilman's elitism was more in evidence than Dana's populism. By the 1920s connoisseurs like Bernard Berenson and educators like Harvard University's Paul Sachs were dominating museum collecting and influencing the training of curators, many of whom now aspired more to scholarship than to public education. Institutions relegated instructional activities to the basement. A well-dressed public was invited to climb the grand sweeping staircases of these ornate public palaces—Buffalo's Albright Art Gallery (now the Albright-Knox) is one example among many—and view the proud new acquisitions of priceless and timeless art. There was a growing high-society interest in American decorative and colonial art. Curators often borrowed techniques from world's fairs, organizing extravagant displays that communicated abundance, wealth and power.

Woman's evening gown, 1925, from the collections of the Chicago History Museum. Courtesy of the Chicago History Museum.

And there was a great deal of it. America was turning into an economic colossus. Signs of its wealth abounded. Automobiles streamed down the new paved highways, skyscrapers towered above the rapidly growing cities, ornate movie palaces sprang up in towns large and small across the land. New museums also were founded in greater numbers. Americans began to realize that museums needn't be only tools for carrying on the traditions of Europe; they could be symbols of an emerging American sophistication. As Alfred C. Parker, director of the Rochester Museum of Arts and Sciences, declared: "Unimportant cities have no museums; great cities have flourishing museums." And flourish they did. During the 1920s a museum building was christened every 11.4 days. Businesses such as Wells Fargo Bank and Crane & Crane Paper Company founded museums to preserve their contributions to American progress and society. By 1933 President Herbert Hoover's administration could proudly report: "Today a museum is found in every city in the United States of over 250,000 inhabitants." Among the influential museums founded during this roaring decade were Colonial Williamsburg in Virginia (1926), the Henry Ford Museum & Greenfield Village in Dearborn, Mich. (1926), the Museum of Science and Industry in Chicago (1926) and New York's Museum of Modern Art (MoMA) (1929).

The Return of Populism

America's era of seemingly boundless prosperity ended almost overnight. With the stock market crash of 1929 and the onset of the Great Depression in the 1930s, the emphasis on serving an elite audience was again called into question by many museum "workers," as they referred to themselves (not "professionals," a term that would come later). In 1931 Philip Youtz, the director of the Brooklyn Museum accused museums of being oriented to "the wealthy collector . . . not the common man on the street . . . who enters its great halls with an initial inferiority complex that leaves him cowed from the start."

Two developments during this era helped remove some of the barriers between "the common man" and the elite class of wealthy collector. The first was the utopian vision of an emerging modern architecture and design that sought to create buildings and exhibitions that were more neutral, more functional and thus less intimidating to the general public. The second was a renewal of the role of education, which the hard times of the Great Depression helped elevate again to a place of importance within the museum.

Public schools, like other national institutions of the day, suffered from a sudden and severe lack of funds. Museums responded to the crisis by offering more classes and other educational services, assisted by charitable foundations that embraced progressive educational values. It was Franklin Delano Roosevelt's Works Progress Administration, however, that made a decisive and lasting contribution. Roosevelt believed that museums, at their best, could be "woven into the very warp and woof of democracy." In addition to

upgrading existing museums and developing traveling shows, the WPA opened 53 art centers with classes in painting, drawing and sculpture. Many of these centers later became permanent museums, such as the Walker Art Center in Minneapolis, the Roswell Museum and Art Center in New Mexico and the North Carolina Museum of Art in Raleigh. The art centers went beyond the WPA's immediate goal of providing employment to teachers and art lessons for citizens. WPA classes were racially integrated, an idea so controversial at the time that it eventually contributed to the demise of Roosevelt's program.

Wars at Mid-Century: The Call to Patriotism

During World War I museums had done little directly to raise morale or influence public opinion save for a few token gestures such as sending newsletters to "homesick soldiers in the trenches." With the onset of the World War II, however, museums, now greater in number and influence, responded with a more vigorous patriotism.

They participated in programs that encouraged military recruitment and supported national security. In the heartland for example, the Walker Art Center created "Halls of Montezuma," a display of modern Marine equipment, while across the river in St. Paul the Science Museum of Minnesota hosted an exhibition about stateside safety. Its display titled "Can America Be Bombed?" appeared on the cover of the AAM periodical *The Museum News* only six days before the attack on Pearl Harbor.

On Jan. 1, 1942, just a few weeks after the attack, a group of prominent museum directors issued a resolution to their colleagues: "If, in time of peace, our museums and art galleries are important to the community, in time of war they are doubly valuable." Museums must "fortify the spirit on which Victory depends" through continuous exhibitions and programs. Art museums converted their regal flowerbeds into patriotic victory gardens, and botanical gardens offered classes that taught citizens how to do the same at home. Museums near military training facilities presented educational programs for the troops on fundamental topics such as the value of democracy. Those in cities popular with off-duty GIs opened members' lounges to men in uniform, serving refreshments and showing motion

pictures. Others showed stay-at-home wives how to prepare food economically despite the limitations of rationing. On the West Coast the San Francisco Museum of Modern Art stayed open to the public until 10 p.m. every night, dutifully blacking out windows as a defense against potential bombing raids. In Hawaii the Honolulu Academy of Arts and the Bishop Museum reopened only days after their city's harbor was bombed. With area schools still closed, the Bishop sponsored classes for children and organized a morale-boosting Christmas carol sing-along for the community.

But in their eagerness to aid the cause, museums sometimes allowed zeal to overshadow objectivity. To aid the U.S. Army, the American Museum of Natural History produced 162 portable exhibits on racial identification to be used by soldiers to help them distinguish enemy troops from allies. MoMA's exhibition "Road to Victory" showed a giant photo of bombs blowing up a ship in Pearl Harbor. Pasted below was a photo of two Japanese diplomats dressed in business suits, their eyes positioned to look directly at the explosion, their mouths laughing with glee. The caption read "Two Faces." Other museums removed all Japanese items from display, sequestering them in storage and replacing them with art and objects produced by American allies.

Elsewhere museums worked to prove that they were truly "doubly valuable" to the nation by serving as hospitals, Red Cross stations, training and research centers, manufacturers and offices. New York's Hayden Planetarium trained 45,000 sailors in celestial navigation. The Kansas City Art Institute and the Franklin Institute in Philadelphia conducted research on camouflage. The California Academy of Sciences manufactured naval optical equipment. One San Francisco museum even played a central role in the post-war peace process. In 1945 the galleries of the San Francisco Museum of Modern Art served as offices for international delegates convened to discuss the formation of the United Nations.

In the post-war years, museum visits exceeded the nation's total population for the first time. Renewed prosperity led to unprecedented interest in education and culture. Refugees from war-shattered Europe streamed into American cities, profoundly influencing the nation's cultural life, sparking new movements in art, science and scholarship. Museums benefited too from the new national focus. Middle-class women increased their involvement in collecting and volunteerism. Teachers looked to museums as field-trip destinations for their classrooms, which were filling rapidly with the first baby-boomers.

But with victory came a sobering aftershock: the emergence of the Cold War with the Soviet Union and China. Like much of the nation, museums became obsessed with protecting themselves from atomic attack, something that many Americans considered imminent. The focus turned now to the precious national legacy that hung upon museum walls or lay within their vaults. Museum charters of the time spoke less of uplifting the citizenry and more about the obligation to protect and preserve art and artifacts. Conservators, many trained as scientists, aided the cause. So did architects. Museum construction projects were increasingly linked not to aspirations of grandeur but to the more concrete concerns of storage, ventilation and security.

The generous educational programs of previous decades received less attention. Cold War paranoia and McCarthyism led to the blacklisting of progressive artists a nd educators. Some museums such as the Dallas Museum of Art were forced to stand up to demands from local "patriotic" committees to censor work by artists suspected of being active on the communist front. Others earnestly organized exhibitions that promoted desirable American values like rugged individualism, motherhood and the nuclear family. Notable among these were "Family of Man," organized by the Museum of Modern Art and "The Farmer's Year," organized by the Farmers' Museum in Cooperstown, N.Y.

During the Cold War, such American values as rugged individualism, ingenuity and self-reliance were incorporated into exhibitions like "The Farmer's Year," which opened in 1958 at the Farmers' Museum in Cooperstown, N.Y.

"Mathematica: The World of Numbers and Beyond" was popular with visitors and critics alike when it opened at the California Museum of Science and Industry (now California Science Center) in 1961. It was the first museum exhibition to use tangible objects and ideas to explain the abstractions of mathematics. Photo by Delmar Watson for the California Science Center.

Schools now widely discredited John Dewey's once groundbreaking work in education as "communistic, atheistic and un-American" and shifted toward teaching "fundamentals" according to "standards." With the notable exception of some children's and science museums, many mainstream museums now also dismissed Dewey's ideas. To connoisseurs, the philosopher was too closely associated with the eccentric Philadelphia collector Albert Barnes, who believed in "Negro" education and possessed other possibly subversive notions about art education.

The 1957 launching of *Sputnik* by the Soviets provided another jolt to America's sense of security. The space race was on and museums quickly joined in. As part of the push to interest a new generation in science, communities founded science museums and planetariums, among them the Oregon Museum of Science and Industry in Portland (1957), the Pacific Science Center in Seattle (1962) and the Miami Planetarium and Museum of Science (1966). The impetus for these new institutions came not from wealthy industrialists as had been the case with art museums and natural history museums earlier in the century, but from the federal government and university educators. Upgraded planetariums were immediately put to use. The seven original *Mercury* astronauts learned star navigation at the Morehead Planetarium at the University of North Carolina in Chapel Hill. Museums also trained teachers and developed groundbreaking science exhibits. In 1961 the California Museum of Science and Industry in Los Angeles (now the California Science Center) unveiled "Mathematica," a show designed to demystify the abstract world of mathematics. It was one of the country's early interactive exhibitions.

"Learning by doing" was back in fashion. It dovetailed perfectly with the scientific method. The hands-on laboratory became the model for a new kind of science museum geared to high school students. Foremost among these was the Exploratorium in San Francisco, founded in 1969 by Frank Oppenheimer, an atomic physicist who had been blacklisted during the McCarthy era. (His brother J. Robert headed the Manhattan Project that developed the first atomic bomb.) In the same vein the Boston Children's Museum, founded in 1913 by natural science teachers, introduced hands-on exhibits for children. The visionary behind this new kind of exhibition was Michael Spock, prominent social activist and son of the era's most famous pediatrician, Benjamin Spock.

A new kind of threat was beginning to emerge for museums during these years, one that few museums recognized. The new mass entertainment of television, popular music like rock 'n' roll, the suburban shopping mall and theme parks such as Disney's Magic Kingdom soon would challenge museums for the attention and leisure-time decisions of the public. Most mainstream museums however viewed themselves as sanctuaries of tradition, unaffected by the hustle and bustle of mass culture. They were content to remain conservative enclaves, preserving Old World values. In 1957 while documenting the vibrant community life on the streets of Pittsburgh, photographer W. Eugene Smith wandered inside the city's Carnegie Museum and later remarked: "Educational television is more imaginative than . . . dusty but sound museums. Museums are stale; they need fresh injections of money, spirit and ideas."

From Civil Rights to Watergate: Growth and Tumult

Like many other national institutions, museums were largely unprepared for the sweeping social changes that began in the 1960s. New science centers and children's museums were founded, but art and history museums lagged behind the times. Outside on the streets, Americans were marching for civil rights. On college campuses students demonstrated for free speech and rallied against the Vietnam War. In galleries and artists' studios in cities across the country new movements in experimental art were beginning to bloom. Yet most museums continued to act like fortresses. They saw their primary duty as one of defending the highest values of Western culture from the destructive impulses of an outside world gone slightly if not frankly mad. Sherman Lee, director of the Cleveland Museum of Art, beseeched his colleagues not to let the art museum become "a whipping boy for a host of extraneous social issues. . . . It is time for art museums and for those genuinely interested in their survival and proper development to resist actively the chaotic demands forced upon them . . . [by] moralizing Maoists."

Founding Director John Kinard (second from right) and Smithsonian Secretary Robert McCormick Adams (far right) at the groundbreaking for the Anacostia Museum in May 1985. The museum's previous home had been a converted movie theater. Smithsonian Institution Archives, Record Unit 371, box 4, image #95-1212. Photo by Rhawn Anderson.

By the close of the 1960s museums had begun to emerge cautiously from their ivory towers. History museums offered outdoor community festivals. Art museums created mobile art vans that allowed works to leave the building and venture to communities without museums. Some institutions actively began to cultivate African-American audiences, a group that historically had been largely ignored by museums. In 1967, the Smithsonian established a branch facility called the Anacostia Neighborhood Museum in a low-income African-American neighborhood in Washington, D.C. Other efforts could only be considered clumsy, at best. The Metropolitan Museum's "Harlem on My Mind: The Cultural Capital of Black America" (1969), for example, was so naïve in its conception that it highlighted the deep communication gap between museums and a large part of the American populace. Community activists began to rally against what they saw as museum paternalism and racism. "Take me into the museum and show me myself, show me my people, show me Soul America," wrote Harlem-born poet June Jordan. "If you cannot show me myself, if you cannot teach my children what they need to know—and they need to know the truth, and they need to know that nothing is more important than human life—if you cannot show and teach these things, then why shouldn't I attack the temples of America and blow them up?"

The rebelliousness and youthful idealism that defined the 1960s inspired a generation not to blow museums up but to found new and innovative ones. The period saw vigorous growth characterized by new kinds of institutions, new kinds of money, a significant leap in new building projects, and new crowds of visitors. The same impulse that wealthy industrialists had felt a century before was now taken up by community activists and educators. They wanted museums to contribute to building community pride. One of their goals was to lift up marginalized ethnic communities. As Washington, D.C., community activist John R. Kinard put it, a museum could "restore a sense of place among [neighborhood] residents" and serve as "a catalyst for social change." Kinard became the first director of the Anacostia Neighborhood Museum, which initially occupied an abandoned movie theater. Other early neighborhood museums founded on the same principles of civil rights and ethnic pride included the Wing Luke Asian Museum (International District, Seattle, 1966) and El Museo del Barrio (East Harlem, New York City 1969).

These new community-oriented museums were buoyed not only by the pride borne of the civil rights movements but also by the availability of government funds and programs. In 1971 the National Endowment for the Arts and the National Endowment for the Humanities, agencies that were formed only six years earlier, established programs specifically designated to provide money to museums. Federal funding opportunities further expanded with the founding of the Institute of Museum Services (later the Institute of Museums and Library Services). New support was offered for exhibitions, performances and educational programs linked to the nation's 1976 bicentennial celebration. Even though these federal agency budgets were modest, their impact was powerful, inspiring a generation of idealistic teachers, artists and activists to devote their energies to museums.

A STUDENT SIT-IN re-created at the National Civil Rights Museum, which aims to help visitors understand a painful yet inspirational period in American history. Courtesy of the National Civil Rights Museum, Memphis, Tenn.

Ironically, it was the influential trustees from major metropolitan museums—the same institutions that initially had resisted change—who lobbied to create the federal agencies that helped bring about that change. A few generations removed from the original founders, many of these trustees began to scrutinize the cost of maintaining collections. They realized that their institutions would not survive financially with the dual mandate of collections care and public service. They turned to the federal government for help. During the 1970s federal funding gave rise to hundreds of community outreach projects— partnerships between museums and senior centers, hospitals, prisons and juvenile justice halls. Museums furthered their visibility, designing elaborate exhibits for neighborhood festivals, YMCAs, local libraries and shopping malls. They reinvigorated their presence in schools. Federal insurance indemnity programs provided the means for importing and insuring valuable artifacts and art works, ultimately making possible such crowd-pleasing shows as "Treasures of Tutankhamen" (1976-79), often called America's first blockbuster exhibition.

By the end of the decade, museum visits had climbed to over 500 million, double the U.S. population. Americans continued to show that they were avid museum-goers, especially those over the age of 65 who were healthier, wealthier and more educated that ever before. The American Association for Retired Persons estimated that between the bicentennial and the end of the decade, the number of people over the age of 65 visiting museums more than doubled. The affordability of commercial flights sparked a boom in cultural tourism, allowing middle-class Americans to travel to the sites and monuments of the world and whetting their appetites for culture at home and abroad. To further cultivate the growing legions of frequent flyers, in 1977 the Fine Arts Museums of San Francisco became the nation's first museum to design exhibitions for airport terminals.

The 1970s and '80s were yet another period of growth for the American museum. More than 3,200 were founded, the equivalent of almost one every other day. (40) Nearly three-fifths of existing museums expanded or undertook major renovations. All told, nearly 2 million acres—the equivalent of the Florida Everglades—was upgraded and added to the museum landscape. Many of these projects were linked to urban revitalization plans, with museums serving as catalysts to help revive sagging inner city neighborhoods. Children's museums too expanded significantly, some founded by parent groups increasingly disenchanted with the public school system, others by parents who valued the hands-on approach to informal learning that flourished in these museums.

During these energetic years, mid-level museum professionals such as educators gained more control over the management and direction of their institutions. The scope and depth of scholarship and exhibitions improved. Training programs for museum staff increased. A national network of professionals revised codes of ethics and established standards for earning accreditation. Yet increased popularity also meant increased public scrutiny. Scandals erupted over insider deals, plundered goods and "deaccessioning," the museum profession's odd, somewhat delicate phrase for divesting itself of its collections—that is, selling or trading its objects. Still, the deaccession scandals at the Metropolitan Museum of Art in the 1970s—when it was revealed that the museum had circumvented two donors' wishes and secretly sold valuable pieces of donated art—led to stricter guidelines that became a model for the field. And the negative publicity the New-York Historical Society received a few years later for its own deaccession practices galvanized its supporters, resulting in new fiscal priorities and a revamped institution.

A Century Ends in Diversity

With the exception of a few pioneering institutions, the exuberant activity of the 1970s had not led to fundamental change throughout the field. In their exhibitions and collections, weren't museums in the 1980s really just better-organized, more popular versions of the museums that existed at the beginning of the century? The typical history museum collection was still narrow in focus, celebrating battles and famous heroes, presenting the hardworking pioneer or colonial family. The typical natural science or anthropology museum was still full of mounted animals in dioramas, dinosaur bones and in some instances human remains and sacred religious objects. Most curators had little idea where the works in their collections had come from and no definitive way of knowing whether they had been legally acquired. Much of the information contained within museums was off-limits to anyone but scholarly researchers.

By the 1980s it had become apparent to many leaders in the field that museums needed to open themselves up to new ways of doing business. The key to survival in the new America was diversity, and not just in terms of audience. Diversity also meant expanding the sources of income. As they looked for additional ways to pay the bills, museums became entrepreneurial, a catch-phrase in Reagan-era America. Effective marketing and aggressive fund raising now were widely seen as essential to institutional survival, especially as federal programs were being cut back or axed entirely. Museums unabashedly approached their own members and corporate sponsors for money. They expanded merchandising efforts, built movie theaters for large-format films and planned even larger, more attention-getting exhibitions. Demographics studies and market research now received greater time and attention from directors and boards of trustees conscious of the bottom line. Audience evaluators emerged as important players, conducting focus groups, and observing and interviewing visitors. Study after study confirmed the profile of the typical museumgoer. She was white, in her mid-to-late 30s, college-educated, more likely to be female than male, and more likely to go to museums if she had visited them as a child.

Yet this composite portrait of the museum visitor did not align with the profile of the average American. The nation's demographics were shifting. Asian and Latino populations were growing, the percentage of whites shrinking. Native Americans and African Americans were gaining new political power. In universities, scholars "deconstructed" American institutions' biases toward the arts and civilization of Western Europe. Educators from kindergarten teachers to dissertation advisors embraced the new multiculturalism.

Mother Maybelle Carter's Gibson L-5 guitar, on display in "Sing Me Back Home: A Journey through Country Music" at Nashville's Country Music Hall of Fame® and Museum.

It survived World War II only to be thrust into the culture wars of the early 1990s: the B-29 Enola Gay, *now on display at the National Air and Space Museum's Steven F. Udvar-Hazy Center. Photo by Eric Long/OIPP, National Air and Space Museum; image # SI2003-29268-5, © Smithsonian Institution.*

They rejected the idea of America as a "melting pot" where different traditions merged into a single identity. Instead they insisted that the nation was a mosaic of distinct traditions and cultures. American society was entering another turbulent era, where categories of race, ethnicity and privilege would be reexamined and contested.

University-based scholars launched stinging attacks against museums. Their past collections and exhibitions practices were signs of "the dread disease of imperialist, capitalist and white culture," in the words of University of California, Santa Cruz professor Donna Haraway. "Colonial," once used to conjure up quaint images of rocking chairs and grandfather clocks, was now a pejorative term. If museums really wanted to reflect America, these scholars argued, it was time to tell, honestly and fully, the stories of those who had been oppressed or ignored by the majority culture.

This challenge to the social order was also a challenge for most museums. Generally they lacked the collections to document America's history from the viewpoints of society's marginalized groups. Nonetheless, the museum field set about the task of staking a place within multicultural America. A taskforce of 25 of the field's leaders produced *Excellence and Equity* (1992), a report that called on museums to emphasize their roles as educational institutions in the largest sense and to reexamine their public dimension to "include a broader spectrum of our diverse society in their activities." Collections expanded to document the growing influence of popular culture and the media. There was a new interest in the diverse cultures and ethnicities of the local community.

Museum educators sought to appeal to new generations of visitors by utilizing technologies such as video and computer screens and new programs such as theatrical performances in the galleries. There were welcome improvements to the museum's physical space brought about by the 1990 Americans with Disabilities Act, which compelled such changes as training docents to give tours to hearing impaired visitors, canting labels so people in wheelchairs could read them and creating audio and touch tours for people with visual impairments.

This was also a time of bitter contention over the museum's role in an increasingly politicized society. The era of the "culture wars" saw pointed debate over who had the authority to interpret the nation's history and the right to display controversial or "offensive" art. Public exhibitions and the institutions that hosted them were suddenly front-page news, often much to the consternation of directors and boards. What a museum curator might see as a thought-provoking challenge to conventional ideas about military history, homosexuality or art scholarship, the media and certain politicians saw as a direct attack on society's core values. Some commentators claimed these skirmishes to be part of a larger battle for the soul of America. Museums found themselves directly in the crossfire.

Notable examples were exhibitions such as "The West as America" (National Museum of American History, 1990), "The Last Act: The Atomic Bomb and the End of World War II," a show about the *Enola Gay* (National Air and Space Museum, 1993), and "The Perfect Moment" (1991), a touring retrospective containing sexually explicit images by photographer Robert Mapplethorpe. As public institutions with their doors wide open to everyone, museums logically became the battlefields where this clash of ideologies played out. Yet despite a good deal of negative press coverage and some barbed commentary by conservative politicians, museums remained as popular as they had always been, with ever larger numbers of people waiting patiently in line to see what all the fuss was about. Membership and attendance numbers continued to grow. Museums emerged from the decade of the 1990s with a weakened level of federal financial support but strengthened in their resolve to be a part of the larger national dialogue about cultural and social issues.

New Challenges for a New Century

Like the rest of the nation, museums lurched into overdrive in the late 1990s, becoming multi-tasking institutions that tried to be many more things to many more people. Collections expanded as museums gathered up popular music, oral history, digital art and websites. Educational programs went digital as educators exploited web technology to post curricula and live data feeds of zoo animals, weather satellites and artists at work. Museums posted online exhibitions and hosted "field trips" via videoconference. They invested in logo merchandise and high-end restaurants and discovered branding and licensing. They also went on another building frenzy. In the 1990s almost every redevelopment zone in a U.S. city or exurb added a museum. A new building or expansion opened every 15 days. But these buildings differed from those of prior decades. They were bolder, flashier projects, intended as icons. Globetrotting architects were commissioned for the next great signature building. Having a "Frank Gehry," a "Renzo Piano" or a "Santiago Calatrava" could add inestimable prestige—and tourist dollars—to a city or region.

But as always there were troubling questions about the future. Was there a vital societal role for an institution associated with slowness and authenticity in an age seduced by speed and artifice? Would emerging technologies and entertainments, especially the Internet, erode people's desire to visit museum buildings? How could museums compete with the stream of information and images emanating from screens that were getting tinier, more portable and more ubiquitous? How would the realities of a global economy affect museums' strategies for collecting, exhibiting and teaching, not to mention funding?

Then came the events of Sept. 11, 2001, and for a brief time the world seemed to slow down and reflect. In the aftermath of a tragedy that would irrevocably change the national focus, museums awoke to the realization that the American public had a new expectation of its museums. In the days following the attacks, hundreds of thousands of people sought solace in museums. The *New York Times* reported that 8,200 people showed up at the Metropolitan Museum of Art on Sept. 13, 2001. Two visitors, painters Helen and Brice Marden, commented, "Today it's comforting to come back and see everything still here. All this beauty. . . . Being in a museum together can feel safe and normal." Across the country museums waived admission fees, invited psychologists and counselors to host workshops for families, sponsored concerts of soothing music, and mounted special exhibitions documenting the event with photographs and artifacts. The South Street Seaport Museum in New York held an exhibition called "All Available Boats: Harbor Voices and Images 09.11.01." The New York Fire Museum presented photographic exhibitions and a changing display of memorials dedicated to the firefighters who lost their lives at the World Trade Center. But programs stretched far beyond New York City. The Japanese-American National Museum in Los Angeles created programs about tolerance and cultural awareness of Arab Americans. The Oklahoma City National Memorial mounted a show that explored the common themes of rescue, recovery and the healing process associated with the events of Sept. 11 and the Oklahoma City bombing. There were many more examples and they came from every state in the union.

Lonnie G. Bunch, then president of the Chicago Historical Society, summarized this new spirit: "Museums all over the country are working to create opportunities that allow visitors to see our institutions as places of healing, education, affirmation and reflection; cultural entities that are ripe with contemporary resonance; and sources for historical knowledge . . . for people wrestling with despair and uncertainty."

During the past century museums transformed themselves every bit as much as the nation itself. The changes did not come without risk or loss, nor did they occur in a smooth or linear fashion. They were the result of tremendous push and pull among opposing forces and competing visions inside and outside the institutions. The same struggle continues in the present day. But of the changes that have occurred, the most profound and encouraging is perhaps that the American museum at last has discovered what it means to be a civic institution. Growing far beyond its early limitations, it has begun to understand its true potential to educate, inspire and lead. It is striving to become what Missouri Historical Society Director Robert Archibald calls America's "new town square, a public institution with the confidence to share authority with the people it serves." It is this transformation that allows the American museum to aspire to be not just another part of the community fabric but a necessary element at the center of the community, a defining place where anyone of any age or background who wishes to enter can be transformed.

THE BUILDING

"...the business of an American architect is to build something that will stand and be fairly presentable for about thirty years."

—JAMES **RENWICK,** THE ARCHITECT WHO DESIGNED THE
FIRST SMITHSONIAN BUILDING IN 1849.

Museums today occupy some of the country's most stunning and creative buildings, proud examples of contemporary and architectural vision and daring. But it was not always this way. The origins of museum architecture are far more humble.

The Metropolitan Museum of Art set up its first exhibit in an old dance academy. The Massachusetts Historical Society shared quarters with butcher stalls in a market hall. The Brooklyn Children's Museum once operated in a remodeled auto showroom; the Oregon Museum of Science and Industry in a hotel room; Chicago's Museum of Contemporary Art in the former Playboy headquarters.

Like each of these venerable institutions, most American museums do not start out with a grand building. They begin with a grand idea.

The realization of a grand idea. View of Baltimore Harbor, featuring the Maryland Science Center (left) and the National Aquarium (right). Courtesy of the Maryland Science Center.

For years, often decades, museum founders and staff gather their wares and wander between spaces. The nomadic existence ends when, after much searching and a bit of politicking, they settle on an address. Only then do they begin to realize their largest physical achievement: a building of their own. In some cases, they settle into historic buildings, turning obsolete structures into vibrant public places. Across the country, there are museums in old mansions, fire stations and factories; in airplane hangars, railroad depots, and naval vessels. A defunct ice house in Cedar Falls, Iowa. An iron foundry in Birmingham, Ala. A storefront shaped like a giant duck in Suffolk County, N.Y. In other cases, museums decide to build from scratch, or add a modern wing to an existing structure. Whether it is renovated or new, each museum building is part of an even larger story: the dramatic fruition of museum architecture set against the changing American landscape.

Museum buildings represent some of our nation's most extraordinary and historic architecture. Yet, as critic Ada Louise Huxtable once said, museum architecture "has been an uneasy, ambivalent, consistently controversial, and passionately debated subject since the first portrait . . . was transferred from a palace or church for the purpose of collection or display."

Translating dreams into bricks and mortar involves an extensive cast of characters. Civic leaders, boards of trustees, directors and the patrons who put up the money all have a say. Architects simultaneously play the role of hero and villain, pursued by a Greek chorus of critics and boosters. Behind the scenes, developers, planners and politicians influence the selection of a site. Scenes play out in ornate palaces in urban parks; restored colonial villages near highways; modern cubic forms nestled on college campuses or between downtown skyscrapers; renovated warehouses on waterfronts; and swanky edu-tainment complexes in locales as diverse as urban renewal districts and rural American Indian reservations.

The story of the modern museum building starts at the end of the Civil War. From the mid-19th century to the beginnings of World War II, museum architects looked to the past. Classical and medieval palaces and colonial buildings communicated permanence and enduring values, antidotes to the fleeting nature of daily life and commerce. Then, with the arrival of modern architecture in the 1930s and until the capital improvement projects of the 1970s and '80s—builders performed an about-face, linking their projects not to past aspirations but to present realities. Practical concerns such as efficiency and urban economic revitalization dominated their agendas. By the 1990s and early 2000s, museums were veering toward sizzle and spectacle. In this era of themed malls and revitalized downtowns, museum buildings have become high-stakes attractions, icons to brand a city or region.

Museum architecture began its symphonic grandeur in Europe. The first public building constructed expressly as a museum was Karl Friedrich Schinkel's Altesmuseum in Berlin, Germany (1830). Schinkel felt that a museum needed the grand presence of a cathedral to assert its cultural and societal importance. He created a grand, central domed hall and an

*The Smithsonian Castle, past and present. **Above:** Strollers on the Mall, c. 1849. Smithsonian Institution Record Unit 95, box 30, folder 4A, neg. #76.4354.*

***Left:** A contemporary view. Photo by Eric Long, neg. #94-5905.*

Ionic colonnade that spanned the entire front of the building. As visitors ascended through the palatial structure to the second-story galleries, they saw sweeping views of contemporary Berlin. Schinkel's goal was to give people a space where they could contemplate works of aesthetic purity without forgetting their obligation to the everyday world. He was inspired by the ancient Greek muses, nine goddesses who presided over the arts and sciences; the word "museum" derives from them.

American museum architecture began a generation later, on a somewhat lesser note. While Schinkel had studied at the prestigious German Bauakademie, early U.S. architects learned their trade via apprenticeship. All too often, 19th-century American museum architects copied European castles and cathedrals, unconcerned about the relationship of a building to its landscape or the nation's citizens. In 1842, the country's first public art museum, the Wadsworth Atheneum, was completed in Hartford, Conn. Its architects, Ithiel Town and Alexander J. Davis, created a forbidding hybrid of Gothic cathedral and Roman fortress, meant more to project power than inspire contemplation. Another early public museum, the 1849 Smithsonian Institution (a building now known as the Castle) was designed by James Renwick. Its bulky forms harkened to the medieval cathedrals of France and England, another reflection of the prevailing attitude about the role of museum spaces.

In the decades after the eclectic Smithsonian Castle opened, American architects professionalized. The American Institute of Architects was founded in 1857, and academies modeled on the French Ecole des Beaux Arts soon followed. Beginning with the Massachusetts Institute of Technology in 1863, these schools taught architects to design in the extravagant style that would dominate American museums for the next few decades—Beaux-Arts classicism. Similar to Schinkel's approach, the Beaux-Arts method combined motifs from ancient Greece (Ionic and Doric columns and pediments), Rome (arches, vaults, thermal windows), the Renaissance (elevated domes) and Baroque palaces (endless enfilade corridors with row upon row of treasures). In the post-Civil War urban building boom, the traditions of Europe appealed to museums' industrialist-founders, who were attempting to re-invent themselves as cultivated aristocrats. They envisioned museums as elevated buildings with grand stairways. Sculptures of lions—those ancient symbols of strength—would guard the entrances. Phrases in Latin—the ancient language of philosophers and statesmen—would adorn the pediments.

The aristocratic pretensions of late 19th-century American museums were tempered by the real-estate adage, "location, location, location." Cities were taking over "undesirable" spaces and turning them into parkland. Museum founders saw great potential in these new green parcels and put their energies into lobbying for space; urban parks were America's closest approximation to European palace grounds. Set back from busy streets, far from the bustle, sootiness and dangers of the city, and surrounded by greenery, a museum in a park commanded a powerful presence. Robert Koehler, the first director of what is now the Minneapolis Institute of Arts, declared that parks were "ideal and practical at the same time." Land was cheap and available, and the "natural setting" enhanced the beauty of the artworks, while permitting expansion that did not conflict with downtown business interests.

New York's Metropolitan Museum of Art was one of the first museums established in a park. In the 1870s, while the institution was still bouncing between rented spaces, its founders were persuaded to build in the recently completed Central Park. This was a significant decision. Cultural life in New York was divided along lines of class, religion and race. Downtown was the place of daytime commerce and nighttime entertainment for the lower and immigrant classes. Central Park lay within New York's wealth corridor, between avenues filling up with mansions. Implicit then in the choice of a location was an expectation about whom the museum would attract and serve. Some founders argued vehemently for a site more accessible to the working classes, but political forces—specifically the Central Park Commissioners—prevailed. The Met would move to the park and have an entrance on fashionable Fifth Avenue. Luring the Met and, later, the American Museum of Natural History (AMNH) was a triumph in the park commissioners' plan for a bucolic area of refined activity, worlds apart from the sooty commercial downtown and cramped immigrant sweatshops.

The Central Park location allowed the new museums to occupy a grand position within the evolving cityscape. But it did not immediately guarantee a grand building. According to the *New York Herald*, AMNH's first building was "hideous . . . half convent, half prison in appearance." The Met's first building fared no better. Completed in the 1880s, its barn-like appearance was criticized as "a forcible example of architectural ugliness . . . fit only for a winter garden or a railway depot." Ironically, 100 years later, some convents, prisons and railway depots would be converted into museums. But at the time, cheap, awkward structures like the Met's were civic embarrassments. Rather than ascending elegant marble steps, visitors toddled over wooden boards, designed to keep mud off their shoes rather than to elevate their spirits. The glass roof leaked on rainy days, forcing staff to cover art with tarps and patrons to step around pails that caught the dripping water. The Met's patrons certainly deserved a more dignified house for their new museum, a promise that would be realized in the coming years.

Still, situating the Metropolitan Museum of Art in Central Park would establish a longstanding pattern of securing grand park locations for art museums. Soon after the Met's decision, the trustees of the Museum of Fine Arts, Boston selected 12 acres in Boston's Back Bay Fens as a permanent site. The Cincinnati Museum Association chose that city's Eden Park. And the trustees of the Art Institute of Chicago accepted the city's offer of a smaller financial contribution in return for a spot in the newly created Lake Park (now Grant Park) when their museum was planned as part of the World's Columbian Exposition of 1893.

Urban park settings and Beaux-Arts architecture met at that 1893 world's fair. Exposition planners wanted the fair's architecture, built on lakefront landfill, to communicate a vision of European culture. They thought the conservative Beaux-Arts style would counter a new commercial architectural phenomenon: bold steel-frame skyscrapers being erected in Chicago's downtown. To the educated upper-classes, the skyscraper was an abomination or, as Henry James put it, "a mere economic convenience . . . a huge, continuous fifty-floored conspiracy against the very idea of the ancient graces." Beginning in 1893 and through the 1920s, Chicago built a series of neo-classical museums in harmony with the fair's classicizing objectives. A building that now forms the nucleus of the Art Institute of Chicago was modeled on a Renaissance revival palazzo. At the time, the institute had no original works of art to speak of—only casts and reproductions. The monumental building, with later additions of bronze lions, a statue-lined staircase and a great fountain, expressed the confidence that some day Chicago would accumulate the fine collections it deserved.

West façade, exterior view, Albright-Knox Art Gallery, 1905: the epitome of the Beaux-Arts museum. Courtesy of the Albright-Knox Gallery.

Chicago's exposition inspired leaders in cities from Buffalo to Saint Louis to San Diego to combine palatial architecture, a park location and the occasion of a world's fair to establish museums. Buffalo's original Albright Art Gallery (now the Albright-Knox) epitomizes the Beaux-Arts museum. Built for the Pan-American Exposition of 1901, it opened as a museum in 1905. The classical Greek architecture took full advantage of the building's location in Delaware Park, connected to nearby Hoyt Lake through a series of platforms and staircases. Visitors entered by ascending a grand staircase and passing through a portico topped by a pediment. Once inside the spacious foyer, marble staircases led them to two symmetrical wings of galleries. Divided by the art of different nations and periods, the galleries encouraged a sense of artistic diversity amid architectural harmony. Such architectural poetry was repeated in a variety of ways in several cities. The cool stone exteriors and the hushed halls created a quasi-religious experience. Like churches, Beaux-Arts museums had little place for visitor amenities, save for a few makeshift sales stands near the cloak room or in the basement, where guards sold leaflets and postcards for a few pennies. Anything more elaborate would have undermined the museum's stature as a place of education and scholarship, far removed from the taint of commerce.

Director John Cotton Dana reviewing the plans for the Newark Museum, c. 1925. Collections of the Newark Museum Archives.

Not everyone rejoiced over these high-minded palaces, which communicated more pomp than circumstance; some thought they were frozen visions of Old World Europe that did not reflect America's vitality. In 1917 John Cotton Dana, visionary director of the Newark Museum in New Jersey, proposed that museum buildings no longer harken to bygone periods but instead represent their times, using contemporary materials such as steel and concrete. Would the Greeks have built with columns of stone in the modern era? Why, then, should contemporary museum architects refer to past styles? "To build first an expensive home, a palace, a temple or any grandiose and permanent structure on the conventional lines of so-called museum architecture [is] . . . to do a foolish, wasteful, antiquated thing; a thing possible only to those who [know] little of modern community life."

Dana criticized not only classical architecture but also park locations as inaccessible to the general populace. In the 1920s, when New Jersey politicians fought to move the downtown museum to an affluent leafy neighborhood, Dana resigned from several civic committees in protest. He held his ground and in 1926, in the city's downtown, the Newark Museum opened one of America's first museum buildings with modern features. As was typical of the tensions between staff and trustees, Dana's enthusiasm for radical ideas was tempered by the building's patron, department store magnate Louis Bamberger. Fearing that the director would go overboard—Dana originally wanted a 16-story skyscraper—Bamberger hired his store's architect, Jarvis Hunt, whose uncle, Robert Morris Hunt had designed the Metropolitan Museum of Art. Bamberger also supervised the entire building process. The result was a compromise between Beaux-Arts and modernism: a stripped down classical exterior nestled into a tight urban lot and a conventional interior courtyard that opened onto a floor plan modeled on contemporary office buildings.

The Newark Museum was part of the larger museum building boom fueled by the strong post World War I economy. The rash of museum expansions, however, did not translate into inventive design. Museum architecture paled in comparison to the concurrent dazzling experiments of modernism seen in skyscrapers, art deco movie houses, suburban bungalows and parkways. For museums, nostalgic visions of a glorious past would continue in most of the nation for at least the next two decades. To house their European masterworks, museum founders continued to commission Beaux-Arts palaces that, to them, communicated wealth, status and longevity. The stately John and Mable Ringling Museum of Art in Sarasota, Fla., typifies the era's spirit. In 1925, circus impresario John Ringling founded this museum to house his collection of Baroque art and circus memorabilia. Using off-season circus performers as his construction crew, he built a sprawling complex on a former alligator-infested swamp—i.e., a brand-new building pretending to be a centuries-old Italianate villa. No one need be bothered by the fact that Florida's real estate boom was less than a decade old.

Even museums about technological progress hid their futuristic exhibits behind fluted columns and frumpy garlands. Inspired by the Deutsches Museum during a visit to Munich in the 1920s Sears and Roebuck President Julius Rosenwald founded America's first museum of science and industry. Highlighting industriousness in the technologies of aviation, transportation and electricity, the Chicago institution often is called the first noisy museum in America, with exhibitions that squeaked, chortled and immersed visitors in a boisterous, activity-filled environment. However, the container for this push-button ode to innovation was old-fashioned: a restored neo-Grecian palace, leftover from the Columbian Exposition. The Museum of Science and Industry opened to the public in 1933, in time for the city's 100th anniversary and in tandem with the Century of Progress World's Fair.

A few years earlier, Sears trustee and stockholder Max Adler had become entranced with a German optical device that created an indoor illusion of the night sky. In 1928 he announced his quest to import this technology and build

In the 1940s the Museum of Science and Industry partnered with B. F. Goodrich to highlight the wonders of rubber. This guillotine demonstrated that car tires can endure far more jolts and shocks than they normally encounter on the road. Archives, Museum of Science and Industry, Chicago.

the nation's first planetarium. Like Rosenwald, Adler looked to the past for a container for his newfangled idea. He commissioned Beaux-Arts-trained architect Ernest Grunfeld, Jr., to design a dressy palace that would display the universe in a classical costume. The resulting Adler Planetarium in Chicago received a gold medal from the American Institute of Architects for resisting the pernicious influence of modern architecture.

Walking the harmonious and repetitious corridors of Beaux-Arts museums was a novel experience for Americans, but it soon wore them down. In 1925, Yale University psychologist Edward Robinson described a phenomenon known as "museum fatigue . . . characterized by aching muscles, tired neck and eyes, and by the vague but insistent desire to escape from too many pictures or too much sculpture." To solve this problem, John Cotton Dana created lightweight "museum fatigue stools" that visitors could carry throughout the museum. Fiske Kimball, director of the Philadelphia Museum of Art, had grander ideas. He envisioned a building to counter this fatigue and invited researchers using new techniques for studying visitor behavior to the museum for five months. Armed with stopwatches, they timed people looking at artwork, discovering that they spent an average of 2.8 seconds looking at each picture. The problem was the architecture. Or, as the researchers put it, "large galleries, high ceilings, oppressive architectural detail combine to diminish people's attention to the actual things on exhibition."

Kimball conceived of three kinds of interiors to slow visitors down and inspire more contemplation: one for the general public that would show the "evolution" of art history; another for scholars that would classify art by its materials; and the period room, which

would show art in a furnished room. He also envisioned garden courts as "rest-places, offering the public relief not only from the strain of constant looking, but also from the drag of standing and slow walking." There would be no numbing corridors or suites of identical galleries. Rather, rooms would be different sizes and shapes (and sometimes reflect the measurements of specific works of art). Instead of straight avenues of movement, frequent turns would create intimacy and a sense of discovery. Electric lighting would combine with outside skylights and windows for brighter viewing spaces.

The new Philadelphia Museum of Art (PMA) opened in 1928. One wonders, however, how Kimball could have felt this building would not overwhelm visitors. Many prominent museums had been built along urban boulevards, but Philadelphia's museum took this practice many steps forward. The building crowns the Benjamin Franklin Parkway, completed just before the institution broke ground. Not until 1997, when the Getty Museum was constructed in Los Angeles, would an American museum loom over its city, physically and symbolically, the way Philadelphia's art museum did.

Many Philadelphians at the time did not appreciate this stroke of monumentality. Nor did the museum's design slow visitors down the way Kimball had intended. Here is how two critics described the building when it opened:

> The architects seem to have gone out of their way to produce an exhausting building. The front presents a hillside with steps more forbidding than those of the Capitol in Rome. At the top of these, one finds an immense court; at the end rises another flight of steps. And within the portals still a third flight of marble stairs leads to the gallery floor . . . the U-shaped plan, around the open court at the center of which is a front entrance, also assures the maximum amount of travel. No *Rundfahrt* [round trip] is possible—one always has to start at the center, go to the end of the wing, and retrace one's steps through the galleries already seen . . . the acuteness of exhaustion [is] produced by the lack of any furniture to sit on.

Psychologists who studied visitors' use of PMA shortly after it opened discovered that people made a beeline for the exit, shortening their visit as much as they possibly could. Perhaps it wasn't until Sylvester Stallone's victory dance on the museum's steps in the Hollywood movie *Rocky* (1977) that most Philadelphians began to fully appreciate the astounding vista that was the reward after all that muscular exertion.

By 1929 the Beaux-Arts formula was growing tired. The Great Depression soon would put it to rest. Museums began to seek new models to communicate their values. Two schools of thought emerged. One, echoing John Cotton Dana's populist ideas, was a call for European modernism. The second, more popular at the time, looked for design inspiration not from Europe, but from America's past.

Above: *The Santa Barbara Museum of Natural History, c. 1924, an example of the Spanish colonial revival in the western U.S.*

Below: *Thomas Jefferson's Monticello was restored as a historic site in the 1920s. Courtesy of Monticello/ Thomas Jefferson Foundation, Inc.*

A keen nostalgia for colonial history arose at the same time America was beginning its love affair with the automobile. Descendents of the earliest European settlers openly feared that massive numbers of new immigrants—notably Eastern Europeans, Italians and Greeks—would undermine traditional American values. They also believed that with the rise of industrial cities, America was in danger of losing its architectural heritage. Reviving examples of colonial architecture could educate the growing nation about how the colonists had civilized the raw continent.

In the western United States, this fear translated into Anglo-Californians copying motifs of the Spanish missions won over from Mexico half a century earlier. As examples of Spanish colonial revival architecture, the Santa Barbara Museum of Natural History (1923) and the San Diego Museum of Art (1926) boast red tile roofs and romantic bell towers. In the eastern United States, colonial buildings and homes of American heroes were restored as historic sites, and automobile travel made them accessible to more than just the local residents. In 1923, for example, the Thomas Jefferson Foundation acquired Monticello, the former president's home near the University of Virginia, with plans to restore it and open it up to tourists from all over the world.

An important Colonial Revival project took place 125 miles southeast of Monticello. In Williamsburg, Va., John D. Rockefeller, Jr., son of America's first billionaire, purchased a group of run-down 17th-century buildings with the goal of re-creating an authentic colonial village. Although, as some pointed out, his money came from the mega-industrial destruction of the colonial past, Rockefeller believed that the values associated with the quaint structures and cobblestone streets of pre-industrial society were superior and worth resuscitating. Colonial Williamsburg opened in 1926 as the nation's first large-scale themed historic attraction. Its most important element was its architecture. Rockefeller did not commission new buildings to house collections and exhibitions; the restored buildings were the collection objects, put on exhibition to educate and transport people back in time. His project inspired other crumbling towns to take action. In 1929, on a wooden dock on Connecticut's Mystic River, citizens founded Mystic

Aerial view of Greenfield Village, c. 1934, showing the placement—though not the names—of the buildings. From the collections of the Henry Ford (P.A.8972).

Seaport, a collection of historic ships, fishing vessels and building and repair shops meant to preserve the rapidly disappearing remnants of America's maritime past.

Like Rockefeller, industrialist Henry Ford believed that architecture could shape the national consciousness. Ford was infamous for his declaration that "history is more or less bunk" as well as for his virulent anti-Semitism. Thus he did not look to the past and chose his "real" Americans carefully. He was inspired by Henry Mercer, proprietor of the Moravian Tile Works in Doylestown, Pa. Mercer's ceramics factory produced handsome tiles for various structures, including, eventually, the Isabella Stewart Gardner Museum in Boston and the Joslyn Art Museum in Omaha. In 1916, Mercer created his own

museum, which told an upbeat story of progress by meshing modern technology with nostalgia, highlighted by more than 50,000 pre-industrial tools. Though the building borrowed Beaux-Arts decorative elements, structurally it was a six-story skyscraper, one of the first American buildings to use reinforced concrete.

Mercer's approach clicked with Ford. In 1929 the legendary industrialist created the Henry Ford Museum & Greenfield Village in Dearborn, Mich., the largest history museum of its time. Rather than painstakingly restoring a site like the one Rockefeller had established or creating an original design in the spirit of Mercer, Ford purchased agricultural, domestic and industrial buildings—such as America's oldest windmill and all the New Jersey quarters (including soil samples) associated with Thomas Edison's invention of the light bulb—uprooted them from their towns and rearranged them in "Greenfield Village."

Colonial Williamsburg, Mystic Seaport and Greenfield Village were milestones in museum history. They used architecture as collections objects and exhibitions in their own right, establishing a trend of preserving historic places and recreating villages from the past as automobile destinations. After World War II, as more and more Americans took to the road with their tourist guidebooks, the number of outdoor history museums grew. Examples include Massachusetts's Old Sturbridge Village (1946), Indiana's Conner Prairie (1964) and Strawbery Banke in Portsmouth, N.H. (1965).

There are probably more square yards of painted canvas, more tons of bronze and marble, more cubic feet of [museum] architecture per person in the United States than in any country in the world. The growth of our museums has been phenomenal.

—HAROLD **STARK,**
ART HISTORIAN, 1934

Until the Great Depression, cities continued to build ornate museums. Unfortunately, the energies devoted to constructing palatial passageways, sweeping staircases and towering vaults left little room for the museum's more practical functions. Architects must have assumed that all collections would be put on display, because none of the new buildings included sufficient storage. Staff frequently criticized the cramped working conditions, while museum-goers complained about poor ventilation, dreadful odors and the exhaustion of laboring up multiple flights of stairs. Who could appreciate the divine realm of culture with swollen feet and aching knees? Directors began to see Beaux-Arts museums as more of a handicap than an asset. Like Newark Museum Director John Cotton Dana, they lobbied their boards for more functional buildings that took advantage of the latest technologies—such as rust-free plumbing and climate control—and new materials and styles. In 1935, the Brooklyn Museum eliminated its steep staircase and relocated the entrance to the first floor. Likewise, in 1934 America's oldest museum building—the Wadsworth Atheneum—completed what is considered the first modern museum renovation in the country. But most museums weren't so lucky. Conservative aesthetic tastes and shortages of materials during the Depression and World War II stymied most pleas for change.

Modern functional technologies may have appealed to those who worked in America's treasure houses, but their industrial aesthetic was not appreciated by those footing the bills. Throughout the Depression years, most museums favored stone materials and Beaux-Arts motifs. Examples include the 1931 Art Deco Joslyn Art Museum in Omaha, faced in 38 kinds of marble and entered through decorated bronze doors; the 1933 classical Beaux-Arts Nelson Gallery in Kansas City; and the 1941 National Gallery of Art (NGA) in Washington, D.C., constructed in pale pink Tennessee marble with Greek columns, shallow dome and an imposing flight of stairs. (NGA's one nod to modernism was a functional basement cafeteria, complete with gleaming steam trays from which cafeteria workers spooned up institutional grub to fill patrons' stomachs, a trend that soon spread to other museums.)

Although these new museums delighted the public and were important additions to their cities, critics continued to sound the calls for modernism. Architectural critic Lewis Mumford dubbed Beaux-Arts museums "imperialist façades" that were "loot-heap[s] . . . for plunder." Several directors called them "'me too' Louvres of the New World." Attacks by critics notwithstanding, three related phenomena pushed museums to accept modern architecture. First, classicism—in its purist incarnation—was associated increasingly with the fascist monuments built by Mussolini and Hitler. Second, in the 1930s collectors, artists, and architects fleeing European fascism began to arrive in the United States, where they influenced tastes in art and architecture. And later, due to war-time industrialization, modern materials were more available (and cheaper) than older ones.

Three museums in New York City—the Museum of Modern Art, the then-called Guggenheim Museum of Non-objective Painting and the Whitney Museum of American Art—seized the moment to develop a new framework for museum architecture. In the late 1920s, as John D. Rockefeller, Jr., was reviving colonial architecture in Virginia, his wife Abby and her collector-friends Lillie Bliss and Mary Quinn Sullivan were organizing a new kind of museum that would become a leading tastemaker for modern architectural ideas. In 1929 they founded the Museum of Modern Art (MoMA). As part of its mission to promote contemporary ideas, in 1932 MoMA organized and toured an influential exhibition of the work of avant-garde European architects. The curators of this show, Henry Russell Hitchcock and Philip Johnson, coined the term "International Style" to describe a new vision for architecture. To International Style architects, like Walter Gropius and Le Corbusier, the Beaux-Arts style was more or less bunk. Rejecting applied historical ornament and symmetrical planning these architects favored a fresh style that focused on a building's function and exploited the qualities of industrial materials and technological advances. Concrete, steel and plate glass were not only more economical than marble and stone, they were "modern" and thus more beautiful.

In 1939 MoMA broke ground for what would become the first building in New York designed in the International Style. Its first director, Alfred H. Barr, Jr., convinced his trustees to build modern, declaring that a conservative building would "betray the very purposes for which the museum was founded." Barr had wanted to hire one of the international architects featured in Johnson and Hitchcock's exhibit. But an American architect, Phillip Goodwin, who happened to be on MoMA's board, won the commission.

Breaking a long museum tradition, MoMA moved toward New York's commercial core— that is, away from Central Park. Instead of vistas of park greenery, visitors would have to make do with a small sculpture garden behind the museum, an exercise in landscape abstraction that paralleled the canvases hanging in the galleries. Goodwin and his protégé Edward Durrell Stone fashioned a six-story building with two rows of horizontal strip windows and a slab cornice that featured punched holes open to the sky. The smooth and uniform façade of white Thermolux (a new translucent cladding) was revolutionary, resembling a department store or office building rather than a palace or temple.

In another break with tradition, visitors entered directly from the sidewalk through a set of glass doors. Rather than climbing giant staircases, they boarded elevators that took them to upper-story galleries. Goodwin and Stone took advantage of steel-frame technology, which allowed them to dispense with immovable interior walls. Within MoMA's columnar grid, exhibit designers could move walls and partitions freely and as needed to compose exhibition spaces. The building concluded in a penthouse rooftop—part of it open to the sky and emblazoned with the words "Museum of Modern Art"—which was used for social events.

With its location and architecture allied to commerce, and its opening broadcast on national radio with tributes from the Henry Ford family and Walt Disney, MoMA sent a strong message to collectors and gallery owners. Calling it "Utopia, Ltd. . . . a colonial complex inflated to prodigious dimensions," satirist Tom Wolfe claims that the building signaled MoMA's intent to colonize the art market from the post-war spoils of Europe. Indeed, soon after the museum opened its doors, New York became the center of the art world.

MoMA paved the way for an even more radical challenge to museum architecture a few blocks away. In 1943 Frank Lloyd Wright was commissioned to design the Guggenheim, his first and only New York building. Reveling in the freedom given him by collector

In his design for the Guggenheim Museum, Frank Lloyd Wright stretched the definition of museum as far as it could go. Interior view of the museum's skylight photographed by David Heald. © The Solomon R. Guggenheim Foundation, New York.

Solomon Guggenheim, Wright stretched the definition of museum further than it had ever gone, even proposing a new name: "Archeseum." He eventually designed one of the most controversial museum buildings of all time: a daring helix containing a gigantic ramp that rises for three quarters of a mile toward a concrete dome punctuated by skylights. Visitors to the Guggenheim need make no tiring decisions about which direction to take; they have only one route to follow, either up or down the spiraling ramp. Wright fancifully envisioned the museum visit as a literary or cinematic narrative, and created a linear path of experience that would forever challenge the ambitions of curators. Completed just after the architect's death in 1959, the museum's exterior was as radical as its interior. The building maximized the possibilities of cast concrete to create a wholly plastic form, a sculptural break in the regular building wall of Fifth Avenue.

On its opening day, all eyes were on the Guggenheim. The building garnered tremendous media attention and became a pilgrimage site for architects. Architectural historian Spiro Kostof praised it as "a gift of pure architecture . . . the great swan song of a great architect." But critic Lewis Mumford declared it a "mischievous failure," and artists protested Wright's scheme almost as soon as it left the drawing board. Leave the art-making to the artists, they begged; give us a workable building. To this day, many artists and critics feel this corkscrew building with its tilted ramp compromises artwork on display. Discussed and debated at length because of the celebrity of its architect and audacity of its design, Wright's Guggenheim foreshadowed the era of star architects creating bold statements that were more about their egos than the art or the visitor.

The last of New York's triad of modern museum buildings was the Whitney Museum of American Art, completed in 1966 by Marcel Breuer, a Hungarian émigré. The museum had been founded in 1930, a year after the Metropolitan Museum of Art refused Gertrude Vanderbilt Whitney's offer to donate more than 500 works of American art. Breuer's building harmonized with the museum's mission to focus on changing exhibitions on the American scene and had a floor plan that resembled MoMA's: an open gallery shaped by movable wall panels and flexible lighting. Its granite-clad façade, however, was sculptural, composed of a series of stepped cantilevers and several oddly shaped windows. At ground level, a dry moat separated Madison Avenue's sidewalk from the lobby. Two decades after MoMA opened, architects were already uncomfortable with museum entrances that too closely met the city street.

With modernism taking hold of New York's museum culture, function dictated form in even the most traditional of buildings. In 1966 the Metropolitan Museum of Art embarked on an architectural experiment of its own that would alter the way Beaux-Arts museums used their classical facades: above its entrance, it hung a massive nylon banner advertising its exhibition of frescoes in a building-as-billboard approach.

Colleges and universities around the nation took advantage of the International Style. Some, like the Cranbrook Art Academy in Michigan, improved the look and feel of interior galleries. The Cranbrook Museum of Art, designed by Eliel Saarinen in 1942,

Above: Carpenter Center for the Visual Arts, Harvard University, designed in the International Style by Le Corbusier. Carpenter Center Archive: Eduard Sekler.

Below: Astronauts White and McDivitt learn about star navigation at the Morehead Planetarium, University of North Carolina, Chapel Hill. NASA; courtesy of the Morehead Planetarium.

featured state-of-the-art incandescent lighting that became a model for the field. Larger universities had experienced tremendous post-war growth, and campus planners were willing to test the tenets of modernism. Campus museums expanded during the post-war period to house researchers and growing collections. The museum planners put their faith in young architects, giving them their first chance to make original statements. In 1951 the Yale University Art Gallery became the first major commission for one of the nation's most important modern architects, Louis Kahn. Distinguished by a hollow concrete floor—which housed mechanical systems—the museum had windowless brick-and glass curtain walls that broke with Yale's conservative legacy of collegiate Gothic design. In 1959 31-year-old faculty member Fumihiko Maki designed his first building, the Steinberg Art Gallery for Washington University in St. Louis, a concrete and glass structure distinguished by its butterfly roof. Forty-five years later the university gave Maki the rare opportunity to update his youthful modernist vision.

Other universities commissioned buildings by the architects who had introduced the International Style to America. At Harvard, 76-year-old Le Corbusier realized his only U.S. building in 1963: the Carpenter Center for the Visual Arts, with floors raised on a columnar grid, a dominating ramp and a roof terrace. Philip Johnson's Sheldon Memorial Art Gallery at the University of Nebraska in Lincoln opened that same year. Characterized by symmetry and allusions to historical forms like the arch, the Sheldon was a harbinger for the postmodern epoch that would soon follow.

Science centers were intrigued by modern materials, such as concrete, and new ideas, such as structuring their spaces as flexible plants. For the most part, they were not as aesthetically successful as the art museums. Between 1951 and 1960, for example, Boston's Museum of Science expanded into a huge nondescript concrete box overlooking the Charles River. In 1957 Portland's Oregon Museum of Science and Industry moved into a utilitarian concrete building, fashioned mostly by contractors

Above: *Buckminster Fuller's geodesic Climatron at the Missouri Botanical Garden. © 2005, Missouri Botanical Garden Archives.*

Below: *Visitors to "Dinosphere" at the Children's Museum of Indianapolis experience a sound-and-light effects show that depicts morning, afternoon and night in the Cretaceous period. The Children's Museum of Indianapolis/A. Overstreet.*

and volunteers from labor unions. Some science centers, however, were inspired works of modern architecture. Built as part of Seattle's 1962 Century 21 Exposition, the Pacific Science Center was fashioned as a graceful, airy structure with stylized arches and a concrete plaza with a fountain. Its young architect, Minora Yamasaki, would achieve fame as the designer of the World Trade Center towers in New York.

The launching of *Sputnik* in 1957 inspired a spate of modern planetariums at colleges such as St. John's College in Annapolis and the University of Nevada in Reno and in cities such as Miami and Dayton. As buildings, planetariums had advanced a long way from Max Adler's Chicago treasure. Modern ones were so unique in their design and functioning that, in at least one instance, their controlled interior settings served as training grounds for astronauts. In 1960 the seven original *Mercury* astronauts learned star navigation indoors at the Morehead Planetarium at the University of North Carolina in Chapel Hill.

Modern architects' ability to manipulate lighting, climate and other aspects of nature also appealed to institutions with living collections. New possibilities opened up for botanic gardens in 1960 when the Missouri Botanical Garden in St. Louis opened a Buckminster Fuller geodesic Climatron, the world's first climate-controlled display greenhouse. Zoos entered the "disinfectant era," experimenting with outdoor concrete and steel, and pale green glazed tile structures that were thought to be more hygienic for animals.

Museum staff reveled in the joys of hygiene and modernization. Up-to-date technologies for plumbing, atmospheric control and lighting promised to make their buildings cleaner and more functional. Humming ventilation systems and sleeker materials promised to end the era of stuffy and dusty exhibit halls. Even Frank Lloyd Wright took to heart the American obsession with ridding the world of germs. He proposed a suction mat system at the entrance of the Guggenheim that would clean patrons' clothes and shoes of loose dirt, all the better to protect the artwork.

Unfortunately, these visions were far beyond the means of most institutions, especially those housed in antiquated structures never intended to be museums. Many buildings were in dreadful

condition, endangering collections. Electrical systems were obsolete. Fire prevention was close to impossible. Many that tried to modernize faced up-hill battles and public outcry against the aesthetic of modern architecture. Government agencies and local residents often took issue with innovative ideas that clashed with surrounding buildings.

The Children's Museum of Indianapolis's late 1940s' run-in with zoning authorities and citizens over a proposed addition is typical of museums' struggles to modernize. On donated space in a leafy upper-class part of Indianapolis, architect Kurt Vonnegut (the novelist's father) proposed a "clean modernistic building" with wide bands of glass block to admit natural light into a gallery and highlight a reproduction of a ground sloth skeleton. Yet, residents protested that such a design would "ruin the neighborhood." Vonnegut's vision was realized when the museum decided to build in the modern style in a less fussy neighborhood. It would go on to become one of the finest children's museums in the world. Elsewhere, citizens felt that they had to protect parkland from the travesties of modern buildings. In 1962, picketers took to the streets of Chicago, calling the Art Institute's modernist addition ugly and demanding the reinstallation of a Beaux-Arts fountain removed for the expansion. Even artists expressed antipathy toward buildings meant to house their masterpieces. Edward Ruscha's mid-1960s painting *The Los Angeles County Museum on Fire* captured many citizens' fantasies of arson for the cold modernist 1964 building.

The most pressing problem facing modernization, however, was not public outcry; it was lack of money. Thankfully, relief was in sight. During the 1960s, changes in federal funding policies channeled money into museums. Half a century after the roaring '20s, museums found themselves once again in a building frenzy. The building boom came in the knick of time: since the end of World War II annual museum attendance had soared to well over 200 million visitors.

With new sources of money and a cadre of trained modern architects at their disposal, museums went on a building spree. The 1970s and '80s saw the establishment of more than 3,200 new museums, the expansion or renovation of almost three-fifths of the existing institutions and nearly 2 million acres added to the museum landscape. Naturally, growth of this magnitude transformed museum buildings as well as their locales. "The museum has become, not only on campus[es] but everywhere, the architectural laboratory of our time," declared *New York Times* architecture critic Paul Goldberger.

Inspired by Wright's Guggenheim and campus museum projects, architects, to borrow a phrase from the times, "did their own thing." Like clothing trends of the 1970s, the resulting museums tended toward the gaudy and clunky, with occasional veers toward brutalism and a few rare nods to elegance. In 1971 Gio Ponti fashioned a 28-sided, grey-tiled structure for the Denver Art Museum. Set in the city's civic center, this fortress-like building was so austere that unsuspecting tourists often mistook it for a prison tower. Houston, a rising metropolis in the heyday of the oil economy, was the site of Gunnar Birkerts's 1972 airplane-hangar-like Museum of Contemporary Art. The interior space was so vast that painters were asked to work on larger canvases so their work would fit the architecture. Elemental geometries inspired Gordon Bunshaft's 1974 Hirshhorn Museum, part of the Smithsonian Institution in Washington, D.C., and across the Mall from the staid National Gallery of Art. Bunshaft believed he could improve on the Guggenheim, declaring that Wright's creation was "no more a museum than I am Napoleon." He fashioned a cylindrical building that rose on concrete piers and featured an interior courtyard in the round. When it opened, critics called it a "defensive pillbox" that had no business housing an art collection.

Crowd control is an issue at popular museums such as the National Air and Space Museum. Photo by Eric Long/OIPP, National Air and Space Museum, Smithsonian Institution, image #SI2005-176.

As an antidote to the now-commonplace use of artificial light, in 1972 Louis Kahn fashioned the Kimbell Art Museum in Fort Worth, Tex.—considered by many architects to be a masterpiece of modern architecture. Its features include a curved concrete vault to filter light through the top of the building and distribute it via stainless steel reflectors. The light streams into small comfortable galleries creating an intimate, richly lit experience with artwork.

Whether their designs were adored or panned, these early 1970s buildings established that museums outside New York could attract attention through bold modern designs. And people flocked to them. After the ribbon was cut at the Smithsonian's National Museum of Air and Space in Washington, D.C., in 1976, for example, more than 1 million people came through the doors in the first month alone. Crowd control was one logistical problem that architects could not ignore. Philip Johnson, using a somewhat unflattering simile, pleaded for large orientation spaces:

> The public, upon entering a museum, and choosing one of six or seven things to do, requires space, like a dog who upon entering a room, will sniff in one or two circumambulations of the room and will at last coil himself in one particular spot. I assure you, orientation space is not wasted.

Other architects were influenced by a new building type sprouting throughout the country—the indoor shopping mall, whose features could be adapted to museums. Institutions began to add atriums to give a sense of roominess, interior escalators to move crowds efficiently and large comfortable eateries to feed the masses. These features were especially attractive to older museums that were expanding. I. M. Pei's 1978 triangular East Wing addition to the National Gallery of Art added an enormous underground shopping and eating concourse. Likewise, Cesar Pelli's 1984 MoMA gallery expansion doubled exhibition space, added an interior escalator, expanded the lobby and cafeterias and included a light-filled glass atrium.

The Museum of Modern Art's 1984 expansion project included another innovation: a neighboring 52-story condominium complex. In an elaborate financial scheme and through the aegis of a trust, MoMA sold its air rights to a developer and generated funds out of the thin air above its building. Three entities profited from the deal. The developer sold the condos. MoMA raised funds for a larger museum. The city gained a private upscale housing development that would change the tenor (and tax base) of the street. MoMA, a pioneer in seeing the link between a museum's building and the commercial life of a downtown, had cut one of the most savvy real-estate deals ever dreamed up by a museum.

By the 1980s it was far more expedient to erect a 52-story building than to expand buildings further into urban parks. With increased environmental consciousness, citizen's groups lobbied against encroaching upon precious green space. Even the powerful Metropolitan Museum of Art faced intense public and legal battles over its 1970s expansions. While the Met was able to grab more parkland to build a wing for the Temple of Dendur, a first-century Roman-Egyptian temple, its building plate was fixed forever: no more expansions into Central Park. To gain more room, many museums adopted a solution similar to the one used by the National Gallery of Art; they put new facilities underground. Some, such as the Brooklyn Children's Museum (BCM), had no choice but to submerge their entire structures.

Founded in 1899, the world's first children's museum finally built a permanent home in 1977. To provide a large continuous space that did not destroy its Brower Park location, the architects built an entire museum underground. Visitors enter via an old trolley kiosk and descend a 180-foot ramp through four floors of colorful exhibits.

What if a museum couldn't find a park to build on (or under)? In the 1970s the Oakland Museum of California devised an innovative solution. The city decided to combine its early 20th-century parkland museums of art, history and the natural sciences into a four-block lot at the edge of downtown. Architect Kevin Roche and landscape architect Dan Kiley created a tiered concrete structure that merged the three museums into one building with five separate entrances that could be approached, up or down stairs, from every direction in the city, or through a parking garage. Flipping the old idea of museum-in-a-park topsy-turvy, they landscaped a park into and onto the museum, fashioning verdant rooftop terraces with splendid views of the Oakland Hills.

Just as museums once added to the luster of urban parks (and not coincidentally to the real-estate values of surrounding neighborhoods), government planning agencies began to see museums as a means for revitalizing faltering inner cities. In the 1970s, older, industrial cities were in dire straits, due to a loss of population and tax revenue to outlying suburbs. Higher-end stores and hotels were leaving the downtown, only to be replaced with parking lots and marginal commerce. Industrial buildings were boarded up. Yet museums still were drawing crowds into the very cities whose populations were decreasing. Planners saw that museum building projects had the potential to inject life into moribund downtowns. Thus began the era of "public/private partnerships" in support of museum building.

In 1977 the city of Dallas established the first downtown arts district in the nation. The Dallas Museum of Art (DMA), founded in 1903, purchased nine acres in a depressed section of the city; this site grew to become a 60-acre arts district of theaters, concert halls and other cultural organizations. The DMA aimed not just to spur economic revitalization but to open its doors to a greater cross-section of the population—not just the elite, but residents from all walks of life. As then-DMA Director Harry Parker noted, "the location is geographically neutral and belongs equally to citizens in all of the city's neighborhoods."

As major museums built new downtown structures, grassroots organizations also were instrumental in revitalization efforts, spreading into abandoned storefronts, warehouses and railroad depots. Alternative artists' spaces, fortified by support from the National Endowment for the Arts, opened up in rough parts of cities such as New Orleans, Atlanta and the Bronx. Transportation museums moved into abandoned railroad depots in smaller communities such as Pendleton, Oreg., Livingston, Mont., and Green Bay, Wis.

Children's museums also were drawn to such "wastelands." For the first 60 years of its life, the Boston Children's Museum was housed in a Victorian mansion in a comfortable middle-class neighborhood. In 1979 the museum relocated to a former wool warehouse in Fort Point, a largely abandoned waterfront area near Boston's downtown. The area was renamed "Museum Wharf." The motivation for the move mirrored DMA's. Fort Point borders South Boston, a neighborhood notorious for its stand against forced integration and school busing in the mid-1970s. Director Michael Spock recognized that by moving to a "neutral zone," the museum could serve as a social catalyst and bring children together in a city rife with racial and class tensions. The experiment paid off. The museum expanded its multicultural programs and exhibitions. Its facility, once in a neglected part of town, now sits among hotels, condominiums and a convention center. In the 1980s and '90s other children's museums would follow suit, setting up shop in abandoned downtown department stores, warehouses and recreation centers throughout the nation—and becoming anchors of redevelopment efforts.

Although location decisions often were based on community needs and a desire to serve local residents, business leaders also were interested in pulling in tourist dollars. As the manufacturing economy declined, the tourist economy grew. To attract this market, cities turned obsolete areas, such as ports or warehouse districts, into themed sightseeing districts. Planners and business leaders argued that museums could benefit the tourism economy by distinguishing regions from one another and championing local customs in a world where different cities were all starting to look the same. Though every festival hall seemed to feature the same franchises, museums always, presumably, would be unique.

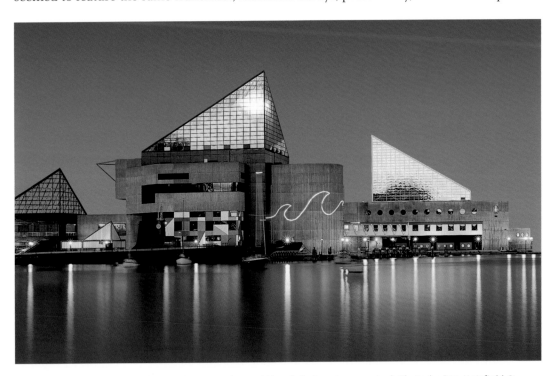

The National Aquarium in Baltimore, a cornerstone of the city's downtown revival. Photo by Ron Haisfield ©
National Aquarium in Baltimore.

San Diego's Reuben H. Fleet Science Center was the first museum to mold its architecture to fit the technical requirements of large-format film. Photo provided by the Reuben H. Fleet Science Center.

They would be able to attract "cultural tourists," travelers who planned their itineraries around historic sites, educational activities and the arts. Appealing to large numbers of people, museums were a logical anchor for the revitalized zones.

One of the first cities to act on this logic was Baltimore. By the 1970s the city was a rustbelt wasteland. Its downtown was sagging; its neighborhoods were depopulating; its inner harbor was blighted. Business and civic leaders sought to pump up the city by creating a tourist zone in the inner harbor that would eventually include the Harborplace festival market and the Camden Yards baseball park. But the first major piece of the revitalization effort was a museum. In 1976 the Maryland Science Center moved from an old library to a brand-new red-brick building in the middle of the inner harbor. It was followed in 1981 by the National Aquarium, designed by Peter Chermayeff, which soon became the largest paid tourist attraction in the state. However, a multi-million-dollar renovation of the Baltimore City Life Museums resulted in failure. The museum had racked up too much debt and couldn't support its expansion, which opened in 1996 and closed a year later.

Even so, the media praised Baltimore for its remarkable comeback, and soon other communities looked to the economic potential of large-scale museum projects, especially aquariums and science centers. Such projects weren't limited to large urban areas. In 1984, marine biologists and philanthropists founded the Monterey Bay Aquarium on the site of a dilapidated sardine and squid cannery facing the Pacific Ocean, sparking a remarkable economic turnaround for the small California coastal community. All told, between 1960 and 2001, 116 cities developed cultural districts to serve their citizens, attract tourists and revitalize their communities. Most of these districts contained museums.

At the same time, science centers invested in a new kind of attraction to liven up their images and attract visitor dollars: large-format film. The hope was that the new Omnimax and IMAX films, which projected jaw-dropping and enormous images of natural phenomena, would encourage audiences to flock indoors to gain a new experience of the great outdoors. However, unlike the motion pictures of the 1920s, the technical extravaganzas of the 1970s did not inspire creative architecture. Starting in 1973 with the Reuben H. Fleet Science Center in San Diego, science centers across the country altered their facilities to fit the technical requirements of large-format film—often pasting on bulbous domed concrete theaters that clashed with the original buildings.

It is fitting to close this section with a discussion of high modernism and its reshaping of urban America in Atlanta. By the 1970s the city had long risen from the ashes of the Civil War and become a thriving airport hub and media center. The High Museum of Art, designed by Richard Meier, put the cultural icing on the cake when it opened in 1983. Although the city possesses bountiful greenery, the museum's planners chose a midtown site connected to plans for public transit, pedestrian access, a cultural district and commercial development. Brought in to design a museum that would stand out, Meier placed dramatic ramps, a direct riff on Wright's Guggenheim, around a high atrium.

This crystalline modernist triumph would open just as modern architecture was going out of favor. Starting in the late 1970s, a broad cultural transformation that would greatly influence architecture was taking hold in other camps. Championed by cultural theorists and linguists in the classroom and progressive architects in the studio, this movement was called postmodernism.

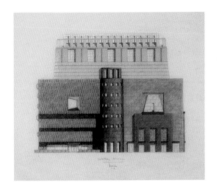
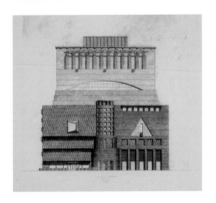
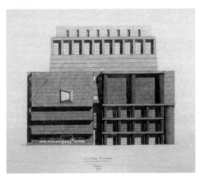

"I am for the richness of meaning rather than clarity of meaning.

—ARCHITECT ROBERT **VENTURI**, 1966

The shift from the Beaux-Arts to the modern style had been high drama, a clash between a longing for the past and a pragmatic approach to the present. But by the 1980s, postmodern museum architects were responding to a different kind of tension: new attitudes to building set against the backdrop of heightened demands from the marketplace. Among theorists and academics at architecture schools, modernism was considered too doctrinaire and insensitive to both its surroundings and contemporary life. Urban renewal efforts based on modernist principles had leveled whole districts of American cities; too many beloved older buildings had been demolished. The sleek and sober buildings that had replaced them fell out of favor. If modernism was epitomized by Mies van der Rohe's dictum, "less is more," Robert Venturi struck the nerve of the times when he chimed, "less is a bore." Postmodernism resurrected ornament, whimsy and more attention to popular taste. America's architectural climate became pluralistic and increasingly wedded to wthe marketplace.

Completed in 1984, the Neue Staatsgallerie in Stuttgart, Germany is considered the first notable postmodern museum. Architect James Stirling incorporated warm-colored stone, classical elements such as architraves and pediments and historical approaches to museum design—including those of Karl Friedrich Schinkel and Frank Lloyd

Designer Michael Graves envisioned a postmodern expansion for the Whitney Museum of American Art. The museum's board disagreed. Photo courtesy of Michael Graves & Associates.

Wright. His building opened the floodgates to an eclectic range of museum ventures, some based largely on the past, others catering blithely to consumer tastes and still others descending into theoretical puzzles.

By contrast, the first postmodern museum in the United States was never actually built. During the late 1980s the Whitney hired Michael Graves to design an addition. Known for his idiosyncratic Portland Building in Oregon, Graves—later Target's in-house designer of teakettles, toasters and other kitchen utensils—was among the flashiest of the postmodernists. For the Whitney, he drew up a companion building, at exactly the same scale as the existing one, but using completely different shapes. Atop both structures, he proposed a clashing form akin to the gigantic toy structures then popular at F.A.O. Schwarz. The Whitney's board rejected the project.

In the early 1990s the architectural firm of Venturi, Scott Brown and Associates put American postmodernism into museum practice. Famed for their 1971 manifesto, *Learning from Las Vegas*, Robert Venturi and Denise Scott Brown realized that most Americans spent their lives on the go, often seeing buildings from automobiles, and that architectural messages were communicated largely through signs. They argued for functional, boxy buildings covered by decoration, signage or anything that would attract the mobile public. When it came to museums, Venturi and Scott Brown turned to classical symbols to get people's attention. Despite 50 years of modernism, weren't most museums still essentially viewed as palaces and temples?

The architects put these ideas into their 1991 design for the Seattle Art Museum (SAM), which 10 years earlier had moved from the city's Volunteer Park to the edge of its downtown area. Creating what has been called "a seriously whimsical building," Venturi and Scott Brown embellished SAM with stylized historical icons. Green, black and mustard leaves crown squat steel columns and arches. The firm then

Top left: *The "seriously whimsical" Seattle Art Museum, designed by Robert Venturi and Denise Scott Brown. Photo by Susan Dirk. Courtesy of the Seattle Art Museum.*

Above: *The kid-oriented design of the Children's Museum of Houston features rainbow-colored arches and cartoon-like "caryakids."*

punned on the monumental staircases of yore, creating an interior flight of steps, visible to the outside through plate glass. "We want [the museum] to be pretty," Robert Venturi commented, "and appeal to children."

In 1992 the Children's Museum of Houston took Venturi at his word. While Brooklyn's children's museum burrowed underground, the booming metropolis of Houston wanted its children's museum to stand high. Driving on Binz or Ewing Streets, it is impossible to miss the building: a buoyant orange and yellow shed with oversized columns, kitschy rainbow-colored arches and bright cartoon-like "caryakids." By distorting traditional symbols from the adult world into giant colorful toys, the architects cracked a wry joke on what it meant to be a museum in the 1990s.

In the sardonic atmosphere of post-modernism, it was now possible to design a museum to test a theory. This was precisely the approach taken by Peter Eisenman. A recognized guru of postmodern architectural theory, Eisenman never had designed a major building until Ohio State University hired him in the 1980s to create the Wexner Center for the Visual Arts on its campus in Columbus. Opposed to modernism, but not content to enliven buildings with garish colors and oversized ornaments, Eisenman created an art center modeled on theoretical ideas about deconstructing the accepted "language" of a building. At the Wexner Center—completed in 1989—he played off the grids of the city of Columbus and the university campus as well as the memory of a demolished state armory building that had once occupied the site. The resulting building sits uncomfortably at the very point that the grids of "town and gown" intersect, framed by an extruded grid of white metal. A portion of the armory is rebuilt as a fake, abstracted ruin. The complicated building jars and confuses its visitors as they walk along a ramp or step via "teensy, narrow stairways" into irregularly shaped galleries (some underground). Eisenman later admitted that his theoretical exercise was mostly an excuse to play with his own ideas about architecture: "I do my work for me—there are no other people."

As postmodernists played with classical symbols and theoreticians played with their own egos, museum leaders sought to solve a more practical problem: meeting the needs and desires of visitors and competing in the marketplace. With government funds waning, marketers and educators were beginning to reach out to visitors, as well as non-visitors, to see what they wanted from museums. As Ohio State University (OSU) was constructing a building that would become a landmark of elite postmodern architecture, an OSU researcher was conducting a landmark study that would challenge museums to pay closer attention to the masses. In the early 1980s, researcher Marilyn Hood studied Toledo, Ohio, residents who chose not to visit that city's art museum. She found that "museum non-goers" valued almost the antithesis of postmodernism: comfortable spaces, familiar surroundings and social interaction. She cautioned museums that if they wanted people to come, they needed to create more inviting experiences and spaces. A 1987 Getty Trust study of people who visited the nation's 11 largest art museums reached the same conclusion. It came as a shock to many in the field that a great many people reported feeling disoriented, intimidated and embarrassed in art museums. "I felt like I was rat in a maze," reported one visitor, capturing the feelings of many.

What did the public want from its museums? Were museums primarily preservers and exhibiters of precious artifacts from the past? Or were they also active educational centers? Were museums anchors for urban transformation and community relations? Or were they sophisticated social centers for eating, shopping and cavorting? What about those commercial forces that had grown more and more influential in setting the direction for museums? Could architects juggle all these diverging identities and come up with a cohesive and memorable building? Could they create buildings that communicated a weighty sense of culture, but at the same time made a bold visual statement and accommodated moneymaking activities? Architect Frank Gehry offered this answer: "The biggest problem is that there is no consensus on what a museum is and what the needs of the museum are."

With these questions looming, museum construction lurched into overdrive. The 1990s unleashed one of the greatest economic booms in American history, driven by emerging digital technologies. Some experts fretted that the Internet—with its stream of information and imagery—would erode people's desire to visit museum buildings. But the public voted with its feet. In 1998 attendance at American museums climbed to an estimated 845 million, more than three times the U.S. population. Museums took advantage of fat economic times to build and renovate at the feverish pace of the 1920s. Nearly every significant museum in the country initiated a capital renovation project in the 1990s, and several urban redevelopment zones added a new museum. In total, a new museum building, addition or renovation opened roughly every 15 days.

Renovation was imperative because modern and even postmodern buildings had aged quickly. Experimental use of light and concrete unleashed conservation nightmares. The Kimbell's streaming natural light threatened artwork. The Oakland Museum's roof-top garden and the Wexner's fabled grid structures leaked water into galleries. The pristine white High Museum was hard to clean. The Denver Art Museum was out of space, as collections and educational programs had grown larger than anyone could have imagined. For others, new departments such as information technology ate up valuable square footage. Entries and exits needed to comply with the 1990 Americans for Disabilities Act (ADA). Increased use by children called for school bus drop-off areas, classroom space and better restrooms. And in some cases, modern buildings had never really functioned all that well, since they were more tied to elaborate mechanisms for wooing donors than to programmatic needs.

As important, museums were becoming cities unto themselves, with their own micro-economies. Despite the internal debates about supporting education, collections and community outreach, the entrepreneurial spirit of the times dictated how new buildings were designed and space was allocated. Making money to cover the rising costs of operations increasingly became the priority. In some cases, collections were moved off-site and staff squeezed into increasingly smaller cubicles. In planning for new museums, prime interior square footage went to restaurants, gift shops and spaces for special events.

"Good things don't end in –eum. They end in –mania or –teria."

—CARTOON CHARACTER HOMER J. **SIMPSON**, 2000

In the late 1960s the Milwaukee Public Museum opened "Piazzo del Museo," an outdoor summer café with white and pink umbrellas, in the only space available—the roof of the museum's parking garage. At that time, most museum food generally was dished out in basement eateries or restaurants restricted to members. But by the 1980s the tables had turned. Across the country, museum food service was no longer a fringe activity or a service for members; it was a profit center. Food franchises saw great potential in cultural tourists, particularly hungry families. McDonald's leased space in the Boston Children's Museum; Pizza Hut came to the National Aquarium in Baltimore.

Art museums recognized that serving cafeteria fare was incongruous with the viewing of fine art. In 1982 the National Gallery of Art (NGA) established upscale sit-down service

Interior view, bridge, San Francisco Museum of Modern Art; the 1995 building was designed by Mario Botta. © San Francisco Museum of Modern Art, photo by Richard Barnes.

on its main floor. Food offerings often aligned with gallery offerings; during an exhibition of 19th-century paintings from Berlin, for example, NGA served Linzer torte and German beer and wine. By the 1990s adding luster to America's newfound palate for cappuccino and lattés, museums were opening Starbucks-like cafes and gourmet establishments. One could meet for coffee or a full meal and never set foot in the galleries. Some art museum restaurants—such as D'Amico & Sons at the Minneapolis Institute of Arts, Palette's at the Denver Art Museum and Patinette at the Los Angeles Museum of Contemporary Art—became gourmet destinations, complete with cookbooks offered for sale. Museums hired celebrity chefs and designed spectacular restaurant spaces that took advantage of dramatic views. The Adler Planetarium's 1990s re-do, for example, gave its prime lakefront view to its restaurant rather than its programs or exhibits. And no wonder: Americans' restaurant spending more than tripled between 1980 and 2000, from $120 billion to $376 billion. Museums sought to get a piece of the economic pie.

America's favorite leisure time activity, however, is not eating but shopping. And by the 1990s museums were hiring retail professionals to help them bring stores out of the basement and into locations that would maximize the bottom line. Retailers almost unanimously blamed architects for not understanding the museum store's role. They advocated for prime spaces at museum exits that emulated themed stores like Niketown and Pottery Barn. They envisioned mini-department stores complete with branded product lines and carefully planned retail shelving and display space. They encouraged architects to create spaces accessible to nonmuseum-going customers who could bypass the admissions gate and exhibits in favor of shopping. Like their restaurant counterparts, these stores have become state-of-the-art destinations in and of themselves, filled with carefully selected mission-related merchandise.

New museums seized upon retail opportunities. In 1995, almost as soon as the San Francisco Museum of Modern Art (SFMOMA) opened its gift shop with a separate entrance at street-level, it was raking in more dollars per square foot than any other retail space in the city. After all, who could resist its exclusive shakable fog-globe desk ornament or custom-made jewelry? Today, the doors of the SFMOMA store are open more hours than the museum galleries. When planning its restoration, the Heard Museum in Phoenix constructed a large and prominent shop of Native American crafts. The Racine Art Museum in Wisconsin went even further. Understanding that shopping opportunities are a draw in and of themselves, the museum inaugurated a street-front store months before unveiling its pristine 2003 building.

A museum certainly doesn't need a spanking new building to establish a spanking new store. Museums located in historic buildings redesigned stores to reflect their collections or their architectural style. In 2000 the Bergston-Mahler Museum in Neenah, Wis.—known for its collection of glass paperweights—created a dazzling Tiffany's-like showroom of glass products. Mystic Seaport's store incorporates materials, such as dark mahogany, that reflect the museum's nautical theme. Some museums made money by reproducing images of their buildings onto postcards, refrigerator magnets and desk ornaments, and the Guggenheim even created ceramic teapots shaped like Frank Lloyd Wright's building. How far museums had come from their earliest days in urban parks, purposefully removed from the temptations of commerce.

After-hours special events also influenced museum architecture; in this case, architectural demands were not add-ons but integrated into the core design of the building. Of course, museums always have used their grand buildings to host events for boards, patrons and even, on occasion, the public. On New Year's Eve 1917, for example, the Minneapolis Institute of Arts threw what was perhaps the nation's first public museum costume ball. Still, it wasn't until 1974 that the Art Institute of Chicago became the first museum to develop a formal program to rent space to other organizations. Around the same time,

COSI (Center of Science and Industry) in Columbus, Ohio, pioneered overnight "camp-ins," turning its interior into a veritable campground and hotel. By the 1990s museums were "hot" spots for all kinds of one-shot events that stretched the traditional use of their buildings: weddings, corporate events, charity balls, bar mitzvahs, birthday parties, festivals, movie shoots and even raves, advertised through the Internet.

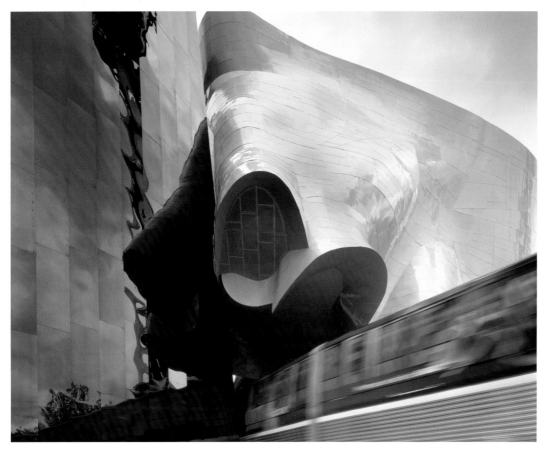

As designed by Frank Gehry, the Experience Music Project's building has a rock-and-roll feel, inside and out.
© Experience Music Project, Seattle. Photo by Lara Swimmer.

Curators and conservators protested; partying in the galleries put precious objects in grave danger. Reports of damage from caterers and rambunctious revelers were common. The solution was not to put an end to this very profitable function, but to design dramatic gathering spaces for special events. Museum spaces now needed to adapt to caterers, dance bands, performers and movie crews, and yet be special enough to attract such rentals. Some museums configured their entire designs around high-ticket rentals. COPIA, the Center for Wine, Food and the Arts in Napa, Calif., opened in 2001 with a lobby for functions that was larger than its exhibit hall. The sizzle was starting to become more important than the beef.

The identification of museums with their most famous [paintings] . . . is being replaced by an association with their high profile architects.

—ARCHITECTURE CRITIC VICTORIA **NEWHOUSE,** 1999

Another way to add sizzle was to hire a celebrity architect to design a "look-at-me" building. Once a museum in-and-of-itself added to the luster of a city; now a famous architect was as important as a workable building, perhaps more so. In 1993 the University of Minnesota gave emerging Los Angeles architect Frank Gehry license to experiment with his design philosophy of deconstructivism. The result was the shimmering Weisman Art Museum on its Minneapolis campus. Four years later, Gehry's billowing titanium spaceship of a Guggenheim Museum opened on the larger stage of Bilbao, Spain. It was a "wow" of a building, as iconic and recognizable as the St. Louis Arch or the Golden Gate Bridge. Architecturally, Gehry had broken new ground, using a sophisticated computer program to engineer previously unimagined shapes and forms. As they had with Wright's Guggenheim, the press had a ball writing about Gehry's creation. *New York Times* critic Herbert Muschamp went so far as to compare it to Marilyn Monroe: "voluptuous, emotional, intuitive, exhibitionist." The building was also an economic triumph, generating $500 million for the Spanish city in its first three years. Like Chicago's late 19th-century museums, Guggenheim Bilbao's architecture was more significant than its collections. Like the cathedrals of yore, it became a pilgrimage site for cultural tourists and a harbinger of a phenomenon now called "the Bilbao effect" or "architourism."

Suddenly everyone wanted a "Gehry." Even before Guggenheim Bilbao was finished, Paul Allen, a collector of Jimi Hendrix memorabilia and co-founder of Microsoft, had commissioned the architect to design the Experience Music Project, a rock-and roll museum in Seattle. In a synergy between celebrity architect, technology guru and mythic

Two views of the Milwaukee Art Museum, designed by Santiago Calatrava and completed in 2001: the exterior bridge (left) and the atrium (right). Courtesy of the Milwaukee Art Museum. Photo by Timothy Hursley.

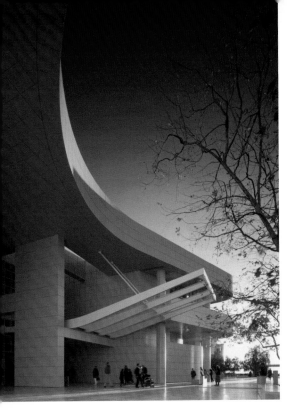

dead rock star, Gehry delivered a striking guitar-like building, which opened in 1999. Its bulging shapes are sheathed in gold, silver and purple stainless steel and in red and blue aluminum shingles. Critics called it an "upside-down jello mold."

In 1997, after 14 years in the making, the most expensive museum in American history—costing more than $1 billion—opened atop a private hillside park overlooking a heavily traveled freeway. The Getty Museum, designed by Richard Meier, borrowed an idea from universities and research centers: the museum as a campus. Not only does the 24-acre complex contain a research center and a state-of-the-art conservation institute, the museum itself is spread over several buildings. The campus affords stunning views, when the air is clear. Indeed, the Getty's manifold viewpoints of Los Angeles are so spectacular that the museum's site rivals its collection.

The 1995 building for San Francisco's Museum of Modern Art epitomized what a striking work of architecture could do for a museum and a city. Previously housed in cramped quarters within a War Memorial building, the new museum joined the ranks of America's top contemporary art museums. Mario Botta's design helped draw in the crowds and created a landmark destination. Because its central tower was an unusual sliced cylinder, people readily remembered the building. Architecture became logo.

Known for his expressive bridges and train-stations, architect Santiago Calatrava brought "high-"design to his addition to the Milwaukee Art Museum, which was completed in 2001. From a distance, the building looks like a bird alighting, the white concrete and glass infrastructure soaring to the sky and establishing a distinctive icon for the Milwaukee skyline. In fact, the museum's geometries were featured in a national ad campaign for the 2004 Toyota Solara, with the tag line "you can't go anywhere without being noticed." Not every city, however, wanted its art museum noticed. In 1999 the Nelson-Atkins Museum of Art in Kansas City chose Steven Holl to design a low-key addition to its 1933 Beaux-Arts building. Holl's building, scheduled to be completed in 2007, adds artistic luster to the Nelson-Atkins without overwhelming its traditions. Likewise, the Joslyn Art Museum in Omaha commissioned British "starchitect" Sir Norman Foster to design a fortress-like window-less addition, built with the same pink marble as its original art deco building.

In the past, architectural commissions had been debated primarily in boardrooms. But the 1990s saw wider involvement from the public, who tried to tone down museums' attempts to make bold statements. Often blaming the "arrogant architect," citizens groups filed lawsuits against projects they considered outlandish. They battled Richard Meier and the Getty over the white hue of the stone he originally proposed and the possibility that museum patrons could peer into their homes from the hilltop location. Eventually, Meier chose beige travertine, and the city planted view-blocking trees and vines around the museum. From 1999 to 2004, citizens groups in San Francisco filed multiple lawsuits against the de Young Museum in Golden Gate Park to reduce the height of a tower, intended to house educational programs. Eventually, the judge fined the plaintiffs for slowing down the project with one frivolous suit after another. In 2005 the stunning new de Young, designed by the Swiss firm Herzog and de Meuron, opened to widespread acclaim.

As museums battled to build, some trustees battled their "starchitects," firing them from commissions—at the Jewish Museum in San Francisco; the Blanton Museum at the University of Texas in Austin; the Smithsonian's National Museum of the American Indian in Washington, D.C., to name a few—and adding even more fervor to headlines. Museums had become central to the civic fabric of a community, and the building process had become more politicized than ever. Were museum projects spiraling out of control? Had the glitz gone too far? Had collections and exhibitions been compromised as museums sought greater sizzle? In 2002 Franklin W. Robinson, director of the Herbert F. Johnson Museum of Art at Cornell University, observed that building projects are seductive and "dangerous and there are other ways to serve one's institution and community. . . . I say no more buildings!"

Almost as if to prove Robinson's point, within a year, the Bellevue Art Museum in a suburb of Seattle became perhaps the first U.S. museum to close down a new building, this one designed by Stephen Holl. The museum had been established in a former funeral parlor, perhaps an unfortunate foreboding of what was to come. In 2001 it reopened a swanky, expensive, high-tech, celebrity-designed building. But the local community hated the building and stayed away in droves, bringing the museum to the brink of financial collapse within two years of the ribbon-cutting ceremony. The board is slowly reestablishing the museum.

Still, the seduction of building is hard to resist. Despite an industry-wide economic downturn in the early 2000s that resulted in significant layoffs and cutbacks in museums across the country, the building frenzy continued with great optimism. In December 2001, just two months after the terrorist attacks, New York opened an elegant new American Folk Art Museum by architects Billie Tsien and Tod Williams, featuring a soaring central stairwell in the small footprint of a 40-foot-wide building. Three years later, MoMA's mega-renovation project—an $800-million, 650,000-square-foot addition designed by Japanese architect Yoshio Taniguchi—reopened to great fanfare. Overall, there were more than 70 major building projects in the works nationally, totaling billions of dollars. Cities continued to peg their hopes on matching a high-profile architect with an ambitious fund-raising campaign. In Atlanta, the High Museum of Art, citing phenomenal growth of both attendance and collections, unveiled a Renzo Piano design for an $85-million construction project. The Telfair Museum of Art in Savannah, Ga., chose Israeli architect Moshe Safdie and commenced the largest fund-raising campaign in the city's history. Ohio's Akron Art Museum hired architectural firm Coop Himmelb(l)au to handle its planned $30-million upgrade. The Institute of Contemporary Art broke ground for its move from downtown Boston to the wharf area near the Children's Museum. And the list goes on, as communities continue to peg their hopes on the flourishing spirit of museums.

A discussion of museum architecture at the start of the 21st century would not be complete without noting the meeting of two odd bedfellows: museums and casinos. In the 1990s these institutions began to mix, toward different ends, in Las Vegas and on American Indian reservations.

The Museum at Warm Springs was one of the first designed to harmonize with the landscape and with native traditions. Courtesy of the Museum at Warm Springs, Warm Springs, Oreg.

At the time, Las Vegas was America's fastest growing city, seeking to change its sinful image to appeal to families and cultural tourists. The city and county invested in a children's museum, a history museum, a natural history museum, displays of aviation history at its airport and a museum that showcased the historical neon signs that had put Las Vegas on the cultural map. One of the most flamboyant, tourist-oriented museums was the Liberace Museum, designed by the firm Leo A Daly. It boasted a huge, outdoor, light-studded portrait of its namesake (bedecked in a sequined tuxedo), a tower crowned with a neon keyboard and an outer wall studded with musical scores. With three incongruous partners—the Hermitage of Russia, the Kunsthistorisches Museum of Austria and the Venetian Casino Resort—in 2001 the Guggenheim opened a flashy Vegas branch, designed by Rem Koolhaus and displaying everything from Titians to high-tech racing bikes. In flyers distributed all over Vegas, the museum billed itself as the "Guggenheim Experience at the Venetian. . . sensationally sensual, showy, sexy, dynamic and dreamy." The over-the-top experiment failed, however, and part of the museum closed down within two years.

As Vegas was going museum, American Indian nations were going casino. The 1988 National Gaming Act permitted federally recognized tribes to run casinos on reservation lands. Soon these gaming establishments were generating tens of billions of dollars—providing both a financial shot in the arm for one of America's most economically disadvantaged populations and a means for reinvigorating cultural traditions. American Indians had long been concerned with how they would pass on their living traditions to a younger generation. The Gaming Act mandated that at least 3 percent of gaming proceeds fund cultural and educational programs. Now there were some serious dollars to meet this goal. In addition, the Native American Graves Protection and Repatriation Act (NAGPRA) of 1990 mandated that museums return certain sacred objects to their tribes of origin. Tribal leaders, in turn, initiated state-of-the-art museum projects to house and care for these items. With their intensive

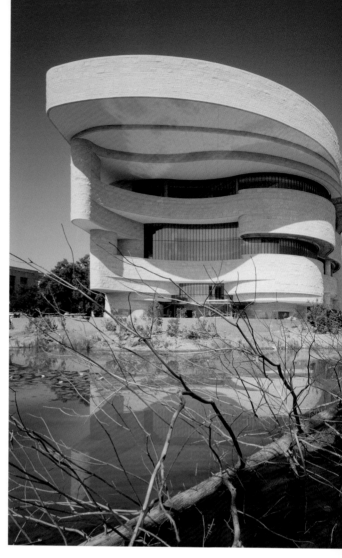

The Smithsonian's National Museum of the American Indian sits beside a tumbling stream and plants selected to evoke a pre-contact natural wonder. Photo by Robert C. Lautman.

attention to the natural environment, the tribal museum projects added a new dimension to museum architecture.

One of the first was the Warm Springs Tribal Museum in Oregon, which opened in 1993. Stastny & Burke: Architecture designed a building to harmonize with both the landscape and the native traditions of the region. The architects described their vision:

> The visitor's journey begins near water in a rock-strewn stream bed. The water becomes polished green slate and leads the visitor through a circular stone drum and into the lobby. . . . Inside the building, columns resemble trees, finished wood is detailed with rough-hewn juniper and bronze door pulls are shaped to mimic feather dance bustles . . . the building forms, materials and details embody traditions evolved over centuries of life in harmony with the earth.

The building won a Merit Award of Excellence from the American Institute of Architects for combining environmental sensitivity with "an emotional wallop all too seldom felt in contemporary public buildings."

Fortified with casino revenues, tribal museum projects continued. In 1998, adjacent to the Wildhorse Casino Resort near Pendleton, Oreg., the Cayuse, Umatilla and Walla Walla tribes opened the Tamastslikt Cultural Institute with a display celebrating past and present native life in the region. That same year, near Mystic, Conn., the Mashantucket Pequot tribal nation—perhaps the smallest tribe in the country—opened the Mashantucket Pequot Museum and Research Center, the largest Native American cultural facility in the country at the time. The aegis was the nearby tribal-run Foxwoods Resort Casino. The museum features a reconstructed 16th-century Pequot coastal village as well as high-tech multisensory displays on eastern woodland and native life. In keeping with Native American philosophies, its building responds to the ecology of its site. By the 2000s, tribal museums were one of the fastest growing segments of the museum community. Michael Hammond, director of the Agua Caliente Museum near Palm Springs, Calif., relays an oft-heard comment: "There are two kinds of American Indian tribes: those who already have museums, and those who are planning new ones."

Tribal museums introduced new ideas into American museums. A movement called "green architecture," gaining popularity in Europe, had garnered little notice in the United States. But to Native American museum planners, studying the ecology of a site, using efficient energy systems and recycled and renewable materials, and other principles of green architecture fit with a spiritual connection to the Earth that was so vital to American Indian religious and cultural traditions. The National Museum of the American Indian, in both its 1997 Cultural Resource Center in Suitland, Md., and its 2004 museum on Washington, D.C.'s mall, was perhaps the first large museum in the country to embrace designs that respect the native habitat.

Of course, the philosophies of green architecture stretch well beyond Native American tribal communities. In 1998 the Madison Children's Museum in Wisconsin designed "First Feats," a wholly "green" exhibition with materials free of pesticide residues, off-gassing particleboard, unstable plastics and toxic carpeting. In 2000 the Architecture League of New York organized "Ten Shades of Green," an exhibition about the principles of green architecture that traveled to several museums. While not meeting the myriad requirements needed to be certified as green, the Nevada Museum of Art's 2003 building defied common honky-tonk building convention in Reno and instead responded to its natural setting. Designed by Arizona architect Will Bruder, the museum's exterior was inspired by the shape of a bluff in the eastern Sierra Mountain desert basin. Bruder used local black stone for the interior and exterior and created a rooftop sculpture garden that allows visitors to see over the tops of glaring casinos and out onto the deserts and mountains beyond.

In 2003 ECHO at the Leahy Center, a science center in Burlington, Vt., became the first new museum building to receive a Leadership in Energy and Environmental Design (LEED) certificate from the U.S. Green Building Council. Built overlooking Vermont's stunning Lake Champlain, it received special commendation for using super-efficient windows and insulation. The California Academy of Sciences in San Francisco also announced an ambitious green building project, hiring Renzo Piano to create a sustainable building that will incorporate the natural world. On what he calls a "living roof," Piano designed a two-acre rooftop garden of native plants that slope into a glass-enclosed piazza. Instead of looking to the past as constructed by humans or to the pragmatic as dictated by the economy, these buildings look to the natural environment for their inspiration.

The Frederick R. Weisman Art Museum, designed by "starchitect" Frank Gehry for the University of Minnesota. Courtesy of the Weisman Art Museum, Minneapolis.

Others have found inspiration in the very concept of "museum," in what award-winning architect Daniel Libeskind calls "the atmosphere a museum exudes." Spearheading such high-profile projects as his stunning Jewish Museum Berlin, the Denver Art Museum expansion, the Contemporary Jewish Museum, San Francisco and the World Trade Center reconstruction in New York, Libeskind is known for incorporating the spiritual and emotional in his innovative designs. "If a certain care has been taken in building a museum," he says, ". . . it glows from within. . . . When everything has been authentically placed in relation to everything else, then the building has its own special quality. That's the soul of the building."

Museum buildings challenge architects, clients and communities to devise forms and spaces that reach as far as the human spirit. And, like the human spirit, they endure. Other types of public buildings—airplane hangars, movie palaces, warehouses—may outlive their original purpose. But while museums may forsake rented spaces for a permanent address, or tear down a building for safety reasons, rarely are they converted to another use or abandoned altogether. The travails of the Detroit Institute of Art illustrate the hopes that museum architecture engenders. In the 1990s, even when its downtown was hemorrhaging amidst severe budgetary woes, the city of Detroit maintained its art institute, resisting the pressure to abandon its 1927 Beaux-Arts building and cede control to nearby wealthy suburbs. The city council felt that "overhauling such a visible symbol" was simply too dramatic. Perhaps the classical building served as a promise that vitality and stability could return someday to that stricken urban core. Rather than close its doors, the institute planned a major expansion into a cultural district for the city.

All over the country, museum buildings continue to uplift and inspire their growing base of admirers and users. Each building reflects the aspirations of its times as well as a universal desire to celebrate culture, community, landscape, and location. In the Beaux-Arts era, museums strove to look alike. Founders were united in their desire to achieve eternal grandeur in the guise of European stateliness. During the modernist era that followed, museum designers worked from a common set of principles based on functional planning and the use of industrial materials. Directors were united in their desire for workable, practical buildings as sites for collections care, visitor centers and urban renewal.

By the end of the 20th century, and into the 21st, the design of the museum had become more diverse, mirroring the clamor and pluralism of the marketplace. Regardless of style or process, the players or the politics, the opening of each museum building is still a momentous event. Moreover, the public's enthusiasm for museum architecture lasts well beyond the ribbon-cutting ceremonies and opening receptions. In fact, even museums that initially were considered eyesores or enigmas have a way of endearing themselves to the public. The vision of a place of permanence has been realized.

THE COLLECTION

After all, not to create only, or found only,

But to bring perhaps from afar what is already founded,

To give it our own identity, average, limitless, free.

—WALT **WHITMAN**

Get an insect, a bird, an animal, a plant, a lithograph, a plaster cast, a spinning wheel, a tea cup, a bit of rock, a mineral, a dozen of the things made commercially in your community. . . . Set your museum brains at work upon these objects and in a few weeks you can open a museum which every intelligent person will rejoice to see.

—JOHN COTTON **DANA**

On April 18, 1906, at precisely 5:12 a.m., a massive earthquake tore through the San Francisco Bay area. Within minutes, downtown San Francisco was in flames. One after another, buildings collapsed. Terrified residents by the thousands fled their burning city. But one woman, a 47-year-old botany curator named Alice Eastwood, was seized by a different impulse. She left the safety of her Berkeley home and, dressed in the long skirt befitting a proper woman of the time, rushed across the bay, toward the raging fires. Her destination was the museum where she worked, the California Academy of Sciences, repository of one of the country's most extensive collections of botanical specimens.

Botany curator Alice Eastwood at Warner Hot Springs, San Diego, c. 1913, a few years after she rushed into a burning building to save her museum's collections. Library/California Academy of Sciences.

By 7 a.m. Eastwood had reached the smoke-filled Academy building. Unable to use the crumbling marble stairs, she painstakingly inched her way along the iron railings until she reached the sixth floor. There she feverishly gathered more than 1,000 records and specimens. For hours, via a makeshift pulley, she lowered items to the street below. "The earthquake didn't frighten me," Eastwood later recounted. "What scared me more was losing my life's work." At last, conditions forced her out of the building and she made a mad dash to join her rescued treasures. By 2 p.m. the Academy of Sciences was completely destroyed. But today those same botanical specimens, saved from a burning museum, can still be viewed. They survive thanks to the heroic efforts of an otherwise anonymous, but most assuredly dedicated, museum curator.

Such devotion is not so unusual in the museum world. Obsession and self-sacrifice lie behind nearly every museum's collection of objects. Individuals with a fierce "collector's passion" shaped the 20th-century museum. They exemplified the American spirit of rugged individualism where the self-made tycoon, not the conqueror or royalty as in the older European model, expressed power through acquisition. Often they were adventurous about it, hunters stalking and bagging their prey, spinning tales of narrow escapes from charging rhinos or storms at sea. Such collectors were highly competitive, even ruthless, repeatedly trying to outdo, outbid and outclass each other. Then, intriguingly, these same individuals often proved to be exceedingly generous, bequeathing their hard-won collections to public institutions in service to humanity—and, let's be honest, their egos. Most important, however, collectors frequently possessed a universal passion that has been compared to falling in love. As the assistant director of New York's Frick Collection observed in the 1940s: "Gnawing obsessions, stealthy pursuits, crushing disappointments, and intoxicating triumphs lie in the background of most beautiful things."

Because of these individuals' incessant drive to amass objects, America's museums possess a universe of fascinating things. And, like the universe, museum collections are continually expanding. With Haiku-like elegance, former Secretary of the Smithsonian S. Dillon Ripley summed up the reason behind this growth: "Culture creates collections; collections create culture."

■   ■   ■   ■   ■

Midway through the 19th century, collections in American museums were embarrassingly inferior to the priceless originals found in Europe. Plaster casts and inexpensive copies of Greek, Roman and Renaissance masterworks. The odd plant, arrowhead or rock that appealed to an explorer or a missionary. A few motley circus animals. Military records of English immigrants. The masterful art and towering dinosaurs that we have come to associate with our nation's museums were virtually unknown.

Ensuing decades, however, would bring an enormous change in quality and quantity to America's museum collections as the nation's wealthiest citizens set their sights on amassing a complete "encyclopedia" of the world. This growth mirrors the nation's economic and industrial rise to power. It also speaks loudly, if not always eloquently, about Americans' proclivity for acquisition, our continuing infatuation with things and our desire to amass and exhibit them. At last count (and this is a conservative estimate), today museums across the nation house some 750 million specimens, objects, artifacts and works of art. Museums possess so much stuff that less than 5 percent can be exhibited at any one time. The rest sits in storage rooms, laboratories or wherever else there is space for one more marble bust, mounted owl or pottery shard. Yet lack of space does not stop museums from acquiring even more things. It is estimated that the aggregate rate of collection growth is 1 to 5 percent annually: millions of additional objects each year.

Behind every great museum collection there are stories, often fascinating ones, about how and why these objects were gathered. Many of these stories are about the influential men and women who used a combination of wealth, willpower, vision and ego to acquire those objects and ultimately bequeath them to us.

As the myth goes, art buying was intuitive to millionaire collectors, a kind of noblesse oblige for the moneyed classes, a cultural pursuit that offered a welcome break from the hard-nosed tactics required to make money. In fact, art buying was always a hard-nosed business, usually conducted with the help of expert advisors and skillful dealers. Typical of these were two prominent early players active at the turn of the 20th century, Harvard-trained connoisseur Bernard Berenson and British dealer Lord Joseph Duveen.

Berenson was a scholar of Italian Renaissance art who believed fervently in the virtues of pedigree, classical beauty and the supremacy of old world values. He was best known to America's elite collectors (whom he called "squillionaires") as an authenticator of masterworks. Operating out of a villa near Florence, Italy, Berenson claimed that it was his life's mission to make sure that all paintings were correctly attributed: "We must not stop till we are sure that every Lotto is a Lotto, every Cariani a Cariani, every Santa Croce a Santa Croce. . . ." An attribution from Berenson could vastly augment the price of a work

of art, much to the delight of the dealers who paid him to study a work with a magnifying glass (later, a flashlight) and then sign a certificate of authenticity.

From 1906 until their highly public falling out in the 1930s, Berenson worked with the legendary dealer Joseph Duveen. Based in London, Duveen was the persuasive voice behind some of the most important American art acquisitions of the early 20th century, including Thomas Gainsborough's *Blue Boy* for the Huntington Library, Art Collections, and Botanical Gardens, *The Resurrected Christ* by Botticelli for the Detroit Institute of Arts, and the *Cowper Madonna* by Raphael for the National Gallery of Art. To find just the right piece for his eager American clients, it is said that Duveen "was at the center of a vast, circular nexus of corruption that reached from the lowliest employee of the British museum right up to the King." The dealer drove up prices by urging collectors to bid against each other. Once a sale was final, however, he then talked the collector into giving the work to a museum.

Although dealers and connoisseurs courted their powerful clients vigorously and advised them freely, when it came to purchasing art the collectors usually prevailed. As museum historian Kenneth Hudson writes of these early collectors, "They knew and loved art and were as savvy and passionate about it as any Renaissance tyrant."

One such collector was the eccentric Boston socialite Isabella Stewart Gardner. In the 1890s, a proper member of Boston high society interested would have collected French academic art, a tasteful and safe choice. But Gardner—a native New Yorker who delighted in rattling the socialites in her adopted city—had other ideas. She teamed up with Berenson and together they hunted down authentic Italian Renaissance masterpieces, combing Europe for Botticellis and Titians.

Even with Berenson's guidance Gardner often made impulsive purchases, driven by her competitive nature. She was reputed to possess an ego so "cosmic and insatiable" that "the hint that anyone else was after an object catapulted her into an immediate purchase." Yet as one former art museum director has noted, "To many people the making of a great collection represents only a combination of money and luck. These elements are usually necessary but there is far more to it than that. To make a really great collection, the collector must have taste, the ability to recognize quality and perseverance in getting the best works of art obtainable." Gardner possessed all of these qualities. In 1903 she built a Venetian-style palace in Boston to display the magnificent

Portrait of Joseph Duveen in the 1920s. Duveen Archives, Sterling and Francine Clark Art Institute Library, Williamstown, Mass.

Art collector and fisherman Thomas Gilcrease, who opened his museum in 1949. Courtesy of the Gilcrease Museum, Tulsa, Okla.

pieces she had acquired. She micro-managed every detail of the construction process, arranged each painting, sculpture or tapestry as she saw fit and then named the museum after herself. "Years ago," she stated when the museum was completed, "I decided that the greatest need in our country was Art . . . we were a very young country and had very few beautiful things . . . so I was determined to make it my life's work." In her will, Gardner forbade any alterations to her precise arrangements of her treasures.

Over the ensuing decades other American collectors would follow suit. Philadelphia's Alfred C. Barnes (1924), Washington, D.C.'s Duncan Phillips (1925), New York's Henry Clay Frick (1935) and Tulsa's Thomas Gilcrease (1949) are a few of the many who established museums in their own names as public monuments to their private tastes.

Not every mansion-museum belonged to an informed collector with a fine eye and impeccable taste. California newspaper publisher William Randolph Hearst was reputed to "represent the *nux vomica* of bad collecting on a grand scale." Between the 1890s and 1930s, Hearst traveled regularly to New York auction houses and bought every "modern gewgaw or ancient tchotchke . . . that drew his eye," stuffing his booty of "fourth-rate paintings of Madonnas," Georgian silver and Grecian urns into miles of railroad cars. The items were crammed into Hearst's garish castle on the Pacific coast, subject of the semi-fictional 1941 film, *Citizen Kane*. In 1942 about $4-million worth of objects from the collection was sold at Gimbel's Department Store in New York. Many objects—including a vast amalgamation of odd lamps, ceramic dogs and portraits of Hearst's mistress—ended up in private collections, although plenty remains at Hearst's San Simeon estate. Today this "Bastard-Spanish-Moorish-Romanesque-Gothic-Renaissance-Bull-Market-Damn-the-Expense" mansion-as-museum is one of the most popular attractions in California.

THE VISITATION, c. 1310, attributed to Master Heinrich of Constance (German, active in Constance, c. 1300). The Metropolitan Museum of Art, Gift of J. Pierpont Morgan, 1917 (17.190.724). Image © 2004 The Metropolitan Museum of Art.

Collectors like Hearst felt that for the right price the world could be theirs. This attitude motivated some dealers to raise prices and move shoddy goods. In the 1920s Italian forger Alceo Dossena became a local celebrity for creating convincing copies of sculptures in styles from Etruscan to Rococo. Fooling both dealers and collectors, many of Dossena's artistic fakes landed on display in American museums. "You can sell anything to Americans," said convicted French forger Jean Charles Millet in the 1920s. "They know nothing about art. . . . All you have to do is ask a fabulous price."

The collector most credited with paying fabulous prices was J. P. Morgan. Between 1902 and his death in 1913, Morgan spent

more than $60 million on art. While some of his purchases lacked authenticity and quality, others were magnificent. Morgan, as legend goes, "would buy a Louis XVI gold box . . . as casually as a commuter picks up a morning paper, and a few minutes later, with the same aplomb, spend $200,000 for the Cellini cup which had come to Adolphe Rothschild via the King of Naples."

At first Morgan's lavish purchases decorated his homes in London and Paris, a practical solution to the burdensome U.S. customs duties that would be imposed on his treasures if he attempted to bring them to New York. Art more than 20 years old was subject to a heavy tax when imported into the United States. But in 1909 Congress passed the Payne-Aldrich Tariff Act, co-sponsored by Rhode Island Sen. Nelson Aldrich. Imported art was now welcomed into the country duty-free. This legislation was to prove of enormous benefit to America's museums and, as some Europeans later bemoaned, of equal detriment to Europe's collections. Several art museum trustees testified in support of the act, and Morgan's influence was decisive. Only two years earlier, he had orchestrated a major bailout of the U.S. banking system and stock exchange, thus helping the U.S. Treasury avert financial collapse. Because he had almost single-handedly rescued the nation from "The Panic of 1907," Morgan was perhaps the most powerful man in America. This was no small factor in the repeal of custom duties that would allow him to import his collection to America and bequeath it to the Metropolitan Museum of Art.

After the Tariff Act Duveen and other international dealers prospered as never before. Using well-oiled connections to continental museums and royalty, they spirited art out of Europe and into the hands of eager American clients—including, within the next few decades, two of Sen. Aldrich's children, Abby Aldrich Rockefeller, a co-founder of the Museum of Modern Art in New York, and her brother William, a trustee of Boston's Institute of Contemporary Art.

In 1913 Congress intervened again, to the enduring benefit of American museums, and softened the Tariff Act to allow contemporary paintings and sculptures, in addition to older ones, to enter the country duty-free. The mechanisms were now in place to stockpile the country's museums with art that would be the envy of any royal court.

That same year also saw the arrival of a controversial new style of artwork from Europe. Works by avant-garde artists like Marcel Duchamp and Alexander Archipenko traveled across the Atlantic and premiered at one

Above left: Collectors like Marjorie Merriweather Post, seen here c. 1950, were accused of draining Europe of its masterpieces. From Mrs. Post's collection. **Left:** NUPTIAL CROWN, *1884, St. Petersburg, Russia. Unknown maker. Accession no. 17.63.* **Right:** CHALICE, *1791, St. Petersburg, Russia, Iver Winfeldt Buch (1749-1811). Accession no. 11.223. Hillwood Museum and Gardens; bequest of Marjorie Merriweather Post, 1973. Photographed by Edward Owen.*

of the most important exhibits of the 20th century: the Armory Show in New York. The first large-scale public showing of modern art in the United States, the Armory Show opened collectors' eyes to radical new images and created a buzz that continued for decades. As critic Calvin Tomkins described it, "Hideous and unspeakable tendencies had been let loose upon the land—blue nudes and nudes that descended staircases, wild beasts and other Parisian monstrosities . . . dangerous breeding grounds for Bolshevism and gross sexuality." It was art as scandal, described by contemporary newspapers as "freakish," "mad" and "inane." The public couldn't get enough. A growing group of American collectors would prove to be eager advocates of this and later radical movements. Inspired by artists like Picasso and Gauguin, they also began to acquire "primitive" art like African ceremonial masks and pre-conquest sculpture from Latin America. In the coming decades, these collectors would found the nation's first museums of modern art.

With the outbreak of World War I, the economic balance tilted further in favor of the United States. War contracts filled bank accounts of industrialists and investors, swelling the ranks of wealthy American collectors. The remnants of European aristocracy meanwhile, desperate for hard currency, were willing to sell their most precious masterpieces. Rembrandts, Tiepolos and Turners crossed the Atlantic. U. S. buyers who couldn't afford paintings lapped up prints, engravings and sketches. In 1916 German museum director Wilhelm von Bode warned that American collectors were draining Europe of its masterpieces. Soon, he decried, America's museums would "equal or surpass the great museums of Europe. . . ."

American collectors also sapped Europe's museums of future masterpieces. Dealers organized "European War Benefit Sales" to provide financial relief to overseas artists. The artists in turn were only too happy to sell their work to eager and rich American collectors.

Throughout the roaring '20s art collecting boomed, benefiting both dealers and museums. By 1923 Americans were spending $250 million annually on art purchases, the American Art Dealers' Association estimated. Even with the onset of the Great Depression, prices for art continued to rise. Some saw the acquisition of art as essential to civic pride and reputation. Said Dallas Museum of Art Director John Ankeney in 1930, "Nature made Dallas rich. Time

Above right: Raphael, central Italian, 1843-1520. **THE ALBA MADONNA**, c. 1510. *Andrew W. Mellon Collection, National Gallery of Art, Washington, D.C.*

will make her powerful. Only Art can make her great." Political turmoil in Europe led to further opportunities for collectors. In 1931 the Soviet government acquired hard currency by putting some of Russia's most treasured paintings on the market. Marjorie Merriweather Post, heir to the breakfast cereal fortune, bought the tsar's Fabergé eggs in addition to Russian icons, textiles, porcelains and silver, which are now at the Hillwood Museum and Gardens in Washington, D.C. Andrew Mellon purchased more than $5-million worth of paintings, including Raphael's exquisite *Alba Madonna* for $1,166,400, setting a record price for a single painting. Mellon's purchases of Titians, van Dycks and Vermeers—sequestered in a safe in the Corcoran Gallery of Art—were great fodder for journalists. While most Americans suffered from economic woes, the former U.S. treasurer was indulging his muses to the tune of millions of dollars. But he had a plan.

In 1936 Mellon made an extraordinary gesture. He gave his treasures to the U. S. government along with an endowment to care for them and a building to house them. "Over the period of many years I have been acquiring important and rare paintings and sculpture with the idea that ultimately they would become the property of the people of the United States and be made available to them in a national art gallery," Mellon wrote to President Franklin Delano Roosevelt. "I have given . . . securities ample to erect a gallery building of sufficient size to house these works of art and to permit the indefinite growth of the collection." The National Gallery of Art was born.

Established on the Mall in Washington, D.C., the National Gallery was intended as a gift to the nation, destined to grow as other collectors came forward: Mellon's son Paul, five-and-dime magnate Samuel Kress, Sears & Roebuck heir Lessing Rosenwald and Philadelphia collector Joseph Widener, much to the chagrin of the leaders of the Philadelphia Museum of Art who had coveted the Widener collection. Still, Mellon's gift, however magnificent, was tinged with scandal. While overseeing the U.S. Treasury, Mellon had been charged with falsifying his personal

Above: Diego M. Rivera, Detroit Industry, North Wall (detail), 1932-33. Gift of Edsel B. Ford. Photo © 2001, Detroit Institute of Arts.

Lower left: Rivera working on the mural at the Detroit Institute of Arts, 1932. Courtesy of the Rivera Archives, Detroit Institute of Arts, © 1932.

income tax returns. He subsequently endured a series of humiliating public trials. Federal prosecutors intimated that Mellon evaded conviction by using his art collection to curry favor with Congress and the American people.

By the 1930s there was an established class of cosmopolitan art patrons like Mellon who had a powerful effect on American tastes in art. They exercised great influence over the kind of art the country's leading museums would acquire and exhibit. Among this class were prominent socialites like Gertrude Vanderbilt Whitney and Peggy Guggenheim. Such patrons did more than collect works by long-dead masters, as their parents had done. They socialized with living artists, acting as modern-day Medicis. Whitney parlayed her fortune and collection into the Whitney Museum of American Art. Guggenheim is famous not only for her financial support of artists but for her numerous liaisons with them. One resulted in marriage to surrealist Max Ernst, whom she helped escape the growing fascist movement in Europe.

Such relationships were not without their problems. In 1932 Wilhelm Valentiner, the flamboyant, German-born director of the Detroit Institute of Arts, met Mexican muralist Diego Rivera and his wife Frida Kahlo at a tennis match in California. Valentiner was taken by this striking couple, especially Kahlo, whom he found "especially charming and typical of modern Mexico." He hired Rivera, an avowed Marxist, to adorn the museum's courtyard with 27 frescos depicting the spirit of industrial Detroit. The frescos were financed by the decidedly not-Marxist Ford Motor Company, under the leadership of Henry Ford's son Edsel, a collector and head of the Detroit Arts Commission. The murals were controversial from the moment they were unveiled in 1933. The press, clergy and politicians complained that the subject—industrial might—was inappropriate for an art museum. Worse, Rivera's nudes

were considered pornographic. Critics demanded the frescos be whitewashed. Ford, it should be noted, had the courage to rally to Rivera's defense, as did many others in the community. Today, the murals are still on display in Detroit, considered to be among Rivera's finest works.

■ ■ ■ ■ ■

Although most U.S. collectors in the 1930s still suffered from an inferiority complex when comparing European works to those created at home, they gradually began to stretch their definition of what constituted art. Prior to World War I, only a few small campus museums, including those at Smith College and the Rhode Island School of Design, had bothered to acquire much in the way of paintings and sculpture by Americans. As early as 1922, though, declaring that collecting European oil painting was a waste of time and money, John Cotton Dana started to build a collection of American art for the Newark Museum. He convinced one of his donors—the wife of a local department store owner—to shift her collecting passion from the art of Italy to the art of New York City. It was a bold and unusual move.

In 1924, the Museum of Fine Arts in Boston became the first major art museum to acquire photography, accepting 27 photographs from Alfred Stieglitz, who insisted that they be framed and treated as works of art. Throughout the 1920s, collectors became interested in other American artists. Fascinated by the notion of "homegrown genius" they purchased works by artists like Edward Hicks and Horace Pippin from dealers in Philadelphia and New York. Taken with local sea- and landscape painting, they set up small museums in artists' colonies in Montclair, N.J., and Ogunquit, Maine. Intrigued by Native American aesthetics, they bought pottery from Pueblos in New Mexico and beadwork from Native Americans throughout the continent.

The Museum of Fine Arts, Boston was the first—but not the last—art museum to acquire the photographs of Alfred Stieglitz (1864-1946). His **HANDS OF GEORGIA O'KEEFFE, NO. 26** *is in the collection of South Carolina's Gibbes Museum of Art. Courtesy Gibbes Museum of Art/ Carolina Art Association. 1974.012.130.*

As the 1930s opened, two trends in collecting were in full swing. Like architectural movements of the day, one looked forward and the other back. In the first, museums of industry began to amass collections of the latest machines. After the Century of Progress World's Fair of 1933, for example, Chicago's Museum of Science and Industry became the repository for such American-made hardware as electric generators, teletype machines and tractors. Even art museums began to collect the nation's technological marvels. In 1935, with leadership from Jock Whitney, an early investor in a three-color film process called Technicolor, MoMA founded a film library—the first archive in the world to collect Hollywood movies. The military also saw the value of preserving evidence of the nation's power. It donated surplus hardware from prior wars to museums, such as the Smithsonian and a newly established Air Force Museum near Dayton, Ohio.

Portrait of Ima Hogg, c. 1898. Courtesy of The Museum of Fine Arts, Houston, Archives.

The second trend was the result of a new fascination among the heirs of the wealthy industrialists for handmade crafts. They scoured country barns and rural attics for such low-tech items as weathervanes, needlework and scythes. Both "collect-American" movements of the 1930s had advantages over museums' earlier collecting methods. American-made items were more available and less expensive and could serve as patriotic counterpoints to items from abroad. American-made objects provided evidence of "native genius and sensibility." They were reminders of the contributions that the United States made to the arts, industry and world progress as well as the humble origins of some of the country's great family fortunes.

By 1930 the term "Americana" was well established in the museum field. Collectors around the nation turned their efforts to hunting down objects made by their fellow citizens. Texas millionaires focused on a specialized branch called "Texacana." In Houston, Ima Hogg—contrary to popular belief, she did not have a sister named Eura—daughter of a Texas governor and heir to an oil fortune, collected American and Texan furniture. "From the time I acquired my first Queen Anne armchair in 1920, I had an unaccountable compulsion to make an American collection for some Texas museum," stated Hogg, affectionately known as Miss Ima. Her pieces went to Bayou Bend, a 15-acre country estate outside Houston, today housing one of the largest collections of Americana in the nation.

An even larger collection of Americana resides in tiny Delaware, at the du Pont family's 983-acre country estate known as Winterthur. Henry Francis du Pont, heir to his family's gunpowder and chemical fortunes, believed that items like finely crafted silver, vases and furniture could offer the public "a new understanding and respect for the integrity of American craftsmanship." He bought more than 85,000 objects, focusing on the decorative arts. As a friend of his once remarked, "It takes a sack of money to collect the way Harry du Pont has done, but it also takes . . . a sure eye for beauty, a perfect sense of balance and an

incredible amount of hard work." In 1930 du Pont established Winterthur as a nonprofit educational foundation. It opened to the public as a museum in 1951.

Other family fortunes also built Americana collections. MoMA co-founder Abby Aldrich Rockefeller amassed a handsome collection of American folk art including hand-carved toys. In 1932 her collection was the centerpiece of the museum's taste-setting exhibition "American Folk Art: The Art of the Common Man in America, 1750-1900." Stephen Clark, heir to the Singer Sewing Machine fortune and a MoMA trustee, also had a penchant for "the plain people of yesterday." He toured the countryside, searching for old spinning wheels, butter churns and similar items. He housed this massive collection in an old stone dairy barn in Cooperstown, N.Y., and called it the Farmers' Museum. Soon it contained all manner of old farm implements—tools, harvesting machinery, ox carts—hauled in by locals. Another notable collector of Americana was Electra Havemeyer Webb, heir to a sugar fortune, wife of a Vanderbilt and a big game hunter (a grizzly bear she shot in Alaska is still on display in Anchorage's airport). In 1947 her collection—including cigar store Indians, hatboxes, hooked rugs and more than a thousand duck decoys—opened to the public as the Shelburne Museum in Vermont, dubbed by one admirer as a "collection of collections."

■   ■   ■   ■   ■

A collection consists of much more than the objects within it. A collection usually reveals something significant about the collector, his or her ideals, and even society at large.

In the years prior to World War II, a chief motive behind natural science collecting was Charles Darwin's theory of evolution. An application, Social Darwinism, asserted that "inferior" species and civilizations were disappearing as more advanced societies were evolving. Collecting was seen as one way of rescuing our natural history from the ineluctable march of progress. Where explorers once randomly plucked items from nature as they traveled the globe, they now worked with universities and natural history museums in pursuit of a mission:

During his expeditions out West, Henry Fairfield Osborn made frequent stops for "tiffin," a term meaning "light meal" that was popular in Britain and India during his day. Courtesy of the American Museum of Natural History.

Left: *Roy Andrews (the inspiration for Indiana Jones, down to the hat) and a colleague examine dinosaur eggs from the Flaming Cliffs at Shabarakh Usu, Mongolia, 1925.*

Right: *Henry Fairfield Osborn collected railway cars full of fossils from Wyoming and Montana and apparently stored many of them in his office at the museum. Photos courtesy of the American Museum of Natural History.*

to assemble a logical order of the world and evidence of biological evolution. They began, naturally enough, with the dinosaur.

Henry Fairfield Osborn, president of the American Museum of Natural History in New York from 1908 to 1933, played a leading role in instigating dinosaur expeditions. The son of a railway magnate and a nephew of J. P. Morgan, Osborn set up a vertebrate paleontology department at Columbia University for the museum's teaching and study purposes. Using his connections to New York's elite, he organized excavations of quarries in the West. As a result, railway cars filled with fossils from the wilds of Wyoming and Montana began arriving in New York.

Osborn soon realized that dinosaurs could play a useful role outside of the laboratory and classroom. He treated museum visitors to exhibits of rigged-up skeletons of such creatures as *Tyrannosaurus rex, Brontosaurus* (now called *Apatosaurus*) and *Triceratops.* Not to be outdone by New York society and fiercely competitive with J. P. Morgan, industrialist Andrew Carnegie financed a dinosaur expedition to "get one for Pittsburgh." The resulting dig in Wyoming uncovered "Dippy," an almost complete 10-ton *Diplodocus* for the Carnegie Museum. Carnegie "was so proud of this specimen, named *carnegiei* in his honor, that he presented 10 life-size replicas to 10 leading world museums," setting off the dinomania that is a part of popular culture to the present day.

All over the country natural history museums began to purchase casts and fossils from dealers, often trading with one another for just the right bone to complete a dinosaur skeleton. Those with access to funds organized their own digs. In 1906 an ambitious, freshly minted graduate of Wisconsin's Beloit College arrived on the doorstep of the American Museum of Natural History, determined to get a job there. Roy Chapman Andrews was hired as a janitor, scrubbing the floors in the taxidermy department. Soon

Above and center: Two views of the Field Museum's famous T.Rex, a superstar named Sue. Photo by John Weinstein (left). © The Field Museum.

Below: "Dinosphere" at the Children's Museum of Indianapolis transports visitors 65 million years back in time with displays of fossilized dinosaur bones and the smell of decaying vegetation. The Children's Museum of Indianapolis/A. Overstreet.

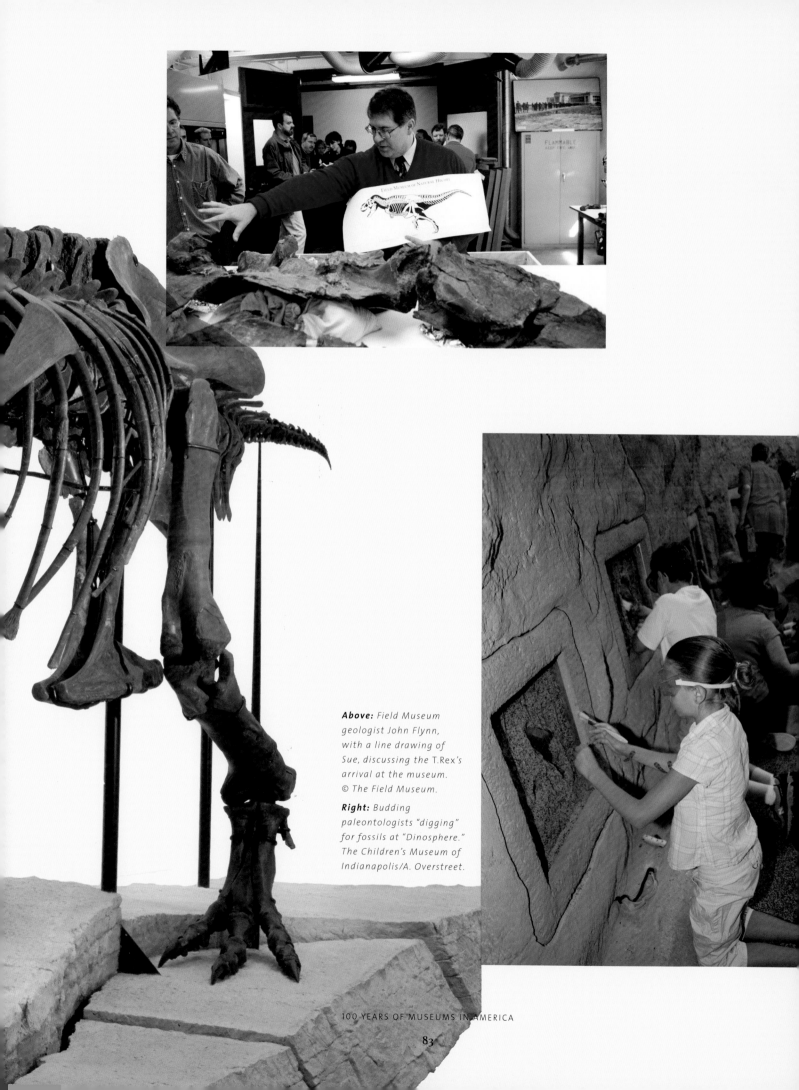

Above: Field Museum geologist John Flynn, with a line drawing of Sue, discussing the T.Rex's arrival at the museum. © The Field Museum.

Right: Budding paleontologists "digging" for fossils at "Dinosphere." The Children's Museum of Indianapolis/A. Overstreet.

he talked his way onto collecting expeditions to Alaska and Japan. He also caught the eye of Osborn, who tapped Andrews for his most celebrated collecting expedition, a 1922 trip across the Gobi Desert, to find the legendary "missing link," that is, evidence that Asia not Africa was the birthplace of humankind. This distinction was important to Osborn, as we shall see. But instead of humanoid skeletons, Andrews unearthed troves of dinosaur fossils. One discovery—unhatched, fossilized dinosaur eggs—captured the heart of the public. In New York, crowds packed the halls of AMNH to get a peek at them. Andrews catapulted to fame and his portrait appeared on the cover of *Time.*

To finance future expeditions to China in the name of "American ideals, American science and the American flag," Andrews invented a clever fund-raising scheme: "The Great Dinosaur Egg Auction." When the Chinese government got wind that a single egg was fetching up to $5,000 (approximately $54,000 in current dollars), officials accused Andrews and his paleontologists of stealing China's treasures to sell them for profit, scouting for oil and mineral deposits on behalf of American industrialists, spying and opium smuggling. The Chinese even arrested a team of Andrews's colleagues. In fact, the suspicions had merit. Andrews was involved in espionage and used his museum missions to gather data for the U.S. government on Chinese industry and military. Strained relations between the two countries prevented further expeditions. But Andrews's fame grew and he is frequently cited as a model for the Hollywood film icon Indiana Jones.

Osborn's own collecting activities generated a different kind of notoriety. Creationists opposed to the teaching of evolution found a visible enemy in natural history museums, with their orderly collections and public displays of antediluvian fossils. In 1922, as the Scopes Monkey Trial loomed in Tennessee, Osborn debated prosecutor William Jennings Bryan in the press and on lecture platforms. Though Osborn eloquently defended science against fundamentalism, the motives behind his collecting expeditions were indefensible. He fervently believed that the principles of "natural" selection applied to human beings. With southern and eastern European immigrants and African Americans from the South streaming into northern U.S. cities, Osborn and his followers sought to use systematic arrangements of specimens to prove the "spiritual, intellectual, moral and physical" superiority of "the Nordic race." He named numerous invalid species simply to support his views of eugenics and eventually was discredited. Today he is known as one of the worst taxonomists in the history of paleontology.

After World War II the study of fossils became more scientifically rigorous, their collecting and exhibition less influenced by social theory. Dinosaur digs continued, under the auspices of university paleontology departments and campus museums such as those at Montana State University, the University of Utah and Texas Tech University. The focus returned to teaching and research.

Today natural history museums remain the venue by which most Americans encounter the fossilized remnants of these giant creatures. Museums have proven endlessly creative in drawing the public's attention to the topic. In the 1980s the Museum of Science in Boston toured "Dinosaur Show," six near-life-sized, computer-operated models of fully fleshed-out beasts that roared and swished their tails. In the 1990s, with the film *Jurassic Park* drawing huge audiences, animatronic models of dinosaurs roared in science museums across the country, including the Smithsonian.

Museums also sponsored digs for more authentic dinosaurs. In the 1990s the Los Angeles County Natural History Museum organized expeditions to Patagonia, Argentina, in search of dinosaur eggs. In 2001 the Field Museum, National Science Foundation, National Geographic Society and the Science Museum of Minnesota cosponsored a dig in Madagascar that led to a spectacular find: a 70-million-year-old, nearly-complete longneck sauropod.

Around this time a museum played an important role in the 20th century's most spectacular dinosaur discovery. In 1990 an amateur fossil hunter named Sue Hendrickson in South Dakota stumbled on the most complete *T.Rex* ever. Press coverage of the 10-ton skeleton rivaled anything stirred up by Andrews's Chinese dinosaur eggs decades before. After a long legal battle between the Native American landowner, commercial fossil hunters, scientists and the U. S. government, the *T.Rex*, now known worldwide as "Sue," was auctioned in 1997 for $8.36 million, a record price for a fossil. The buyer was the Field Museum in partnership with McDonald's Corporation and Walt Disney resorts. Although purists decried the commercialism of this price-spiking deal, visitors were wildly enthusiastic. Attendance at the Field increased by 30 to 40 percent in the first five years following Sue's debut.

Striving to stay current with our age-old fascination for dinosaurs, many museums such as the Philadelphia Academy of Natural Sciences and Denver Museum of Nature and Science retooled their exhibitions to reflect the latest fossil research. In 2004 the Indianapolis Children's Museum opened "Dinosphere," a huge enclosed dome filled with the 65-million year-old fossilized bones of juvenile dinosaurs. The biosphere includes the smell of decaying vegetation, various Cretaceous-era sounds and, in a touch of whimsy, mini-dioramas with toy dinosaurs dressed up as museum workers. The museum's goal is to combine scientific research and advanced educational and exhibition techniques in placing the visitor inside the world of the paleontologist.

In recent years, dinosaur collections have remained lightning rods in the controversy over evolution. With the rise of religious fundamentalism in some parts of the country, zealous visitors who held that their information was "biblically correct" sometimes confronted museum workers. At the same time institutions like the Museum of Earth in Ithaca, N.Y., and the University of Nebraska State Museum in Lincoln developed ways to train docents and other educators how to explain the scientific method and the validity of evolutionary biology.

It's a question of only a few years when everything reminding us of America as it was at the time of its discovery will have perished.

—ANTHROPOLOGIST FRANZ **BOAS**, 1898

A century ago, part of the dinosaur's allure was the mystery of its extinction. Americans were becoming increasingly fascinated by vanishing worlds. They were intrigued not only by fossils but also by the nation's disappearing indigenous cultures and its receding flora and fauna. And with good reason. This was a time of rapid industrialization and urbanization. Ranchers, cowboys and miners, settlers, speculators and railroad tycoons had bulled their way westward for nearly a half century. No one of the day saw the irony in the fact that Americans had been the destroyers of the land and way of life they now scrambled to preserve. Symbolic of the destruction were the immense herds of buffalo slaughtered to the point of extinction. More tragic was the systematic destruction of the American Indians and

William Hornaday, taxidermist and planner of the National Zoo, envisioned the zoo as a refuge for the country's vanishing species, such as the bison. NZP Archives © Smithsonian's National Zoo.

their way of life. By the early 20th century the "Native American population was about 2 percent of what it had been [before the arrival of the Europeans]," notes James Nason, former curator at the Burke Museum, University of Washington, and a member of the Comanche Nation. "Scientists said 'if we don't do something right now to study these people, we will have lost our chance. They will be gone.'"

Driven by a perceived urgency and perhaps also by a mixture of guilt and nostalgia, Americans began feverishly to collect specimens of their natural history, both at home and abroad. Museums gladly embraced the movement.

Explorers uprooted plants from the rainforests of Latin America and the valleys of Alaska. They deposited the flora at museums and botanical gardens, where the plants were dried, pressed and transformed into "botanical specimens." To botanical gardens they brought live trees, shrubs, flowers, seeds and bulbs that were propagated, hybridized and transformed into glorious assemblages of "exotic species." From the mountains of Canada to the deserts of Africa, hunters "bagged and tagged" thousands of lions and tigers and bears. Scientists poached hundreds of thousands of bird eggs and nests or ventured to the wilds of Nebraska and Wyoming to "collect" the great buffalo. While taxidermists mounted buffalo hides for display, zoos tried to perpetuate the species in captivity. The founder of the Smithsonian's National Zoo, William Hornaday, envisioned the zoo as "a city of refuge for the vanishing species of the continent." An early champion of animal conservation, Hornaday organized the transport of bison from the Great Plains to Washington, D.C., and co-founded the American Bison Society to help preserve these great beasts of the American wild. By the 1920s the collecting of smaller specimens like plants, birds, insects and snakes was so popular, the Brooklyn Children's Museum was distributing butterfly nets and "killing bottles" to eager children. Boy Scouts were trained in taxidermy so they could earn merit badges and start their own "Scout Museums" of mounted birds and small animals.

The popularity of the emerging scientific field of anthropology furthered interest in "dying" civilizations. Sponsored by world's fairs and museums, anthropologists strived to collect as much as they could about so-called primitive and vanishing tribes—even, in some cases, the tribal members themselves.

Native American household, ceremonial and sacred objects were highly sought after, and museums acquired them in a variety of ways. In some cases Native Americans who needed money sold items to dealers, collectors and anthropologists. But often they were unwilling to part with objects. George Dorsey, an anthropologist who directed expeditions for the Field Museum, instructed one of his assistants: "When you go into an indian's house and you do not find the old man at home and there is something you want, you can do one of three things; go hunt up the old man and keep hunting until you find him; give the old woman such price for it . . . running the risk the old man will be offended; or steal it. I have tried all three plans and have no choice to recommend." Sometimes looters, seeing a quick way to make an easy dollar, dug up unprotected areas. In one infamous example, they removed hundreds of sacred wooden statues guarding Zuni shrines in New Mexico and sold them to collectors and museums. They did this despite the fact that the Zuni believe that removal of the *Ahayu.da* war gods meant to decay naturally in the outdoors, will lead to war, violence and natural disaster.

Above: LAKOTA SIOUX DOLL, *c. 1890. Southwest Museum of the American Indian Collection, Autry National Center.*

Left: MIXTEC-AZTEC SHIELD, *15th century. © National Museum of the American Indian, Smithsonian Institution.*

In other cases tribal elders asked museums to safeguard sacred objects. In the 1890s the Omaha Indians of Nebraska loaned sacred poles and medicine bundles to the Peabody Museum of Archaeology and Ethnology at Harvard University with the understanding that someday their tribe would reclaim and care for them. In many instances anthropologists simply took items, believing they were rescuing them from mistreatment or destruction by the primitive and uneducated peoples who had made them. An early manual for museum workers published by the American Association of Museums offered the prevailing view in rationalizing museums' rights to these items: "Most history museums require some anthropological material to represent the red man's part in the story of the white man."

The 1906 federal Antiquities Act, signed into law by President Theodore Roosevelt, was the government's first attempt at historic preservation. Its goal was to protect historic and prehistoric sites on federal land, such as Chaco Canyon and Mesa Verde, which had been vandalized by grave robbers. It also expressly allowed the gathering of Native American artifacts and remains "for the benefit of and permanent preservation in public museums." Now archaeologists, working in tandem with museums, could legally unearth sacred graves and gather bones, relics and funerary objects. And they did, by the thousands. Between 1906 and 1907 one archaeologist named Gerard Fowke unearthed hundreds of Comanche remains in central Missouri. These eventually were acquired by the Missouri Historical Society.

The Antiquities Act was devastating to Native American culture. "Native American remains were no longer their own," says Nason. "The bodies of the dead became property like baskets or bowls in a collection."

Explorers and anthropologists went so far as to collect living people. In 1897 arctic explorer Admiral Robert E. Peary gave the American Museum of Natural History in New York "material" that included several barrels of human bones retrieved from a graveyard in Greenland and what he called six "faithful Eskimos." The captured people were relegated to the basement, where four of them, including a man named Qisuk, soon died of tuberculosis. Though the museum staged a fake funeral for the benefit of Qisuk's son Minik, the young boy later stumbled upon his father's skeleton, carefully skinned, prepared and placed on exhibit.

In 1910 a "wild man" who would come to be called Ishi suddenly appeared in the small town of Oroville, Calif. His tribe, the Yahi-Yana, had been wiped out by disease and massacre. Alfred Kroeber, a professor of anthropology at the University of California in Berkeley, persuaded the Bureau of Indian Affairs to permit him to move Ishi into the university museum's basement. Ishi lived for years at the Phoebe A. Hearst Museum of Anthropology, working as a janitor to earn his keep. He became a must-see sensation. Crowds watched him make arrowheads and hunting spears that eventually became part of the museum's collection. After Ishi died of tuberculosis in 1916 his brain was removed, despite Kroeber's protests, and sent to the Smithsonian, where it was kept in a glass jar in storage, forgotten for more than 80 years.

■　■　■　■　■

Before World War II, the overwhelming sentiment was to amass as much as possible. Museums, whether dedicated to art or science, flora or fauna, were essentially in what museum scholar Stephen E. Weil called "the salvage and warehouse business." The war years had a profound impact on collectors' attitudes and practices, characterized by a heightened protectiveness. Fearing an attack on U.S. shores, some museums squirreled away their most precious objects in basement vaults or far off-sites. The very different conditions in Europe also would have dramatic consequences for American museums.

With the Nazis' rise to power, the movement of art across borders became frantic, in many cases the result of collectors' efforts to save their own lives. In Switzerland in 1939, the Nazi Party auctioned off modern artwork from leading German museums. The stated goal was to rid Germany of work by "degenerates," namely Bolsheviks, Jews or anyone critical of the Reich. Rather than destroy these works, the Nazis sold them to raise foreign currency. Many American collectors boycotted the sell-offs, but some participated, including publisher Joseph Pulitzer and Maurice Wertheim, a progressive Jewish philanthropist and one-time publisher of *The Nation.* In the words of Pulitzer, they acted to "save the art."

The war years in Europe witnessed what author Lynn Nicholas later identified as *The Rape of Europa*, the title of her prize-winning 1994 book. It was systematic, widespread state-mandated theft. The

After World War II, American museum specialists traveled to Europe to assess the damage to the continent's works of art. National Archives 206314.

Nazis looted European museums, bullied dealers and Jewish collectors into forced sales far below value or simply commandeered what they wanted. Many records were lost or destroyed. Works "vanished" into the hands of dubious owners, sold by dealers with ties to the Nazis. (In the post-war years, some of these works entered American museums. Usually such sales were the result of technically legal transactions. But just as often, there was inadequate documentation about previous ownership—known to the art world as "provenance"—which further confused the situation. Not until the 1990s would researchers such as Nicholas, Konstantin Akinsha, Hector Feliciano and Grigorii Kozlov publish extensive documentation on this shameful chapter in world history.)

After the war, through a federal agency called the Commission for the Protection and Salvage of Artistic and Historic Monuments—known as the "Roberts Commission" and housed at the National Gallery of Art—American museum specialists traveled to Europe to assess the war damage to the continent's monuments, masterworks and archives. They were horrified at the destruction. With the dawn of the nuclear age, museum directors became increasingly concerned about security. The United Nations Educational, Scientific, and Cultural Organization (UNESCO) published a guide that showed museums how to protect collections from nuclear annihilation, earnestly recommending the use of metal-slatted Venetian blinds to counter the light from an A-bomb explosion and "fairly thick cellophane tape" to seal windows and prevent the seepage of radiation. In 1951 the director of the Corcoran Gallery of Art went so far as to propose that because of "the threat of atomic missiles," museums should remove their entire contents to a "separate building located . . . well beyond the potential [enemy] target area." He suggested the so-called targeted museum buildings be used instead for public lectures or concerts. Presumably, in the event of a nuclear attack, audiences would just duck and cover, comforted by the fact that the museum's collections were safe from the threat of obliteration.

Meanwhile, U.S. museums discovered that while European art prices were still relatively high, works from Asia were widely available. Asian craftsmanship and aesthetics had been greatly admired by collectors in the United States since at least the 1880s, when zoologist Edward Sylvester Morse gave Boston's Museum of Fine Arts Japanese pottery he had acquired during a scientific expedition. In the early 1900s, Boston was a center of Asian art collecting, and scholars and collectors traveled there to view the MFA's growing collection of Japanese, Chinese, Indian and Korean art. Between the two world wars, several prominent collectors gave Asian art to museums around the nation. Flour executive Alfred Pillsbury gave his particularly fine collection of Chinese jade and terra cotta figurines to what is now the Minneapolis Institute of Arts. And Harvard-trained scholar Laurence Sickman helped gather one of the best collections of Chinese landscape painting outside China for the Nelson-Atkins Museum of Art in Kansas City.

Collecting from Asia extended beyond art museums. In 1927 more than 40 children's and public museums, the Boston Children's Museum and the Charleston Museum, acquired exquisite Japanese "friendship" dolls, complete with elaborate kimonos, as part of an international "Friendship" campaign between U.S. and Japanese cities.

World War II changed Americans' attitudes toward Asia, especially Japan. Many Japanese collections were removed from display or mysteriously disappeared. After the war, however, museums reactivated their interest in Asian art. Sometimes G.I.'s who had served in the Pacific presented their local museums with "souvenirs" from their tours of duty. Other museums sent curators to comb the black markets of Tokyo for bargains on lacquer items, jade and statues. Curators at the Cleveland Museum of Art were advised to buy especially valuable objects, such as screens, as quietly as possible, lest the Japanese government declare them national treasures and prohibit exportation.

At the same time European dealers and artists flooded into the United States, and the fine arts scene exploded. Galleries in Manhattan attracted a whole new generation of wealthy collectors whose fortunes were growing in the postwar economy. Among the many who caught the bug were Chicago's Mary Block and her husband Leigh Block, vice president of Inland Steel; Houston's John and Dominique de Menil, whose fortunes dovetailed with the Texas oil boom; New York's Barbara Duncan, wife of W. R. Grace executive John Duncan; and Detroit's Lydia Kahn Winston, daughter of industrialist architect Albert Kahn. The Blocks purchased Impressionist paintings that eventually went to the Art Institute of Chicago and Northwestern University in Evanston, Ill. The de Menils were drawn to Surrealism; they eventually founded an entire museum in Houston. Duncan, a major collector of Latin American art, later donated to the Jack S. Blanton Museum of Art at the University of Texas, Austin. And Kahn became the first private collector to purchase a work by Jackson Pollock—for $275, in 1946.

Homegrown artists such as Pollock and movements like Abstract Expressionism were a boon to private collecting. Dealers promoted art as carefree financial investment; simply hang a canvas by an up-and-coming artist on your wall and watch it double in value before your eyes. Or befriend a museum director, let him advise you, unofficially; then promise the pieces to his museum, take a tax deduction and hang them in your house until death do you part.

In 1946 the San Francisco Museum of Modern Art opened the nation's first art rental gallery. Its goal was to promote collecting to an even wider field of potential art buyers: the growing middle class. Art collecting also was promoted in magazines like *Good Housekeeping* and *American Home* and by department stores. Sears and Roebuck shoppers could buy a real Picasso lithograph for $300 and get a chance to meet the art showroom spokesperson, T.V. personality Vincent Price. Those who couldn't afford an original work could purchase a "paint-by-number" kit and fashion their own Rembrandt or Michelangelo.

Postwar interest in the fine arts spread far and wide, from the suburban shopper to artists' colonies (Provincetown, Mass.) to college communities (Black Mountain, N.C.). Victor D'Amico, MoMA's head of education, surmised that the turn to aesthetics was related to a "spiritual hunger" that arose during the nuclear age: "One wonders whether there is not a relationship between the growing power of destructiveness on the part of our scientific genius, and that indescribable urge for creation on the part of the general public."

Educator Paul Sachs trained scores of future museum professionals how to care for priceless works of art. Photographed by George S. Wooddruff, 1943 or 1944. Courtesy of Fogg Art Museum, Harvard University Art Museums.

Ironically, the Cold War had the opposite effect on museum acquisitions. Amid the explosive scientific discoveries and vibrant art scene of the 1950s, most museums abandoned voracious collecting. Gone was the obsession with swash-buckling dinosaur diggers, eccentric millionaire art collectors and oddball amalgamations of local bric-a-brac. It was time to protect and preserve.

■   ■   ■   ■   ■

Collections faced more tangible threats than Cold War paranoia. Museums were bursting at the seams. Many objects were in poor condition. Early explorers and science curators often yanked natural materials right from the ground. Once in museums, these items received little care beyond perhaps an application of a pesticide like arsenic. Artwork from abroad frequently arrived in poor condition—grimy, cracked, discolored. Some objects were subject to even more damage from intensive day-lighting, forced heat and cramped storage. As conservator Sheldon Keck observed, "We have learned from sad experience that [art and other precious objects are] subject to the ravages of time, climate, chemistry and micro-organisms." Not to mention the scourge of museum basements: vermin that happily nested among the treasures and chewed to their hearts' content.

In addition, many objects had only vague paper trails, even though a cataloguing system of neatly filed blue index cards devised by librarian Henry Watson Kent had been in use since 1910. Directors and trustees comprised an old-boy network, with collections sometimes used as private playthings. Cutting inside deals was common practice. There are tales of directors who would phone a director-pal at another museum and ask to borrow a European masterwork. The desired painting would be loaded into the back of someone's car and driven to its new destiny, backed up by a handshake or verbal promise. In these years, museum vaults, supposedly established in the public trust, were sometimes unguarded from both the natural elements and human temptation. As the United States snuggled into a suburban lifestyle, museums also turned inward—toward the matters of conservation and documentation.

Operating in a world where collectors value their objects almost as much as life itself, the museum conservator is like a medical doctor, saving a damaged treasure through a proper treatment. In the 1920s museums adopted promising medical technologies to care for collections. Field Museum scientists used X-ray machines to examine mummies without unwrapping them. Art museums, cautious about an influx of counterfeit art, turned to X-rays and microscopes to help identify forgeries. A leading laboratory for this work was housed at Harvard University's Fogg Art Museum, where educator Paul Sachs trained students to learn the anatomy of a work of art—its materials, chemistry, application techniques and the signature flourishes of important artists.

In the 1950s the Public Museum of Grand Rapids started sending programs and materials—including the mounted animals pictured here—to schools throughout the region. Courtesy of the Public Museum of Grand Rapids.

In the 1950s two of Sachs's alumni, Carolyn Kohn Keck and Sheldon Keck, helped transform the art of restoration into the science of conservation. Whereas restorers altered works of art by applying and manipulating materials, conservators like the Kecks sought to repair objects and return them to their original state. In 1955 Carolyn taught the first course in painting conservation at the New York State Historical Association in Cooperstown. In 1959 Sheldon opened the first training program for art conservators at New York University. With the emergence of a trained corps of conservators, larger museums invested in full-scale laboratories, while smaller museums relied on regional facilities, like the one founded at Oberlin College in 1952, to care for their works.

If conservators took on the role of doctor, registrars became the accountants. Until World War II recordkeeping was primarily the responsibility of curators, often referred to as "keepers," a title still used in Great Britain. It was their job to keep collections in some kind of order. But curators hadn't kept pace with the influx of items. They had other things to think about, such as acquiring more objects. In the 1950s a new kind of keeper—the professional registrar—emerged. The registrar was charged with tracking collections and documenting their condition and provenance. Rising art values and the increased number of traveling exhibitions made this task a specialty. Insurance firms were entering the fine arts business, and required accurate records, especially when art traveled between museums. In the 1960s registration became more specialized with the introduction of computerized databases.

During the same period, the field of conservation also advanced considerably. The American Institute for Conservation of Historic & Artistic Works was founded in 1972, and the field developed new ways to deal with the chronic problem of treating, conserving and preventing further deterioration of collections. Led by dedicated professionals like the Smithsonian's Carolyn Rose, conservators asserted their voices, advising the field on such details as climate control and filtering systems. Put a humidifier next to that armoire or it will crack. Lower the light level on that engraving or it will fade. Don't serve dessert in that gallery unless you want ants crawling up your Renoir. Conservators became "institutional gadflies," holistic practitioners dedicated to maintaining the health of collections.

Still, many museum closets remained a mess, with a few skeletons hidden inside. In the late 1960s and early 1970s, as museums lobbied for federal monies and tax advantages, the outside world began to sniff through those closets. Two insider practices emerged from the mothballs and into the headlines. The first scandal involved deaccessioning, museums disposing of collections they no longer wanted. The second involved museums acquiring antiquities they had no business owning.

Every newlywed has exchanged that extra coffee maker, every gardener understands the importance of pruning. Likewise, nearly every museum has weeded through its collections and at one time or another disposed of, traded, transferred or sold unwanted things. Deaccessioning is a legal and often sensible way to manage the vast quantity of objects that sit in collection vaults. But getting rid of collections is a tricky business. There are the legalities of bequests and donors' stipulations. There are the politics of informing donors or their progeny without hurting feelings or financial loyalty. And there is the matter of public perception. Is the object so historically or artistically important that it must remain in the public trust—and therefore in the museum? Who says so? How will a community react when it discovers that its museum is disposing of objects from the collection?

In 1942 the Illinois State Museum's mounted elephant Charlie had become a "white elephant." The museum found Charlie a new home at the Decatur Illinois Republican Headquarters, and no one batted an eye. It seemed perfectly appropriate for a museum to give another worthy cause first dibs on its unwanted collections. The Minneapolis Institute of Arts, however, drew ire in the 1950s when it sold 4,500 works to raise funds to buy a few first-rate masterpieces from Europe. But the Minneapolis trustees were not aiming simply to make money. They understood that if an object went on the market, proceeds should not pay the day-to-day bills but rather should be used directly for collections care or to acquire objects more in keeping with the institution's mission. Collections must beget collections, a recommendation now articulated in the American Association of Museums' *Code of Ethics for Museums.*

The stakes began to rise in the 1970s. Art sitting in storage skyrocketed in value. A Matisse worth $30,000 in 1957 could garner up to $500,000 by 1972 (and $14.8 million by 1995). Operating costs also were rising, and inflation was high. It was increasingly expensive to run a museum, let alone maintain a collection. A scandal at a New York museum brought these issues to the fore.

In 1971 Thomas Hoving, the brash and controversial director of the Metropolitan Museum of Art, presided over the sale of French modern art given to the museum by Adelaide Milton de Groot. According to legend, since the 1940s the Met's curators had considered de Groot a difficult personality and her paintings second-rate. Gradually, they transferred her collection to the storerooms. But knowing that de Groot would eventually bestow a large cash gift to the museum, they cared for the works and courted their donor. When she died in 1967, the Met got its donation and more. Her paintings weren't second-rate; in fact, they were worth a fortune on the market. De Groot's will stipulated that if the Met didn't want the paintings, they were to go to the Wadsworth Atheneum in Hartford, Conn. But Hoving was not about to send them to a rival museum. He wanted to use the de Groot "sludge," as he called it, to "raise a twenty million dollar war chest." Through a series of undercover transactions between an international network of dealers and curators, the Met sold one of the works, Henri Rousseau's *Tropics.* To the chagrin of American art connoisseurs, the work landed in a private office in Tokyo. The next year, the Met secretly sold another donated work: Dorothy Bernhard's gift of Vincent van Gogh's *The Olive Pickers.*

Henri-Julien-Félix Rousseau (le Douanier) (French, 1844-1910), **TROPICS,** *formerly in the collection of the Metropolitan Museum of Art, present location unknown. Image © The Metropolitan Museum of Art.*

This Akkadian seal, ca. 2334-2154 B.C., beside its modern impression, depicts a water god in his enclosure. Cylinder seals were worn on a string and then rolled over clay to leave a design or "signature." Approximately one-third of the Iraq Museum's collection of more than 15,000 cylinder seals were looted. © Lynn Abercrombie.

When the Met's undercover transactions became public, art experts and the media were outraged. They questioned how the prices were set, who benefited, why the sales were necessary (the Met was not hurting for money) and the impact this would have on other museums. New York's attorney general launched an investigation. In a scathing article in *Art in America* titled "Should Hoving Be De-accessioned?" art historian John Rewald assailed the Met for arrogance: "Has it occurred to anyone at the Metropolitan that its high-minded practices can backfire and hurt other museums? . . . Immediately after the Rousseau/van Gogh deal became known, a former benefactor of the Metropolitan put a highly important, historic and magnificent Impressionist painting on the market instead of willing it to the museum. A fundraiser for at least one American museum has already been told by a prospective contributor: 'Why come to me if you need money? Do what Hoving does and sell some of your pictures.'"

But this cautionary tale did end on a positive note. In response to the de Groot scandal, the Met's trustees created strict deaccessioning procedures that would become valuable models for other museums.

From the 1970s to the 1990s other acts of deaccessioning made headlines in their communities. The financial, ethical and legal dimensions of deaccessioning were examined by judges, accounting boards, curators, scholars, directors, boards of trustees, registrars and conservators. Museum professional associations revised their codes of ethics with such non-ambiguous statements as: "Funds obtained through disposal [of collections] must be used to replenish the collection."

■   ■   ■   ■   ■

A lintel from Thailand. A statue from Nigeria. Mosaics from Cyprus. Textiles from Peru. Museums have always been destinations for pilfered treasures, probably even before Napoleon's war trophies wound up in the Louvre and Lord Elgin's Parthenon friezes entered the British Museum. Today the Museum Security Network estimates that almost $10 billion in art is stolen and laundered around the world annually. War, of course, only worsens the situation. During three days in April 2003, an estimated 15,000 objects were looted from the Iraq Museum, Baghdad. Three years later less than half had been recovered.

The illicit trafficking of cultural property—the looting of antiquities from archeological sites and museums in poor countries for the benefit of museums and collectors in wealthier ones—has been a problem for decades. Archaeologists, government officials, dealers, journalists, auction houses, the military and even tourists are complicit. Before the 1970s, if the contraband happened to be an important antiquity or work of art, it stood a good chance of drifting into a museum collection, especially one in the United States.

Two international organizations—the United Nations Educational, Scientific, and Cultural Organization (UNESCO) and the International Council of Museums (ICOM)—had long been concerned about the illicit international traffic of art and antiquities into American museums. (Founded in Paris in 1946, UNESCO promotes the advancement of education, science and culture, and the preservation of world heritage. ICOM was formed at the same time, also in Paris.) The U.S. State Department also issued warnings that art plundered by Nazis was being smuggled into the country, possibly through Latin America. And beginning in the 1970s, delegates at international gatherings began to pose uncomfortable questions. By coveting art and antiquities, were museums supporting the trafficking of plunder? Should they demand better documentation before accepting an object of dubious origin? What should they do about contraband that was already in their collections?

If the answers to these questions seemed clear to international agencies, discussions within museums were cloudy. Scholars frequently argued that antiquities were safer in a museum in an "advanced" country than buried underground in "the third world." One American committee went so far as to plead "cultural poverty," arguing that the United States was a relatively young nation and thus needed antiquities from "culturally rich" but "financially poor" nations. To the committee, antiquities' role in scientific inquiry and public education trumped the means by which they were obtained.

The debate over one case changed the course of museum collecting forever. In 1947, as interest in pre-Columbian antiquities was growing worldwide, the Guatemalan government passed a law restricting their export, hoping to protect the country's cultural heritage. It did little good. During the 1950s and '60s archaeologists at Harvard and the University of Pennsylvania set up large-scale projects to study Mayan relics and ruins throughout Mexico and Guatemala. They hired locals to clear-cut paths through dense jungles and do the heavy manual labor involved in excavation. Soon organized groups of thieves (called "pothunters") began smuggling artifacts off the sites, now more accessible due to the paths archaeologists had funded. Using power saws and other crude methods, the robbers hacked away at pyramids and temples. No site was immune; even national monuments were mutilated. Smugglers slipped fragments—sometimes as large as 10 by 30 feet—across borders and through airport customs. Dealers sold the goods on the international art market, asking as much as $500,000 for a single piece. Many were then given to museums.

Initially the universities sponsoring the digs did not intervene. But in 1968 the International Congress of Americanists unanimously passed a resolution condemning the looting of pre-Columbian antiquities and requested that museums refuse to acquire such artifacts. In 1969 Clemency Coggins, a doctoral student at Harvard University, published a detailed description of the systematic theft of Mayan relics in Guatemala and Mexico, complete with maps and photos. With her colleagues at the Harvard's Peabody Museum, she documented 15 sites where vandals had sawn off or smashed to bits ancient stelae carved with "extraordinarily beautiful" Mayan hieroglyphics and masks. Coggins provided evidence that, despite the plea issued by archaeologists, much of the plunder resided in U.S. museums. Years later, she would receive a gold medal from the Archaeological Institute of America for her work.

The outside world was beginning to take notice of the illicit import and export of world art. *Washington Post* staff writer Karl Meyer published a list of looted South American cities in an exposé titled *Plundered Past*, which became a book in 1973. A number of actions followed. ICOM issued an "Ethics of Acquisition," stating that before adding something to its collection, a museum was ethically bound to find out who had owned the object, where it had come from and whether it was exported under the letter of the law. In the United States, Froelich Rainey, director of the University of Pennsylvania Museum of Archaeology and Anthropology, took the lead with a 1970 statement known as the Philadelphia Declaration. He condemned the "wholesale destruction of archaeological sites" and urged wealthy nations to introduce "more rigid import controls." The museum's curators pledged to "purchase no more art objects or antiquities for the Museum unless the objects were accompanied by a pedigree."

Perhaps most influential was the 1970 *UNESCO Convention on the Means of Prohibiting and Preventing the Illicit Import, Export and Transfer of Ownership of Cultural Property*. It specifically called on museums to "ensure their collections are built up in accordance with universally recognized moral principles," which included taking actions against "theft, clandestine excavation and illicit export." The UNESCO convention eventually went to the U.S. Senate, which ratified a statement prohibiting museums from receiving any more stolen goods. In 1983 the United States became the first major art-importing country to sign the convention into law. The issue was no longer a debate over ethics.

Even though looting and illegal trafficking continue to be worldwide problems, the museum profession took an important ethical step with this debate. Now the museum's duty was not only to safeguard its own objects but to safeguard cultural heritage in a broader, global sense.

■   ■   ■   ■   ■

A skateboard. An ATM card. A souped-up Harley Davidson motorcycle. A bottle of Goya brand picante salsa. A costume worn by hiphop artist Run D.M.C. How have these items, all made post-1970 and connected to popular culture, come to be collected alongside Renaissance paintings and colonial-era furniture?

Slave shackles. Armbands emblazoned with the Star of David. The door from the Birmingham jail cell that imprisoned Martin Luther King, Jr. A songbook with racist drawings of Chinese immigrants. A briefcase found in the rubble of the World Trade Center. How did these items, evidence of evil, come to be collected alongside works celebrating the best of humankind?

Beginning in the 1970s the protective bubble around museum collections slowly dissolved, as curators and collectors adjusted to political and social change. Rejecting the idea of a "melting pot" where different traditions merged into a single identity, they saw the nation as a mosaic of distinct traditions and cultures. How would these increasingly multicultural viewpoints influence museums? What kind of objects could represent the new America? How could collections more effectively serve all of society?

Museums took three big steps. First, they began to do a better job documenting the lives of all Americans, not just those in positions of influence. Second, they began to research and return looted objects, managing their collections more ethically. Third, they looked more closely at the relationship between people and objects. Why have a collection if it isn't accessible and meaningful to the public for whom it is held in trust?

A picture speaks a thousand words: close-up view of a metal ring inside a slave pen. Collections of the National Underground Railroad Freedom Center.

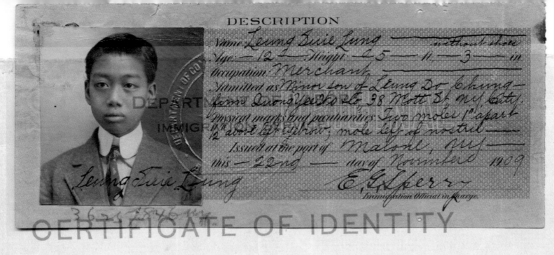

CERTIFICATE OF IDENTITY

NAME *Leung Suie Lung*

NO. *5 76*

The drive to collect objects that reflect the full range of human experience grew out of 1960s social activism. In 1967 G. Ellis Burcaw, director of the University Museum of Idaho, observed that the nation's museum collections were limited in scope. He implored museums to tell a fuller story, to begin "actively collecting [objects of] the poor, the working classes, the minority groups," instead of passively cataloguing whatever collectors chose to bring in the doors.

Such sentiments found a ready audience. American museums began to amass two new types of collections. The first focused on documenting contemporary times and the rise of mass media culture. The second reflected the country's changing racial, ethnic, religious and social character, as well as evidence of past acts of oppression.

Art institutions were the first museums to collect contemporary items and, by the 1970s, the collecting of art by living artists was in full swing. Contemporary art collecting allowed art museums to grow. First- or even third-rate works by the Old Masters were increasingly scarce—"endangered species," one museum director called them. But contemporary art was in continual production.

During this period the National Endowment for the Arts' (NEA) Museum Purchase Plan, launched in 1968, enabled more than 50 smaller regional museums—including the Arkansas Art Center in Little Rock, the J. B. Speed Art Museum in Louisville, Ky., and the Amarillo Art Center in Texas—to buy works by living artists. The late 1970s also saw a surge of interest in contemporary Latin American artists—although museum departments devoted to that genre would not come into their own until the Museum of Fine Arts, Houston led the way in the 1990s.

Collecting faced a new challenge—the transformed nature of artworks. Unlike the art of the past, easily mounted on pedestals or stretched onto frames, contemporary art adopted a bewildering number of guises. Some works were so enormous or heavy or reliant on

Certificate of identity for Suie Lung Leung, issued on Nov. 22, 1909, in Malone, N.Y. Lois Leung Collection, Museum of Chinese in the Americas.

electronic technology they warranted special rooms, entrances and floors. Others existed only as sounds, and still others as ideas. Many were constructed from materials that decayed easily or were meant to erode. Others occurred as performance, involving the audience and spaces outside the museum. Yet while artworks dramatically changed, the nature of collecting them did not. Art curators persuaded collectors and artists to make donations. They purchased art from artists, dealers and auctions. They commissioned artists to produce new works. They read journals and listened to the opinions of a vast number of critics and experts. And, as they had since the end of World War I, they operated in a well-honed marketplace, set up for the buying and selling of art.

Outside art museums, collecting methods were different. In university history departments, the new field of social history was looking away from "great men and great deeds" toward long cycles and day-to-day life. The new narratives of history stressed the emergence of new technologies, patterns of work, arrangements of domestic living and interactions among social groups. Social historians argued that U.S. history must tell the stories of all Americans, from rural laborers to the urban working classes, from slaves to immigrants. As Thomas A. Livesay, then director of the Museum of New Mexico put it in 1996, "The bottom line begs the question, 'Who owns history?' The answer must remain, 'None of us and all of us.'"

With populist motives and small budgets, social historians rummaged through the material culture of American society. Like raccoons, they raided attics, garbage dumps and abandoned buildings. Like scavengers, they shopped everywhere—at flea markets and supermarkets, in product catalogues and eventually on eBay. Like peddlers, they knocked on doors, collecting

oral histories, sifting through photo albums and watching endless reels of old home movies to capture an aural and visual record of the extraordinary moments of ordinary life.

Curators felt a sense of urgency. Objects needed to be preserved now, before they reached the landfill. Collecting today would give present generations more control over the way curators of the future interpreted the 20th century. American historians began to set their sights on documenting the popular culture of baby boomers.

An icon of baby boomer culture sits in Washington, D.C. In 1978 Edith and Archie Bunkers' easy chairs—along with a doily, an ashtray and two mock beer cans—from the set of the hit 1970s T.V. show *All in the Family* joined the collections of the Smithsonian's National Museum of American History

Xul Solar (Argentinian, 1887-1963), **JEFA/PATRONESS***, 1923. The Museum of Fine Arts, Houston; museum purchase with funds provided by the Latin American Experience Gala and Auction.*

Left: "Sand, Sun, and Fun" in the 20th-century gallery at the Oakland Museum—one aspect of the museum's examination of how people achieve the California dream. Courtesy of the Oakland Museum of California.

Center: Seeking to attract the baby boomer generation, in the 1990s the Strong Museum began to collect 1960s Barbie dolls and G.I. Joes. Courtesy Strong Museum, Rochester, N.Y.

Above, right: Archie and Edith Bunker's chairs from the set of **ALL IN THE FAMILY**. Courtesy of Smithsonian National Museum of American History, Behring Center.

Below, right: Elvis Presley's "Solid Gold" Cadillac and the gold-plated piano he received from his wife Priscilla on their first anniversary. Photo by Tim Hursley. Courtesy of the Country Music Hall of Fame and Museum.

(NMAH). These $8 thrift-store chairs, upholstered in dowdy fabric, were acquired within days of the show's last filming, donated by the show's producer Norman Lear at the request of curator Ellen Roney Hughes. "On their own merit, the chairs—lacking in provenance, beauty or distinction—would never have been accepted," noted Hughes. "The [museum's] Community Life Division acquired them because they were central props in a television show that was significant on a number of levels: as a leading situation comedy, a dominant type of American television show; as a pivotal show that caused changes in the genre; as revealing of common beliefs, values and behaviors in American life during the 1970s; and as a widely shared American cultural experience with passionate fans and detractors."

NMAH elevated the junkyard chairs to museum quality, caring for them in keeping with the highest standards of registration and conservation. They went on display along with another prop of immense meaning to baby boomers: the ruby slippers Judy Garland wore in the 1939 movie *The Wizard of Oz*. Smithsonian Secretary S. Dillon Ripley presided over the exhibit's opening, joined by a parade of T.V. stars and curators. As the Smithsonian added other iconic T.V. and movie props to its collections, an outpouring of pro and con reactions flowed into its mailroom. Many critics, including Ripley's successor Robert McCormick Adams, slammed the museum for adding such "trivial" artifacts to its august collections, "exaggerating their importance" and promoting the harmful activity of television viewing. "If the relics of T.V. are accepted as additions to permanent collections of museums," said Adams, "is there not a danger that we will contribute to the ongoing erosion of vital standards of judgment and performance in the society at large?"

But the Bunkers' chairs appealed to Smithsonian visitors. Nearly 25 percent of visitors specified that they had come to NMAH specifically to see the chairs. Hughes argued in favor of collecting popular culture. "The forms of American popular culture—movies, television programming, country music . . . are products of American creativity," she said, "with worldwide impact and recognition . . . in its totality and diversity, popular culture is highly significant." Thus emerged museums devoted solely to collecting and exhibiting media culture, including the Museum of Television and Radio, founded in 1975 by CBS executive William S. Paley, and the Museum of the Moving Image in Astoria, N.Y., founded in 1977.

Around the country, museums consigned objects of the moment to their collections vaults. In effect, they were curating time capsules for the future. In the 1980s Philadelphia's Please Touch (Children's) Museum worked with toy manufacturers to collect each year's top-selling toys, along with accompanying advertising. Some day they would shed light on growing up in America during the age of mass consumerism. In Boston, various computing machines were enshrined in a Computer Museum, now part of the Boston Museum of Science. When these bulky machines became obsolete and their parts unattainable, the museum's collections would give scientists a complete set of hardware and software to study.

Historical societies focused their efforts on documenting how local events—a new transportation system, a fire, a presidential visit—had shaped their communities. The Oakland Museum of California gathered artifacts from surfers, hippies, yuppies and black power and gay rights activists—examples of late 20th-century youth and political culture in California. Along with the objects, the museum collected the owners' stories. "While it is possible to conduct the collecting of objects and documentation as a close-ended process, terminating with interviews with the donor or seller and the physical transfer to the museum," noted L. Thomas Frye, the museum's emeritus curator of history, "it is equally possible to consider the relationship to be open-ended, with a continuing dialogue between the source person and the museum. I have sometimes loosely referred to this phenomenon as collecting the people along with their objects." Contemporary collecting thus wasn't only about documenting the recent past. It was about building relationships with the public—in the present tense.

Proponents of contemporary collecting pitched nostalgia to baby boomers and Generations X and Y. A leader was the Strong Museum in Rochester, N.Y., originally a repository for Margaret Strong's immense collection of 19th-century dolls. In the 1990s the museum began to collect and exhibit 1960s Barbie dolls and G.I. Joes, 1980s *Star Wars* Halloween costumes and a 1990s Wheaties Box sporting an image of an Olympic gold medalist. Curator Scott Eberle and Director G. Rollie Adams explained their reasoning for broadening the timeframe of the Strong's collections: "Outside the museum's walls, American culture was making room for body piercing. Could we blame our visitors for thinking of us as detached, fussy, or unspontaneous? Could we blame them for staying home?"

The beat of contemporary collecting picked up when museums became repositories for something near and dear to the hearts of most Americans: popular music. The Country Music Hall of Fame and Museum in Nashville opened in 1967 and grew to include more than 200,000 recordings as well as associated ephemera, such as Elvis Presley's gold Cadillac and Patsy Cline's cowboy boots. The Smithsonian purchased items related to jazz great Duke Ellington and hip hop pioneer Grand Master Flash. A few years later historical societies were acquiring objects associated with local musicians who had made it big, such as Prince (Minnesota) and Mahalia Jackson (Chicago). Documenting the roots and history of rock and roll, the collections of the Rock and Roll Hall of Fame and Museum in Cleveland (opened 1995) include curiosities like John Lennon's granny glasses and Jim Morrison's Cub Scout uniform. In 2000 Seattle's Experience Music Project dove into edgier tastes with its Jimi Hendrix collection and instruments smashed in concert by grunge artists Pearl Jam and Kurt Cobain. A chorus of smaller grassroots museums continue to pop up around the country, playing to Americans' love affair with music and celebrity.

Exploring contemporary history in [museums] is a dark, bloody, and contested ground, not for the faint of heart.

—LONNIE G. **BUNCH**, DIRECTOR,
NATIONAL MUSEUM OF AFRICAN AMERICAN HISTORY AND CULTURE

In more than a century of frenzied collecting, few people had thought to save items that represented America's ugly side. "Why would anyone save artifacts from such humiliating experiences like the Chinese Exclusion Act?" asked John Kuo Tchen, describing his difficulties in finding materials about Chinese immigration for the Museum of Chinese in the Americas in New York. Social historians and curators such as Tchen argued that collecting these experiences was important to opening up a dialogue about American history. Part of a museum's purpose should be to preserve and present evidence of a community's travails.

Anonymous, **UNTITLED (ALLEGORY OF THE LIFE OF ST. FRANCIS)**, *c. 18th century. Mexican Fine Arts Center Museum Permanent Collection, 2000. Gift of Daniel and Mary Healy. Photo by Kathleen Culbert-Aguilar.*

One of the first museums to collect the experiences of immigrants was the Norwegian-American Historical Association, founded at St. Olaf College in Minnesota in 1925. It not only collected nostalgic items from the old country, it documented "the tangled problems involved in the adjustment of [Norwegian pioneers] to their new environment." The Jewish Theological Seminary in New York and the Hebrew Union College in Cincinnati engaged in analogous efforts, collecting Jewish ceremonial objects to "illustrate the life of the people" and "counteract . . . prejudice against Jews." The collections grew during the ominous years preceding World War II, as European synagogues sold objects to finance Jewish emigration. The Theological Seminary's collection formed the basis for the Jewish Museum, which opened in Manhattan in 1947.

It wasn't until the 1960s that other marginalized ethnic communities in urban neighborhoods began to found museums that documented their immigration, cultural heritage and contributions to America, as well as the stumbling blocks encountered along the way. Chicano and Latino activism gave birth to El Museo del Barrio (East Harlem, New York, 1969); Mexican Museum (Mission District, San Francisco, 1975); Mexican Fine Arts Center Museum (Pilsen District, Chicago, 1982); and the Mexic-Arte Museum (Austin, Tex., 1983). Asian-American activists founded the Wing Luke Asian Museum (International District,

Seattle, 1966); the Museum of Chinese in the Americas (Chinatown, New York, 1980); and the Japanese American National Museum (Little Tokyo, Los Angeles, 1982). The gay community, persons with disabilities and other disenfranchised groups collected materials about their history and struggles. Edward T. Linenthal, author of a history of the U. S. Holocaust Memorial Museum, calls this kind of collecting "a vibrant form of memory work."

Like other history museums, the Japanese American National Museum documents the nation's triumphs and its tragedies. The Heart Mountain Barracks pictured here help tell the story of the government's internment of Japanese Americans during World War II. Photo by Norman Sugimoto. Japanese American National Museum (94.105.1).

The collecting of the history of one group —African Americans—illustrates how difficult and fraught with emotion memory work is. In the 1970s African-American collections grew in two ways. First, mainstream museums worked with social historians to incorporate black history and culture into their collections. Second, black community leaders started their own institutions as part of the wave of American ethnic museums.

Novelist and folklorist Zora Neale Hurston at the New York Times Book Fair, *1937. Library of Congress, LC-USZ62-126945.*

The first collection of African Americana, however, had been organized decades earlier by Puerto Rican intellectual Arturo Alfonso Schomburg. In the 1910s Schomburg moved to New York and began to collect books, art and other materials with the goal of disproving the myths of racial inferiority espoused by people like Henry Fairfield Osborn and affirming African people's role in the making of world civilization. Too challenging for a museum at that time, the Schomburg collection was acquired by the New York Public Library, where it has since grown to more than 1 million records and objects. Likewise, in the late 1920s, working under the supervision of anthropologist Franz Boas, novelist Zora Neale Hurston compiled extensive collections of Southern "Negro folk expression," including songs, children's games, "hoodoo spells" and "black magic." These collections are now part of the Library of Congress.

Not until well after the Civil Rights Movement would traditional museums collect black history in the context of American culture. In the 1970s the Smithsonian's National Museum of American History gathered material from the movement, including buttons, banners, tapes of speeches, oral histories, clothing of marchers and eventually the "Whites Only" Woolworth's lunch counter from Greensboro, N.C. The task was relatively easy. The movement was only a few years old, with many participants still alive and willing to contribute mementos and stories.

But collecting the physical evidence that had led to need for a movement in the first place—the objects related to slavery, the Jim Crow era and the Underground Railroad—proved to be more difficult. Out of fear and a desire to forget, these materials had largely been destroyed, save for a rare item of clothing or diary of an escaped slave hidden in an attic. Stories had been passed down orally. With popular successes like the 1977 T.V. mini-series *Roots: The Saga of an American Family* and the growth of African-American studies in universities, historic houses found that visitors were often more interested in the daily lives of servants and slaves than the wealthy homeowners. In 1979—to the dismay of nervous tour guides—social historians at Colonial Williamsburg declared that it was time to tell visitors who had really worked in the fields and kitchens at Williamsburg during the colonial era. Museum leaders agreed to expand the narrative, but there was a major impediment. In all its rooms of carefully restored pieces, Colonial Williamsburg possessed no objects related to its slaves. Thus the museum's first programs on slavery relied on actors and inventive theatre techniques rather than on physical artifacts.

Theatrical programs like Williamsburg's coincided with a movement to unearth and reconstruct a three-dimensional story of slavery. In the mid-1970s archeologists started to dig around 11 former slave dwellings on the grounds of the Hermitage, Andrew Jackson's Tennessee home. Meat bones, ceramics, religious charms, coins and weapons led to conclusions about slaves' diets,

Above: *Excavation of one of four field quarter slave cabins at the Hermitage. Each one was 40 feet by 20 feet with a dividing wall and housed two families. The Hermitage: Home of President Andrew Jackson, Nashville.*

Below: *"Jumping the Broom" wedding ceremony re-enactment at Carter's Grove Slave Quarter, Colonial Williamsburg. Courtesy of Colonial Williamsburg Foundation.*

beliefs, economy and power relations with plantation owners. The Stonewall Jackson House in Virginia and Drayton Hall, a restored rice plantation in South Carolina, hunted down archives and oral histories, anything that could provide a fuller story about the slaves on their sites.

In 1988 Colonial Williamsburg re-constructed its 18th-century slave quarters at Carter's Grove, about eight miles from its main site. It even re-enacted a slave auction in 1994, complete with a reconstructed trading block. The visceral reaction of visitors created controversy and made newspaper headlines. In 1998 Thomas Jefferson's home, Monticello, added an audio tour that identified Jefferson's slaves by name and told some of their individual stories. In the meantime other historical societies slowly dug out slave auction flyers, bills of sale, flyers offering bounty for captured escapees and other evidence of slavery buried deep in storage areas.

Of course, some African Americans didn't trust mainstream museums to collect their history. How could a collection assembled by well-meaning but detached professionals and academics tell a community's true stories? Shouldn't African Americans take charge of how their history was being collected and interpreted? Activists initiated a black museum movement. In 1961 Margaret Burroughs founded the DuSable Museum in Chicago and in 1965 Charles Wright began a small mobile museum in the basement of his Detroit obstetric practice. In the Anacostia neighborhood of Washington, D.C., and in New York City's Harlem, black leaders began to work with their communities in the late 1960s to develop art and cultural exhibits to advance black consciousness and pride. By the 1980s groups in many cities—Los Angeles, Philadelphia, Austin, Tex.—had organized museums of black culture and history.

This slave pen (seen here in its original location) was preserved and added to the collections of the National Underground Railroad Freedom Center.

Like the earliest American museums, these institutions often were founded before they had collections or even buildings. Community members charged with developing collections operated under a sense of scarcity and duty that echoed the urgency of 19th-century collectors. In 1982 Byron Rushing, then-director of the Museum of Afro-American History in Boston, called on black Americans to start collecting their heritage right away: "Collecting black material culture is . . . not a game or a hobby. It is part of a life-and-death struggle . . . to control what is collected about us [and] to take a step closer to independent interpretations of our historical condition."

Curators from black-run museums searched local churches, barbershops and businesses. They asked for objects like scrapbooks, quilts, photographs and baseball uniforms. To get

Museums all over the country pay tribute to Rosa Parks, the woman who launched the Civil Rights Movement. **Above:** A re-enactment of her famous bus ride at the National Civil Rights Museum, Memphis, Tenn. **Below:** The bus itself. From the Collections of The Henry Ford Museum (2001.154.1 / B.1158381).

what you need, Rushing suggested, "Invite yourself, get invited, to look through attics and cellars. Call people when you hear they're moving. Read obituaries. Let lawyers, ministers, undertakers know you are collecting." In addition to gathering what they could about family and community life, activists saved buildings and burial grounds that were valuable artifacts of black history. In 1981 a coalition lobbied to save the Lorraine Motel in Memphis, site of Martin Luther King, Jr.'s assassination, from demolition and turn it into a memorial museum. Citizens in Henning, Tenn., founded the Alex Haley Museum, saving the *Roots* author's boyhood home, where he listened to his grandparents tell the stories that inspired his masterpiece.

Recent years have witnessed a surge of African-American collections and the blossoming of institutions, such as an expanded Charles Wright Museum of African American History in Detroit; Birmingham Civil Rights Institute; National Voting Rights Museum in Selma, Ala.; and the National Civil Rights Museum in the restored Lorraine Motel. African-American archaeology projects spread to historic museums in northern and midwestern towns that had been active in the Underground Railroad movement.

Yet artifacts are still extremely rare, and all museums compete fiercely for them. In 2001 an online auction website announced that the Montgomery, Ala., bus on which Rosa Parks had launched the famous boycott was for sale. For years the bus sat in an Alabama field, storing rusty tools; now its owner wanted to cash in. Bidding was fierce. The Henry Ford Museum

& Greenfield Village in Dearborn, Mich., won out to the tune of $492,000, plus the costs of restoration. Steven Hamp, the museum's director, declared his prize acquisition to be the single most important artifact of the Civil Rights Movement.

Not possessing the Ford Museum's budget, African-American museums relied on their connections to add artifacts. In 2002 the Civil Rights Museum in Memphis received from the Tennessee Legislature the right to display 200 pieces of unsealed police evidence from King's assassination. Items such as a bullet found in King's body and a gun seized from assassin James Earl Ray packed an emotional wallop. At the Birmingham Institute an amateur collector donated shards of glass he had gathered off the street after the 1960s racist attack at the 16th Street Baptist Church that killed four young girls.

In 2002 a Kentucky farmer donated a slave pen from his property to Cincinnati's National Underground Railroad Freedom Center. The two-story log building in which escaped slaves had been shackled to the floor was re-built inside the museum. "The first time I entered it I cried," said Rita Organ, the museum's former director of exhibitions and collections, "It's almost like the walls were talking. Once you know what it is, and how it was used, you can't not feel the emotion."

The struggles and emotions of collecting recent history also were experienced by other ethnic museums. Using photographs and historical documents, Japanese Americans sought to reconstruct the history of their internment during World War II. The Japanese American National Museum in Los Angeles acquired a barracks from the Heart Mountain War Relocation Center in Wyoming, which was reassembled for the museum by former camp prisoners, their families, and other volunteers.

Some of the thousands of shoes that were confiscated from prisoners arriving at the Majdanek concentration camp. United States Holocaust Memorial Museum, courtesy of the State Museum at Majdanek, Lublin, Poland.

In San Francisco, the Gay, Lesbian, Bisexual and Transgender Historical Society archived the underground publications that had helped the gay community to communicate with each other before some cities became more tolerant of gay rights. They developed exhibitions of these collections for Gay Pride parades and public libraries.

The difficulties of piecing together objects that documented past tragedies only underscored museums' resolve to be more proactive in the collecting of pivotal historical events. In 1978 a group of Holocaust survivors, politicians, and educators announced plans for a museum about the Holocaust in Washington, D.C. They worked with the same sense of urgency that spurred other collectors. "The evidence [of the Holocaust in Europe] is disintegrating," stated

Martin Smith, who became the exhibition director of the U.S. Holocaust Memorial Museum, which opened to the public in 1993. "Everything is rotting away. Somehow or other these things need to be seized."

Researchers traveled to Europe to visit concentration camps, ghetto sites and survivors' homes. They saw that the camps, now state museums in Poland, possessed horrific evidence: bags of human hair, victims' suitcases, items used to torture people and leftover canisters of Zyklon-B gas.

They asked for a dismantled barrack from Auschwitz. They learned that Majdanek had hundreds of thousands of shoes that had been ripped off the feet of victims, so they asked for 4,000. At a railroad depot near Warsaw, Jacek Nowakowski, later the museum's director of collections, found a former cattle car that had transported victims to their deaths. It was important to the collectors that all of the items be donated, not purchased. They didn't want to create a market for the evidence of evil.

Caring for such objects was "overwhelmingly painful" to museum staff. "Professionally, I had been used to dealing with beautiful things," said Registrar Emily Dyer. "We [the collections staff] had to try to steel ourselves from becoming emotionally involved, but of course that was not always possible." There were delicate conservation challenges as well. Artifacts often arrived battered and dirty, but it was not appropriate to restore them to their former pristine condition. For example, the museum acquired a filthy milk can in which archives had been buried so they would survive the war. Conservation consultant Steven Weintraub developed a special process to preserve the mud that clung to the can, since the poor condition was important to its story.

As historian Edward Lilenthal has observed, "No longer is there a lengthy period between events and the urge to memorialize." Potent memory work in the form of museum collecting began to take place in the immediate aftermath of calamity: the AIDS crisis; the Oklahoma City bombing. In 2001, within hours of the Sept. 11 terrorist attack, the Library of Congress began to collect websites and blogs commenting on the event; a day later, staff launched a project to collect oral histories. New York museums immediately began to archive the experience with makeshift exhibitions of photographs. Other museums collected comments from visitors stranded in their travels, still in shock and streaming into museum galleries to

seek solace. Within days, with the support of New York Port Authority, curators showed up at the Fresh Kills landfill in Staten Island, where debris from the World Trade Center was being piled. They tagged melted steel, airline chunks, a stairwell sign, carbonized furniture—anything they felt was worthy of being preserved as "a tactile, three-dimensional expression of the unspeakable scale" of the disaster.

Their reactions were as charged as those of the collections workers at the U.S. Holocaust and Underground Railroad museums. As the *New York Times* stated, "curators began the physically and intellectually exhausting work [of collecting] even as the firefighters were still battling fires. . . . Relying on a mixture of professional experiences, aesthetic judgment and a strong dose of gut reaction, they picked out objects from amid the 1.4 million tons of debris to save . . . computer keyboards, pages from wall calendars, a file cabinet and dozens of other items that are valuable by virtue of their connection to cultural history, like Judy Garland's ruby-red 'Wizard of Oz' slippers at the Smithsonian."

It may seem hard-hearted to compare rummaging through the Sept. 11 landfill to collecting popular culture. But the *Times* had a point. So many Americans experienced the terror attacks through the lens of television. Many turned to museums to help make sense of these events. Museum collections were now expected to document the full spectrum of the human experience, from the sublime to the tragic—and to do so almost instantly.

■　■　■　■　■

The forefathers shot the Indians, or poisoned them with bad whisky . . . all that remains of them are the few tools and stone implements which they carried, and which we find in their graves.

—W. J. **HOLLAND**, DIRECTOR, CARNEGIE MUSEUM, 1902

For Native America, NAGPRA provides a new sense of empowerment under which long-lost items can be repatriated, and it means that Native Americans can be active participants in the museum community.

—ROGER **ECHO-HAWK**, ASSISTANT CURATOR, DENVER ART MUSEUM, 2002

In the 1990s museum collecting took a major step forward with the passage of the federal Native American Graves Protection and Repatriation Act (NAGPRA) and new guidelines on Nazi-era provenance from the American Association of Museums. Museums were ready to make amends for mistakes that tainted some collections.

Enacted in 1990 NAGPRA requires museums that receive federal funds to inventory their collections of Native American sacred and funerary objects, human remains and objects of cultural patrimony; send summaries of these inventories to Indian tribes; and repatriate items if tribes with appropriate cultural affiliation to the objects request it. NAGPRA is "the single most important piece of national cultural property legislation ever adopted in the United States," writes James Nason. "[T]he passage of this legislation . . . was a stunning victory for Native American communities."

The victory was long in coming. Since the massive anthropological collecting of the late 19th century, museums and Native Americans have had what anthropologist James

Clifford describes as a "charged set of . . . asymmetrical power relationships." Museums harbored many ancestral remains and sacred objects while Native Americans struggled to honor their ancestors and maintain their traditions. In the 1970s, inspired by civil rights movements, the 1970 UNESCO convention and successful repatriations of aboriginal objects by Australian and Canadian museums, American tribes asserted their rights to their heritage. They questioned museums about displays that presented Native Americans as "savages." They asked for the return of pipes, medicine bundles, ceremonial masks, funerary objects and human remains. Some museums responded callously, either ignoring the requests or refusing them outright. Tribal leaders persisted. A breakthrough came in 1978 when Congress passed the American Indian Religious Freedom Act (AIRFA), establishing Native Americans' rights to use and possess sacred objects necessary to ongoing religious practices. According to Nason, AIRFA "sent shockwaves through the museum community," which feared the day when tribes would come to them, law-in-hand.

Above: In the 1980s Omaha leaders asked the Peabody Museum of Archaeology and Ethnology to return their Sacred Pole, given to the institution for safekeeping a century earlier. Peabody Museum, Harvard University Photo N32151.

Left: The repatriation ceremony marking the return of the pole. Peabody Museum, Harvard University Photo N31958C.

Throughout the 1980s tribes put pressure on museums. Omaha leaders approached Harvard's Peabody Museum and declared that they were ready to take care of their sacred pole, loaned to the museum for safekeeping a century earlier. The Missouri Historical Society helped purchase land for the reburial of the Comanche remains unearthed after the Antiquities Act. The board of the Denver Art Museum authorized the return of war gods to the Zuni and helped arrange for a secure shrine for the objects' placement. By 1989 several states had passed repatriation laws and many museums had quietly returned items to tribal communities. The federal government also ordered the Smithsonian to survey its Native American holdings, authorized the creation of the National Museum of the American Indian (which would open in September 2004) and began to debate the passage of NAGPRA.

When museums became aware that repatriation could become federal law, they began to worry aloud. Aren't these objects safer in a museum? What do Native Americans know about proper care? How will tribes prove that an object is really sacred? How will they prove ownership? Won't they simply drain museum collections, and then turn around and sell objects for profit to private collectors? And how will we pay for all the extra work this is going to create? In its 1988 annual report, the American Association of Museums boasted of "slowing the process on the Native American Museums Claim Commission Act." Similarly the American Association of Anthropology argued for anthropologists' right of scientific inquiry and research. How could museums return skeletal remains for reburial, when there is much to learn about them that could benefit science? Attorney Walter Echo Hawk countered, "What Europeans want to do with their dead is their business. We have different values."

Siding with Native Americans was the U.S. Congress. After all, families who had lost young men in wars were asking for their remains; why shouldn't Native Americans be granted this same basic right? Qisuk's skeleton still sat in a storeroom at the American Museum of Natural History, Ishi's brain in a glass jar on a shelf at the Smithsonian. Didn't rights regarding human remains supersede the right of scientific inquiry?

Led by Arizona representatives Morris Udall and John McCain and Hawai'ian Sen. Daniel Inouye, and after heated negotiations between Native American activists and the museum community, NAGPRA passed. President George H. W. Bush signed it into law. "It is the hope and commitment of AAM and Native American leadership that, having dealt with this issue in the political arena, we can now, together turn to the much more exciting and important promise of establishing a new and dynamic relationship between Native Americans and museums," wrote AAM President Ellsworth Brown.

Museums scrambled to create inventories and decode NAGPRA's legal jargon. "The intent of the law was very good, but compliance turned out to be difficult," says Peter Tirrell, associate director of the Sam Noble Museum of Natural History in Norman, Okla., which held 4,500 sets of human remains and about a million Indian artifacts. Museums found themselves caught in tribal politics when more than one group claimed the same object or people belonging to the same tribe disagreed.

Museums also became involved in politics when Native American beliefs about the living power of spiritual beings conflicted with museum practice about hermetically sealed storage and object conservation. According to American Indian traditions, sacred objects require special care. Some must not be handled by women. Others must be fed organic materials. These requirements baffled museum administrators, who still managed to hammer out compromises that allowed for private sacred ceremonies within collections areas.

Baskets in the ethnology collection at the Sam Noble Oklahoma Museum of Natural History, University of Oklahoma. Photo by Linda Coldwell.

Many objects collected in the field had been preserved with toxic chemicals, making them potentially harmful both to museum workers and the people to whom they were repatriated. In 1996 lawmakers added a clause to NAGPRA that required museums to disclose information on the chemical treatment of repatriated objects. By 2000 almost half of museums with Native American collections had repatriated or were in the process of negotiating the return of objects. Both Ishi and Qisik finally were laid to rest in their homelands.

NAGPRA transformed museum practice on many levels. With government support museums developed comprehensive inventories and trained staff, which benefited them far beyond the law's requirements. The Arizona State Museum in Tucson established programs to assist tribes in the technical aspects of repatriation. Others created programs, recorded oral histories and learned the stories and significance of collection objects. Museums' fears about losing vast amounts of their collections were unfounded. "What better contribution to a people can a museum provide," notes curator George Horse Capture, "than to help them survive."

■　■　■　■　■

From the 1940s to the 1980s many of the details of World War II looting were obscured. Succumbing to what art restitution expert Constance Lowenthal called "collective amnesia," the world let the issue of unclaimed Nazi plunder remain dormant. But with the fall of

Communism in 1989 records in Russia became available to researchers for the first time. In 1994 Lynn H. Nicholas published *The Rape of Europa*, an account of how and why the Nazis had hijacked art. Around the same time, Paris-based investigative journalist Hector Feliciano's *The Lost Museum: The Nazi Conspiracy to Steal the World's Greatest Works of Art* was released in the United States. Both authors revealed that some looted artwork was now owned by American museums. Usually the works had been bought through perfectly legal transactions. But inadequate documentation about previous ownership—i.e., an artwork's provenance—confused the situation. The revelations shocked the American museum community. "These looted artworks are the remnants of a lost museum destroyed and scattered around the world by Hitler's murderous attempt at changing history," wrote Feliciano, "By tracking these works down and bringing their stories back to life, the shadows created by all these years of oblivion will, hopefully, dissipate at last."

To provide greater access to its collections, the New-York Historical Society opens its storage facility to the public. Joshua Silk Photography/NYHS.

That same year Henri Bondi, nephew of deceased Viennese collector Lea Bondi Jaray, wrote a letter to the Museum of Modern Art (MoMA), noting his concerns about a painting on display there. Egon Schiele's *Portrait of Wally* had been loaned by the Leopold Foundation of Austria as part of a traveling exhibition. Bondi claimed Nazis stole *Wally* from his aunt in 1939; thus it was rightfully his. MoMA refused to turn it over, stating it did not belong to the museum. The district attorney of Manhattan stepped in and seized the painting. The museum community was unnerved. Were museums now responsible for researching the provenance of works on temporary loan? What did the seizure mean for future exhibitions? Would other collectors be reluctant to lend works with incomplete provenance to museums? Within months MoMA's worst fears were realized when two lenders opted out of an upcoming Pierre Bonnard exhibition. Like much disputed work from the Nazi era, *Wally* turned out to have a convoluted history involving many unclear transactions. But one thing was clear. MoMA's legal obligation was to the Leopold Foundation, not Bondi. The museum was directed to send the painting back to Austria.

Bondi's fight opened a door for the heirs of Nazi victims. More claims materialized. After a series of complicated investigations and negotiations, the Seattle Art Museum and National Gallery of Art returned paintings to the heirs of Nazi victims. With the awakened interest in Nazi-era looting and the likelihood of even more claims, President Bill Clinton formed an advisory commission in 1998, chaired by Edgar Bronfman, head of the World Jewish Congress. Museums chose to be proactive. Both the Association of Art Museum Directors and the American Association of Museums issued guidelines. Research methodologies were developed, press releases written, websites created. "Red flags" were placed around artworks with spotty paperwork from the war years and posted on the Web by organizations like the International Foundation for Art Research (IFAR) and the Getty Information Institute. Still, newspapers and heirs of Holocaust victims accused museums of not going far enough. In 2001 AAM published a detailed methodology to help museums research suspect art. Two years later the organization unveiled the Nazi-Era Provenance Internet Portal, a gateway to digitized information about collections in U.S. museums. At last it was becoming easier to get answers to questions that had remained unanswered, deliberately or inadvertently, for a half century.

NAGPRA and the Nazi-Era Provenance Internet Portal sent the message to the public that most museums are willing to apply present-day standards to help correct errors made in the past. In 2004 AAM and ICOM released the *Red List of Latin-American Cultural Objects at Risk*, a step toward curbing the illicit traffic in pre-Columbian and Colonial objects from Latin American archaeological sites and churches.

But the issue of repatriation will not go away. In 2002, 18 prominent museum directors in the United States and Europe issued a statement affirming their right as "universal museums" to transcend borders and keep long-held antiquities. "Objects," the directors said, "should be viewed in light of different sensitivities and values, reflective of the earlier era [of collecting]. . . . They have become part of the museums that have cared for them, and by extension part of the heritage of the nations which house them." The statement indirectly referred to the Greek government's repeated demands for the return of the Elgin Marbles, held by the British Museum since the 19th century. Yet in 2006 one of these "universal museums," the Metropolitan Museum of Art took the unprecedented step of agreeing to return six contested antiquities to the Italian Cultural ministry. Today looting of cultural heritage continues around the globe and more claims surface daily. Indeed, repatriation of collections continues to be an unresolved issue in the museum community.

KWAKWAKA'WAKW (KWAKIUTL) MECHANICAL MASK, *late 19th century. © National Museum of the American Indian, Smithsonian Institution.*

■　■　■　■　■

Since anything is a collectible, anything can become the subject of a museum collection.

—WILCOMB **WASHBURN**, *MUSEUM NEWS*, 1996

In the 1970s the popularity of youth museums and science centers advanced the idea that museums did not need collections to serve the public. Traditionalists cringed. Wasn't the phrase "non-collecting museum" an oxymoron? Art historian Alma Wittlin argued, "A place in which people are exposed to changing lights or to a galaxy of light and sound unrelated to objects may offer a new kind of symphony or carnival . . . but it is not a museum. Objects have to remain the stars of the cast." Yet by this time the idea of what constituted an object had changed.

Museums had gained an immense amount of knowledge about culture in their century of collecting. They had learned that one person's treasure is another's white elephant, and vice versa. They had learned that possession is not nine-tenths of the law. They had learned that the meaning of things changes over time. They had learned that it is these meanings, not the objects themselves, that drive a museum. James H. Duff, director of the Brandywine River Museum in Chadds Ford, Pa., put it this way: "Our objects live. Through them we reveal history, process, action, emotion. When we succeed at that task . . . we stimulate the potential in this world for beauty, for invention and for understanding."

Like a child advancing into a new developmental stage, museums also had learned the value of sharing their treasures with all the people who cared about them. Museum theorist Elaine Heumann Gurian postulated, "Not meaning to denigrate the immense importance of museum objects and their care . . . they, like props in a brilliant play, are necessary but alone are not sufficient." Gurian meant that museums' value to society had shifted from housing and caring for collections to serving as public places that gather people, tell stories and evoke memories. Accessibility, education, interpretation and exhibition were the keys to keeping objects and the ideas they embody alive.

Yet as author David Carr reminds us, museums "build collections because we strive to keep and preserve evidence of human continuity, and in order to sustain remembrance. We strive not to forget how we have become who we are . . . cultural institutions hold artifacts and their legacies, when our memories as humans cannot. This makes possible the transmission of meanings among distant generations." In other words, the urge to collect is tied to the very essence of what it means to be human. As long as artists create, scientists discover, adventurers explore the universe and humans tell stories, there will be collections. These collections will find their way, in one form or another, to museums.

THE EXHIBITION

At the 1879 Philadelphia Centennial, Americans flocked to see the latest sensation from Paris: Jules Verreaux's life-size recreation of two ferocious Barbary lions in mid-attack, their prey a doomed Arab courier and his terrified camel, helpless to escape certain death. Spectators were fascinated and horrified by the intensely dramatic scene. It proved so popular that the Carnegie Natural History Museum, duly impressed, eventually bought it for $50, transported it to Pittsburgh and put it on display. It can be viewed there to this day.

Verreaux's creation broke new ground. Before its arrival in the United States, the public had been accustomed to crude exhibitions of taxidermy featuring animal hides stuffed with straw or lumpy rags, their legs propped up with rods and nailed onto wooden planks. Exhibited as curiosities, a giraffe from Africa, a bear from Alaska and a kangaroo from Australia might share the same glass and mahogany case—a scene of course, that could never occur in reality. Verreaux, on the other hand, had posed four carefully chosen figures in a way that told a gripping story, giving spectators a vivid lesson about life in a faraway land.

This dramatic scene of a doomed Arab courier has fascinated and horrified visitors for more than 100 years. Photo by Melinda McNaugher. Courtesy of the Carnegie Museum of Natural History.

Visitors had a very different experience at other exhibitions of the day. Most late 19th-century museums exhibited *all* of the objects in their collections. (To put that in some perspective, consider that today most display only about 5 percent). Their goal was not to tell a dramatic story, as Verreaux had done, but rather to show off sheer numbers of objects. Some displays were so exhaustively and colorlessly systematic—drawer after drawer of hand-labeled seashells or arrowheads, for example—that they must have induced a feeling of drowsiness in all but the most ardent naturalist. Others were eclectic to the point of confusion, cluttered with unrelated objects and artwork from a dizzying array of periods and styles. Nineteenth-century American displays mirrored the collections in European cathedrals and palaces, which had been designed to impress the public with their owners' wealth and power. This was in keeping with the times: museums were established in part to show that America was becoming a cultural and economic powerhouse.

As the 20th century approached, American museums began to develop new approaches for exhibiting their collections. The reason for the change was clear. Aiming to become more educational, a number of institutions had been working with local boards of education and settlement houses (organizations founded to help immigrants adapt to the "American way of life"). But exhibitions had a long way to go if they were to fulfill the museum's nascent educational mission. Inventive curators turned to the original environments— the landscapes, villages and homes—from which collections were first acquired. They borrowed techniques from the era's wildly popular world's fairs and international expositions and composed objects into habitat dioramas, life groups and period rooms. The goal was scientific accuracy and attention to natural details. Exhibitions would tell a new kind of story—one that used a carefully crafted setting to show how objects related to each other in the outside world. Before the advent of color cinema and long before television and transatlantic air travel, these mini-environments offered a glimpse into strange and exotic worlds that had been accessible to most people only through fiction.

About this time a taxidermist named Carl Akeley began his museum career. In 1886, after achieving fame for preserving the skin of Jumbo, circus impresario P. T. Barnum's beloved elephant, Akeley left a commercial studio in upstate New York and joined the staff of the Milwaukee Public Museum. He wanted to create displays that were both life-like and beautiful, to instruct an increasingly urbanized public about life in the natural world. At the Milwaukee Public, Akeley created America's first museum habitat diorama: the famed "Muskrat Group." He studied and dissected the animals and meticulously sketched their anatomy. He then modeled them in clay, positioned them in realistic poses, and carefully attached hides to the clay models.

Akeley was interested in the artistic as well as the scientific, drawing inspiration from a pre-movie form of entertainment called the cyclorama. This was a public theater with an enormous circular canvas that, when accompanied by special effects, illustrated a story, usually a war battle. Cyclorama painters moonlighted at the Milwaukee Public Museum, where they shared ideas with Akeley. In 1890 he placed a miniaturized version of the cyclorama's curved backdrop in a wood-framed case; the canvas depicted the muskrat habitat, a river bending into the horizon. In front of the river, he placed his anatomically correct models, a colony of muskrats, in various poses—swimming, eating, sleeping. Instead of freezing one dramatic event as Verreaux had done, Akeley created an entire story that incorporated many moments of a muskrat's day into one physical space. The result was so life-like that it thrilled museum visitors. Still on view today, "Muskrat Group" became the prototype for what would be known as "the Milwaukee style" of exhibit design. Akeley would go on to produce larger and more elaborate habitat dioramas for other natural history museums, introducing visitors everywhere to a view of life in the wild.

A related innovation was taking place 90 miles to the south, in the city of Chicago. This one involved posing models of human figures to tell a story about "primitive" life. World's fairs regularly had displayed live native peoples in "faithful environments" of their villages, attracting crowds of spectators. At the 1893 Columbian Exposition, sculptors attempted to make these popular temporary exhibitions more permanent by borrowing life-casting techniques from Scandinavian ethnology and British wax museums. Using live people as

their models, sculptors created costumed mannequins, paying careful attention to the clothing, hairstyles and other ornamentation specific to different tribes. Then they positioned the mannequins in life-like poses, performing daily activities such as cooking. The scene was encased in glass, allowing visitors to walk around the display, as if they were visiting the actual villages.

The "Muskrat Group," America's first museum habitat diorama, 1890. Taxidermist Carl Akeley designed the life-like display to teach urban residents about the natural world. Courtesy of the Milwaukee Public Museum.

Smithsonian curator William Henry Holmes, one of the innovators of this "life-group" design approach, explained its practical advantage. Mannequins, he pointed out with implacable logic and no touch of irony, didn't need to be fed and housed. They could live on in perpetuity to "form a permanent exhibit, which, set up in the museum, continues to please and instruct for generations."

Life-group sculptors paid faithful attention to detail, but they relied on their imaginations, too, perhaps to create a more heightened sense of drama. Artistic license, however, sometimes perpetuated stereotypes about Native Americans. In 1901, at the Pan-American Exposition in Buffalo, Holmes unveiled 12 meticulously crafted dioramas of native people from the Arctic to the Antarctic and everywhere in-between. The best known of the Buffalo life groups featured an Inuit family from Smith Sound, Greenland, laughing as they harpoon a seal. Called "The Happy Eskimos," it was created in part to communicate that "the Eskimos . . . are the most cheerful and mirth-loving people you ever saw," Holmes explained. "The Happy Eskimos" created a sensation at a time when the public was fascinated by arctic exploration. The life group was transferred to the Smithsonian and remained on display there for more than 80 years.

Anthropologist Franz Boas insisted that his life-group of a Kwakiutl family at the American Museum of Natural History be based on actual field research. Neg./Trans. no. 338764s. American Museum of Natural History Library.

Science, artistry and stereotypes also influenced the spectacular "Hopi Snake Dance Group," created by Theodore A. Mills in 1901 for the Carnegie Museum of Natural History. While many life-group creators conducted their own fieldwork, Mills had never actually witnessed a snake dance. Instead, he worked from photographs, dressing the mannequins in real ceremonial clothing purchased from a trader in Arizona. He then composed a scene featuring a curling serpent slithering through the mouth of one dancer, as others "charm" it with feathers. Mills's use of drama and real artifacts influenced exhibit designers in natural history museums for decades.

Life groups would become more realistic thanks to anthropologist Franz Boas of the American Museum of Natural History (AMNH) in New York. Boas took a decidedly scholarly approach. As he organized AMNH's North Pacific Coast Hall in 1899, he insisted that costumes, ornaments and tools be displayed "correctly" and with reference to their actual use based on field research. The best-known group in this extraordinary hall depicted the Kwakiutl people of Northern Vancouver, with whom the anthropologist had lived and studied.

But even Boas recognized that life-group exhibitions had an artificial air and could be more confusing than instructional for visitors. "It is an avowed object of a large [life] group to transport the visitor into foreign surroundings," he said, "[but] the surroundings of a Museum are not favorable to an impression of this sort. The cases, the walls, the contents of other cases, the columns, the stairways, all remind us that we are not viewing an actual village . . . and spoils the whole effect."

Nonetheless, life groups and habitat dioramas were popular with the public and spread to museums across the nation. Inspired in part by innovators like Akeley, Holmes and Boas, the fields of anthropology and taxidermy were growing in influence. Curators exchanged information about new exhibits at professional meetings. University and art college students actively sought museum apprenticeships, hoping to join collecting expeditions sponsored by wealthy patrons. This influx of talent, as well as steadily expanding collections, led to larger and more elaborate displays. In 1910 AMNH suspended a 64.5 foot Haida canoe from the ceiling of the North Pacific Coast Hall and filled it with mannequins of a Chilkat (Tlingit) chief and dancers in ornate ceremonial costumes, being rowed to a Potlatch feast. A highlight of school field trips, the scene was described by J. D. Salinger in *Catcher in the Rye* as "this long, long Indian war [sic] canoe, about as long as three goddam Cadillacs in a row, with about twenty Indians in it, some of them paddling, some of them looking tough. . . ."

In 1914 the State Museum of New York in Albany unveiled six depictions of local Iroquois culture, designed by Arthur C. Parker, an archaeologist of Iroquois descent. Parker added theatrical lighting, darkening the hall and illuminating each case from within. The effect must have been as dramatic for visitors as entering a movie palace, one of America's newer forms of entertainment.

Designers of habitat dioramas were not about to be left behind. They added curved ceilings and skillfully crafted props, like fake rocks and grass, to their recreated environments. Some built towering displays, featuring big-game trophies from hunting safaris in Africa. Others perfected the mini-diorama, a small-scale version that fit into nature centers and smaller museum buildings. By the 1930s, as artists supported by the Works Progress Administration began to work in museums, the number of habitat diorama projects increased. Influenced by the public's growing interest in Americana as well as the rise of the national park system, diorama designers positioned mounted North American

mammals like bison and antelope against painted images of national parks, such as the Grand Canyon and Yosemite.

■   ■   ■   ■   ■

While natural history museums played to museum-goers' fantasies of exotic people and the great outdoors, art museums and historical sites provided a glimpse into the indoor lives of the wealthy in period rooms. These became the indoor version of the habitat diorama. Instead of painted backdrops and mounted animals, period rooms displayed the real thing, with framed paintings on the walls, household items and authentic furniture.

Curators took their cues from preservationists and world's fair planners. As far back as the 1860s citizens groups had organized restorations of the homes of national heroes—starting with George Washington's home in Mount Vernon, Va.—and along the way launched America's historic preservation movement. Such efforts communicated patriotic pride. Children and adults were educated about the nation's founders, while a style of architecture and design that dated back to the American Revolution was preserved.

World's fair planners re-created colonial New England kitchens with more commercial goals in mind. These kitchens functioned as profitable "ye olden tyme" restaurants, serving American Yankee cuisine to fairgoers. Museums saw the educational potential of these displays. At Memorial Hall in Deerfield, Mass. (1891), the de Young Museum in San Francisco (1896) and the Oakland Museum of California (1910) colonial kitchens were furnished with authentic crockery and butter churns rescued from "forsaken corners of attics, cellars and barns" in New England. At a time when the immigrant population was growing rapidly, curators sought to give visitors an appreciation of

Living history museums like Colonial Williamsburg **(top)** and Old Sturbridge Village **(below)** use architecture, props and costumed actors to animate the past for visitors. Courtesy of Colonial Williamsburg Foundation; Old Sturbridge Village.

Yankee thriftiness. At settlement house museums, such as Hull House Museum in Chicago, colonial kitchen exhibitions served as backdrops for modern kitchens, where cooking classes were taught to the nation's newcomers.

Carefully composed kitchens and the pristine colonial bedrooms that usually accompanied them raised a few problems. They often looked more like stage sets than actual living quarters. As historian James Deetz has observed, "period rooms give the impression that all Americans sprang into existence at the age of twenty-one and were very neat."

In 1907 in Salem, Mass., George Francis Dow broke new ground when he curated a 17th-century bedroom, parlor and kitchen for the Essex Institute (now part of the Peabody Essex Museum). Unlike prior efforts, Dow's rooms looked like they were inhabited by real people. Knitting needles dangled from an unfinished stocking. A pair of eyeglasses rested on an opened newspaper. Like diorama designers, Dow wanted to tell a story that would stir visitors' emotions. Going for a theatrical effect, he trained three women, dressed in home-spun costumes from the era, to greet visitors and show them around the house. This use of costumed actors to animate a historic recreation came to be called "living history." In the decades that followed, it would be adopted on a much larger scale at Colonial Williamsburg, Old Sturbridge Village, Conner Prairie and similar historical sites.

Art museum curators also were intrigued by period rooms, using them to arrange collection objects within a context. Some period rooms were works of art in-and-of-themselves, purchased intact by collectors fascinated by aristocratic lifestyles. In 1904 Sen. William A. Clark of Montana purchased the Salon Doré, a gilded 18th-century parlor that had belonged to a Parisian count, and installed it in his New York City mansion. When Clark died the Salon was transferred to the Corcoran Gallery of Art in Washington, D.C., where it opened to the public in 1925. Detroit railway magnate Charles Lang Freer bought the Peacock Room, a 19th-century dining room that once graced the home of an English shipping magnate. Designed by James McNeill Whistler as a "fantasy view of the 'Orient,'" the extravagant room was painted with blue and gold peacocks. The Peacock Room opened to the public at the

Above, right: The Salon Doré, an 18th-century parlor, was moved from France to a New York mansion before it arrived at its final home, the Corcoran Gallery of Art, in 1925. Collection of the Corcoran Gallery of Art.

Below, right: Designed by James McNeill Whistler, the Peacock Room inspired other peacock rooms, including one at Elvis's Graceland. Freer Gallery of Art, Smithsonian Institution, Washington, D.C.: Gift of the Estate of Charles Lang Freer.

Smithsonian's Freer Gallery of Art in 1923 and is said to have inspired other peacock rooms, including the one at Graceland, Elvis Presley's mansion in Memphis.

With the public's interest in the colonial past and the growing market for antiques and Americana, curators in U.S. art museums focused their attention on this side of the Atlantic. They started developing exhibitions to promote American aesthetics, in the words of historian Gary Kulik, "investing early American objects with the aura of art." Paintings and sculpture were coordinated with furniture and decorations that reflected the revival of a colonial American style. The Metropolitan Museum of Art opened its American Wing in 1924, 17 elegant rooms of decorative arts and furniture from the nation's mansions. Designer R. T. H. Halsey arranged the rooms in chronological order, from a 17th-century Ipswich, Mass., parlor to an early 19th-century Baltimore dining room. Halsey, a stockbroker by trade, believed that his period rooms would serve as "tastemakers" for members of the public, who then would exhibit their own "good taste" by purchasing reproductions of the objects in department stores.

Throughout the 1920s the popularity of period rooms exploded. Decorated rooms became popular features in art museums around the nation, a way of informing the public about the history of the decorative arts. Influenced by displays in German and Swiss museums, curators arranged period rooms from different eras in a chronological progression of historical styles. Impressive examples are on view today at the Brooklyn Museum, which between 1918 and 1929 installed 21 rooms that were acquired intact from various parts of the country. At least one community, however, didn't want to see its design heritage uprooted. When Brooklyn purchased the entire first-floor interior of the Cupola House in Edenton, N.C., locals formed their own museum association to keep the rest of the house in North Carolina. Years later preservationists copied the Cupola rooms and put the imitations back in the original house in Edenton.

Ever prudent and economical, curators at the Philadelphia Museum of Art devised a less expensive and less controversial method. During the 1920s, they "rescued" items from homes slated for demolition, restored the mantelpieces, fireplaces and paneling, and arranged the resulting period rooms cohesively. With the addition of paintings and sculpture, a visitor could experience a little of "old Philadelphia," and see how a wealthy collector might decorate his or her home. Yet another kind of period room, seen chiefly in the western United States, was a recreation of an artist's studio, such as the "cowboy artist's" log-cabin studio that opened in 1930 at the Charles M. Russell Memorial Museum in Great Falls, Mont.

Staff at Chicago's Museum of Science and Industry took the idea of period rooms below ground for a 1933 exhibit called "Coal Mine"; museum founder Julius Rosenwald had seen a similar show at Munich's Deutschesmuseum. Using equipment acquired from a defunct Illinois coal operation, MSI staff sought to simulate a real mining experience. With extensive input from retired miners, the museum painted a room in its basement to resemble a mine interior, even scenting the space with a special perfume that mimicked coal's distinct odor. Visitors boarded a miner's elevator cage, which creaked down rollers, plunging them down a shaft fashioned out of canvas. Inside the semi-darkened "mine," visitors watched machines extract "seven tons of coal" from the earth, as water trickled in through ditches. The exhibit even had a touch of taxidermy: a canary, which miners traditionally had relied on to warn of hazardous air quality.

Enthusiastic former miners donned mining gear and staffed the exhibit, becoming the museum's most popular tour guides. "Real?" exclaimed Waldemar Kaempffert, MSI's proud director, "It is impossible to distinguish reality from illusion here." Even so "Coal Mine" failed to mention real but controversial issues such as union-management conflicts and miner safety. "Coal Mine" was built as an ode to technological progress and, as its original catalogue states, to inspire an appreciation for energy sources that will "lead to the end of social ills . . . [to] national wealth, [and] domination of world markets. . . ."

Some scholars and connoisseurs considered simulated environments like "Coal Mine" a counterfeit approach to exhibition design. They believed that artificial sets and dramatic vignettes of period rooms and dioramas did not reflect what Princeton University art historian Frank Jewett Mather called an object's "museum values," that is, its aesthetic and spiritual qualities. Recreations were misleading because they froze objects in the past instead of relating them to the present day, noted Alexander Dorner, who directed the museum at the Rhode Island School of Design in the 1940s. "[A] museum that tries to separate the past from the present," he said, "is indeed like a head without a body or a body without a head."

"Coal Mine" offered everything associated with a real mining experience, including a perfume that mimicked coal's distinct odor. Courtesy of the Museum of Science and Industry, Chicago.

Outside the museum's walls, the arts and sciences were becoming more abstract. The roaring 1920s had introduced Americans to jazz music, Surrealism and new scientific ideas like Einstein's Theory of Relativity. Thanks to expanded public education, America's literacy rates were increasing dramatically. In 1880, 20 percent of the U.S. population was unable to read or write in any language. By 1930, 95 percent of Americans were literate. Curators could now convey information through text rather than elaborate stage set. It was time for museums to depict a new kind of story: one that reflected the language of modern times.

Katherine Dreier's "International Exhibition of Modern Art," at the Brooklyn Museum, 1926-27, was influenced by the streamlined approach of the Bauhaus artists. Katherine S. Dreier Papers/Societé Anonyme archive, 1818-1952. Yale Collection of American Literature, Beinecke Rare Book and Manuscript Library.

Much of the impetus for modern exhibitions came from Germany's Bauhaus. Founded by German artists and architects shortly after World War I, the Bauhaus school believed a utopian society could be achieved by ridding buildings and interiors of fussy ornament and focusing on sleek new technologies. In the 1920s, teams of Bauhaus artists developed a streamlined approach to exhibitions using eye-catching industrial materials such as cellophane and wire netting and creating linear paths that directed people from display to display.

Profoundly influenced by Bauhaus, four key players took the lead in reshaping museum exhibition design in the United States: collector Katherine Sophie Dreier and wunderkind museum directors Alexander Dorner, Everett "Chick" Austin and Alfred H. Barr, Jr.

The daughter of German immigrants, Katherine Sophie Dreier often traveled to Europe during the 1920s. The Brooklyn resident spent a great deal of time with Bauhaus artists, whose ideas inspired her to organize the first modern art installation in a U.S. museum. For nine weeks in 1926, "International Exhibition of Modern Art" presented more than 300 works from 23 countries at the Brooklyn Museum. It was a smash hit, attracting 52,000 visitors and generating provocative reviews in the national press.

Dreier wanted the show's design to reflect the spirit of modern art. Rather than stack every inch of wall space with art, she positioned the paintings against plain walls, leaving blank spaces between the works. In a nod to the museum's period rooms, but mindful of the modernists' emphasis on the present, she displayed four domestic rooms with purchases from a local department store. Her aim was to promote modern art as an essential item for the modern home. The Brooklyn show also featured a scale model of a "television room," consisting of a "small dark room" where visitors would "turn a button" to rotate European masterworks onto a screen. "Some day, all the important museums will have their own real television rooms," Dreier predicted. "Through art the world will indeed be one." An active suffragist, she organized one of the nation's first shows devoted to contemporary woman artists (1934). She eventually donated her extensive early modern art collection to Yale University, where it remains today.

Another pioneer of modern exhibitions was Alexander Dorner, the German-born director of the Museum of Art, Rhode Island School of Design (RISD). Before he came to the United States, Dorner had directed the Landesmuseum in Hanover. There, he commissioned artist El Lissitsky to create *Abstract Cabinet,* a modular room for the display of modern paintings (1927). To view the art contained in the cabinet, visitors rotated differently sized cases and panels made of corrugated tin and other shimmering industrial materials. The installation changed constantly, depending on how visitors arranged the art inside.

Abstract Cabinet created an international buzz, and several U.S. museum directors traveled to Hanover to see it. Through his connections with these Americans, Dorner was able to leave Nazi Germany in 1938 and move to Rhode Island. At the RISD museum, he created five "atmosphere rooms" for the display of ancient art. Unlike period rooms, these spaces contained neither antiquated furnishings nor brocaded wallpaper. Rather each room was painted a different color to evoke the "aesthetic and philosophical essence" of the artwork on display. Dorner placed colored transparencies of architecture in the windows—one for ancient Egyptian architecture, one for Mesopotamia and so on. Below each transparency was a case of objects from the era, arranged to mimic the shape of the buildings that shone in the light of the windows above. To create more "atmosphere," Dorner piped liturgical music into the galleries via earphones for individual listeners and created a push-button device that allowed visitors to turn selected objects on their sides.

More than 60 years ago, innovative museum director Alexander Dorner was piping music via earphones into the galleries of the Museum of Art, Rhode Island School of Design.

Dreier and Dorner's experiments attracted the attention of two classmates in Paul Sachs's legendary museum training course at Harvard University, Everett "Chick" Austin and Alfred Barr, Jr. Austin was a prodigy who "did things sooner and more brilliantly than anyone," Barr once said. In 1927, the 26-year-old Austin moved to Hartford, Conn., to take over the directorship of the staunchly traditionalist Wadsworth Atheneum. There he staged controversial exhibitions and programs, deliberately choosing "Distinguished Works of Art" as the title of his first show because, he said, only a few of the Wadsworth's works were "distinguished." He believed the key to a good show was not to stack the walls with second-rate works but to separate quality from mediocrity and choose only art with the greatest aesthetic value.

Austin had a penchant for elaborate costume balls, opening galas and magic shows, which he liked to perform at the museum. For "Distinguished Works," he placed a mysterious curtain at the center of the exhibition. At a choice moment on opening night, Austin pulled back the curtain to reveal the museum's new prized acquisition, a painting by Tintoretto. He went on to organize America's first exhibition of surrealist art in 1931 and its first Picasso retrospective in 1934.

The influences that guided these experiments in Germany, Brooklyn and Hartford also made their way to Manhattan, where Alfred Barr, Jr., would institutionalize modern exhibition design at the Museum of Modern Art. Like Dorner, Barr believed that art has

For his first exhibition, "Distinguished Works of Art," museum director Chick Austin organized a spare display to highlight the beauty of the works on view. Wadsworth Atheneum Museum of Art, Hartford, Conn. Courtesy of the Wadsworth Atheneum Archives.

a timeless quality; there was no need to put works in the historical context of a period room. Like Dreier, he felt that artworks should be spread apart; there was no need to cover the walls, top to bottom. Like Austin, he believed in spare displays of outstanding pieces. There was no need to show the museum's entire holdings. These techniques have become so standard that today most visitors don't even notice them.

In the 1930s as MoMA was erecting its first building, Barr called for interior galleries to be open and loft-like. As exhibitions changed, moveable partitions could be inserted to create new room shapes, sizes and patterns of circulation. Barr also thought about how to explain abstract art to visitors. Until this time, most U.S. art museums provided little written information; a work's title, the artist's name and perhaps the medium were printed on a small label centered in the bottom of a frame. The idea was to let the art—or the context in which it was displayed—speak for itself. Barr pioneered a different approach: lengthy text, with information on country of origin, the artist's biography and how the work related to others in the room, typewritten onto labels and thumb-tacked to walls.

To enhance the viewer's experience of art, Barr searched for a "neutral" wall color that would create minimal distraction and show paintings at their best. After some experimentation with various shades and textures of beige cloth, he turned to the famous Bauhaus credo, "white, everything must be white." White was the color the Bauhaus disciples associated with hygiene, purity and sun-bleached Mediterranean architecture. It evoked both the classical past and new beginnings. White paint became the standard background for exhibitions, and gallery spaces came to be called "white cubes," which were heralded by the art world as a glorious innovation. "The development of the pristine, placeless white cube is one of modernism's triumphs—a development commercial, esthetic and technological," art critic Brian O'Doherty wrote later. "In an extraordinary strip-tease, the art within bares itself more and more."

MoMA's stripped-down galleries freed both artists and curators. Visitors no longer were distracted by fussy wallpaper but could focus on the canvas. Throughout the ensuing decades curators would mount a wide range of adventurous shows on the ubiquitous white walls: abstract, cubist, Dada and surrealist paintings; African masks, East Indian textiles and pre-Columbian carvings; and Americana and household items elevated to high design.

Art museums also had a practical reason for streamlining exhibition design. As museums became more interested in touring shows, they adopted MoMA's flexible method of presentation—ideal for traveling exhibitions. In 1932 MoMA established a Department of Circulating Exhibitions, the first museum department dedicated to developing shows that would tour to other institutions. By 1939 there was a marked rise in frequently changing installations in large urban museums as these institutions competed for audiences. Most directors believed that the most practical way to accommodate a constant stream of changing exhibitions was to have "a neutral setting for exhibits without decorative effects of any kind."

One of most creative art installations of this era was MoMA's 1939 "Indian Art of the United States," which brought Native American objects out of the natural history museum and into the art museum. Unlike Barr, curator and future MoMA director Rene d'Harnoncourt felt that exhibitions could never be neutral. He believed that by exhibiting Native American objects such as Mimbres pottery as art pieces rather than as primitive tools, he was "elevating" their value in the eyes of museum-goers and bringing them to life. For "Indian Art," d'Harnoncourt hired Navajo artists to demonstrate sand painting. Colorful

"Races of Mankind," an unscientific comparison of the races of the world organized in the 1930s, was dismantled 30 years later following protests from Civil Rights activists. Photo by Charles Carpenter; CSA77747. © The Field Museum.

Navajo ponchos and blankets were artistically draped over cylinders, "arranged on orange-colored platforms of varying heights set against a sky-blue background wall . . . creating an abstract tableau."

Modern design was not limited to art museums. Starting in the 1930s anthropology and science museum curators found that industrial materials and "neutral" backgrounds could help them better convey the theories of the day, especially scientific progress, human control of the natural world and racial hierarchy. Carlos Cummings, a curator at the Buffalo Museum of Science, urged the field to think of exhibitions as textbooks that proceeded in a crisp, logical order: "The individual rooms, each of which refers to a different branch of nature science, are regarded as chapters; and the individual exhibits, carefully selected to complete the narrative, are considered as paragraphs or pages . . . the plan affords a logical basis for arrangement from every standpoint." In 1937 staff at the Milwaukee Public Museum rearranged a collection of 3,328 birds' eggs. Instead of following Akeley's naturalistic "Milwaukee style," curators grouped eggs onto geometric cylinders resembling canister tops, sorted them by color and size and arranged the egg-filled cylinders in six equally spaced rows in a wall-sized case. The exhibition looked more like a modern-day grocery store aisle than nests in the wild.

In Chicago, the Field Museum broke with its tradition of life groups in a landmark anthropological exhibition called "Races of Mankind" (1933). Its aim was to allow visitors to compare racial features from around the world in a systematic way. The aim may have been scientific, but in the same year that the Nazis rose to power in Germany, such racial categorization could hardly have been neutral or harmless. The museum commissioned Malvina Hoffman—a student of sculptor Auguste Rodin—to model 98 different kinds of "racial stock" in bronze. Rather than organizing the sculptures into life groups, Hoffman reconfigured the Field's long hall of Greek cornices with partitions and screens. She arranged the sculptures to progress from "Neanderthal to Nordic" on eye-level wooden pedestals set into lighted niches. For this "avenue of man," she chose the background colors carefully, "pale golden beige" for the walls and modern linoleum for the floor. A side gallery featured a map of "racial stocks" as well as charts of different kinds of eyes, hair and skin color. This very unscientific science exhibition endured for three decades, finally being dismantled in 1968 following a letter-writing campaign by Civil Rights activists.

During World War II, museums realized that maps, charts and globes were useful visual devices for explaining national security and military strategy to an increasingly nervous public. "Can America Be Bombed?" a 1941 exhibit at the Science Museum of Minnesota, featured a globe flanked by large bombs, with one missile positioned to hit the southeastern United States. The show was designed by Works Progress Administration artists and traveled throughout the country. In sad irony, it was featured on the front page of *The Museum News* one week before the bombing of Pearl Harbor.

After the United States entered the war, the number of "map and globe" exhibitions grew dramatically. The Newark Museum used designs by renowned engineer R. Buckminster Fuller to build "Dymaxion World," (1943) a geodesic globe-like structure meant to show how the war was impeding the flow of "vitally important drug plants" into the country.

Maps were also a prominent feature of the Museum of Modern Art's 1943 "Airways to Peace: An Exhibition of Geography for the Future." It was designed by Bauhaus typographer Herbert Bayer who turned the museum's galleries into a cartographic journey that displayed the new kinds of mapping being employed in military campaigns. Its main feature was a giant transparent globe, surrounded by charts, maps, Mercator projectors and aerial photographs. The exhibition also featured text written by Wendell Willkie, a former presidential candidate and a prominent opponent of American isolationism.

With the end of the war came renewed attention to life here at home. The internationalist approach that dominated the war years soon was overtaken by the paranoia of the Cold War era. Sen. Joseph McCarthy achieved national attention with his anti-communist "witch hunt." Some artists and intellectuals were blacklisted for their political beliefs. Even the most innocent exhibition theme could infuriate McCarthy's followers. In 1956, for example, when the Dallas Museum of Art agreed to host "Sport in Art," an exhibition sponsored by *Sports Illustrated,* the "Dallas County Patriotic Council" demanded the museum cancel its plans. Council members were offended by four works—including one of an ice skater and another of a fisherman—that had been painted by alleged "reds."

Other less "subversive" exhibitions were far more successful and popular. Key among them were the Museum of Modern Art's "Family of Man" (1955) and "The Farmer's Year" (1958) at the Farmers' Museum in Cooperstown, N.Y.

"Family of Man" remains one of the most well-attended photography exhibitions of all time and, in the words of historian Eric Sandeen, "one of the most significant cultural

"Family of Man" was on view at the Museum of Modern Art, New York, from Jan. 24, 1955, through May 8, 1955. © The Museum of Modern Art/Licensed by SCALA/Art Resource, N.Y.

productions of 1950s America." It was described by photographer
Minor White as "a jolly good show, a statistical stopper, a box-office
success [that] proves how quickly the milk of human kindness turns
to schmaltz."

The show was influenced by photojournalism and large-format
photography magazines such as *Look* and *Life*. Its curator, 76-year-
old Edward Steichen, had been chief photographer for the fashion
magazines *Vanity Fair* and *Vogue*. In 1952, inspired by a photographic
series in *Ladies Home Journal* that attempted to illustrate the universal human experience,
Steichen issued a worldwide call for photographs that documented the "gamut of life from
birth to death." From more than 4 million submissions, Steichen and his assistants selected 503
photos by 257 photographers from 68 countries. He divided the photos into themes—lovers
caressing, couples bickering, mothers nurturing, children playing, mourners praying—and
asked his brother-in-law, poet Carl Sandburg, to write a prologue to pull the photos together
with one central focus. "A camera testament," Sandburg wrote, "a drama of the grand canyon of
humanity, an epic of fun, mystery, and holiness—here is the Family of Man."

The exhibition is noteworthy not just for its universalist theme but for its design by
architect Paul Rudolph. At the entrance a new transparent material called Lucite®
displayed the photographs so that they seemed to float in the air. Rudolph grouped them
according to Steichen's vision of the human life cycle and painted the walls different colors
to emphasize a progression from birth to death. Photos of women giving birth were hung
in a white-curtained womb-like "pregnancy temple." One of the show's most controversial
images came near the exit: a giant color photo of an A-bomb exploding, juxtaposed with a
semi-circle of photos of children from around the world, playing ring around the rosy.

Scholars and artists debated the merits of "Family of Man."
Was it art or propaganda? But the accessibility of the
message and layout and the emotional tug of the photos
captivated the public. In the 1950s and '60s, it traveled the
world, setting attendance records from Pittsburgh to Paris,
from Minneapolis to Moscow. Today it is on permanent
display in Luxembourg, Steichen's birthplace.

The rural counterpart to "Family of Man" was "The
Farmer's Year." Farmers' Museum Director Louis C. Jones
was an accomplished folklorist and knew how to tell a

good story. Working with curator Per Guldbeck, he arranged the museum's collection of agricultural bric-a-brac according to easily grasped themes in order to tell an uplifting tale of 19th-century American rural life. "From a knowledge of the resourcefulness," Jones wrote, "the ingenuity, the courage and laughter of our people comes a lift of the chin, a confidence in our hearts that we too shall solve our problems and look forward to the tomorrow of our children's children." "The Farmer's Year" opened in 1958 and remained on view until 1982. It depicted 12 months in the life of a 19th-century "common man who, through the sweat of his brow, self-discipline, rugged individualism, and common sense, was able to transform the howling wilderness into a productive garden, thereby laying the foundations for the greatness of America. . . ."

To organize this story visually, the museum turned to a familiar format: the picture calendar. Twelve earth-toned panels, each titled with the name of a month in large letters, contained short captions written in a conversational tone. Below each panel, a few carefully chosen objects illustrated a theme. In "Fixing and Sharpening Tools," for example, five sentences explained how in February the thrifty farmer prepares his tools for the coming spring. Below, six sharpening devices of different shapes and sizes were displayed as artfully as a Japanese flower arrangement. The museum also created special areas where children could use old-fashioned tools like treadmill churns and piggots.

The audience for "The Farmer's Year" was diverse. Local farmers wanted to teach their children how new technology was improving life on the farm. Urban tourists visiting

A 1951 game show called **WHAT IN THE WORLD** *featured curators using their "remarkable museum mentalities" to identify "mysterious" artifacts. University of Pennsylvania Museum (neg.#139460).*

Cooperstown to see the Baseball Hall of Fame were drawn to a romantic vision of rural life in times past. The exhibit featured stories and concepts that were reassuring to a public perhaps puzzled by a steady stream of post-war lifestyle innovations.

Among the many innovations of this period was broadcast television, which began to mesmerize the nation in the 1950s. Restaurants, movie theaters and libraries all reported diminished business. Museum attendance continued to rise but curators were concerned about the impact this new medium would have on visitors. Exhibitions that once seemed daring suddenly looked mundane when compared to the marvels of viewing moving pictures at home. Worried that television would erode their appeal, museums responded by producing their own T.V. shows and adding new technology into their galleries.

In 1951, the same year *I Love Lucy* premiered on network television, families could also tune their black-and-white sets to a game show called *What in the World*, hosted by the University of Pennsylvania's Museum of Archaeology and Anthropology. It featured such "mysterious" museum artifacts as a petrified gourd and an antique cooking utensil, which then would be identified before a stumped audience by guest curators using their "remarkable museum mentalities."

Throughout the 1950s and early 1960s, museums across the nation sponsored weekly shows on local networks, achieving minor celebrity status for their directors and curators. Science

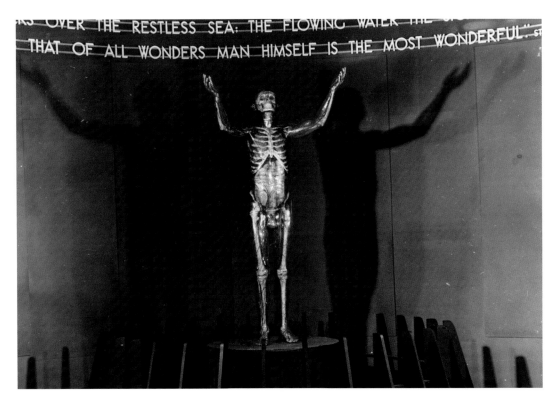

To compete with television, science museums focused on the public's fascination with the human body. At the Cleveland Health Education Museum in the late 1940s, visitors could gaze upon the organs, veins and teeth of a giant transparent woman named **JUNO**. *Courtesy of HealthSpace Cleveland.*

museums such as the California Academy of Sciences aired shows featuring "friendly scientists" conducting experiments in a "museum lab." The Indianapolis Children's Museum hosted a local children's hour. In 1956 the American Association of Museums partnered with CBS to produce *Odyssey*, a short-lived, hour-long Sunday afternoon show. *Odyssey* sent television cameras across the nation to exhibitions that told heroic stories, including tales about Julius Caesar's Roman legions and Japanese samurai warriors.

Museums had been broadcasting lectures on radio since the 1920s. But they soon found that the visual nature of television held greater promise for replicating the exhibition experience. Television could "tell the museum story with immediacy, dramatic focus, high interest and broad appeal," said Robert E. Dierbeck, who served as the Milwaukee Public Museum's television coordinator during the 1950s. Some curators, however, were appalled at the thought of condensing their life's work into television sound bites and, worse, competing with performers like Lucille Ball. One museum director lamented, "The day is not too far away when . . . museum personnel will have to be actors as well as scientists."

But at other museums, staff worked to help promote television to an increasingly curious public. In the mid-1950s Chicago's new educational television station, WTTW, established its fledgling operations at the Museum of Science and Industry. The broadcast studio doubled as a public exhibition where visitors could watch television production in action, years before interactive T.V. studios would become popular exhibitions in children's museums.

Museums adjusted their exhibitions in other ways. Twenty years after the Muzac Corporation began to pipe music into commercial spaces, art museums added sound to their galleries. In 1942, with its curators leaving to join the war effort, the Saint Paul Art Gallery in Minnesota recorded their art lectures onto vinyl records and provided record players so that a visitor could "help himself to a gallery tour." In 1957 a private company called Acoustiguide introduced a reel-to-reel tape recorder, hooked to a thick leather strap that visitors could tote through galleries. According to an early Acoustiguide ad, simply by pushing a button museum-goers could listen to experts "present authoritative information exactly as the director wants to have it presented."

Science museums produced unique exhibits that surpassed the limitations of a small black-and-white screen. Some focused on the public's fascination with human bodies and advancing medical technology. In the late 1940s the Cleveland Health Education Museum (now HealthSpace Cleveland) unveiled *Juno*, a giant transparent woman based on *Der Glaeserne Mensch* in Dresden, Germany. Visitors could gaze upon Juno's organs, veins and teeth—everything but her soul. Juno and her German counterpart traveled the country, appearing at world's fairs and museums and popularizing the use of transparent mannequins to teach human biology.

Combining transparency with size and movement, Chicago's Museum of Science and Industry in 1952 and Philadelphia's Franklin Institute in 1954 constructed multi-story plaster hearts that visitors could step into, early versions of the gigantic human jaws and other body organs seen in science museums around the country today. One young visitor to the Franklin Institute commented, "Thank you for the Heart exhibit. I learned so much. I never knew my heart had stairs in it."

Still, most museums were content to rely on more traditional exhibition techniques. They reflected the ethos of the 1950s, described by journalist-historian David Halberstam as an "orderly era, one with a minimum of social dissent" where "the traditional system of authority held." Many exhibitions of the day consisted of row upon row of static glass cases, pictures and sculptures. "Everyone is familiar with the neglected museum, with its badly lit, inadequately labeled and jammed exhibition cases," Lothar P. Witteborg, chief of exhibitions at the American Museum of Natural History, wrote in 1958. "Many museums were and still are being designed and the exhibits installed according to traditions established before our Industrial Revolution."

Of course, the old-time exhibitions did have their charming qualities. Visitors often would return years later to a museum they had visited as children. To their delight they found that, as novelist J. D. Salinger described, "you could go [to the museum] a hundred thousand times, and nothing would have changed . . . the only thing that would be different would be you." But exhibition designers understood that America's museums needed to move beyond nostalgia. They needed "fresh injections of money, spirit and ideas."

■　■　■　■　■

As the 1960s began, American society was about to experience radical change. Postwar affluence coupled with the remarkable communicative powers of television contributed to a new era marked by "a vast and surprisingly broad degree of dissidence," in which people began to "question the purpose of their lives." Within this social climate, industrial designers, avant-garde artists, educators, social activists and market-savvy directors began to question the purpose of museums. They questioned whether the public got anything out of exhibitions that relied on a passive viewing of objects. They wanted exhibitions to engage the public and become more relevant to people's daily lives. In the words of designer Alexander Girard, they wanted to create shows that were "a joyous spectacle, a dance."

Avant-garde artists led the way. In the early 1960s, influenced by experiments in European galleries, they began to rebel against what artist Allan Kaprow called the "shhh—don't touch" atmosphere of art museums. They criticized white cubes as being too institutional. Artist Robert Smithson declared that white walls "murdered and entombed art," separating it from life, much the way prisons or hospitals separated inmates and the ill from humanity. In private galleries and other alternative spaces, Kaprow, Smithson and others began to stage their own installations, which they called "happenings." Sometimes they painted the walls black; other times, they encouraged visitors to become part of the art-making by writing on the walls or even stomping on artwork placed in the middle of a room.

At the end of the decade, adventurous curators brought the spirit of these radical installations to museums. In 1969 Chicago's Museum of Contemporary Art hired environmental artists Christo and Jeanne-Claude to wrap the entire museum building, inside and out, using cloth, plastic and twine. Only the white walls of the interior were left bare. The Whitney Museum of Art organized "Anti-Illusion: Procedures/Materials" in which artists parodied the shape, size and proportions of white rooms. Sculptor Robert Morris, for example, placed large L-beams at odd angles in the museum, demanding that visitors weave their path through the works and experience a cube-shaped room in an entirely new way. That same year, at the Museum of the Rhode Island School of Design, Andy Warhol created "Raiding the Icebox," a pun on the term "white cube." Warhol took eclectic items—parasols, shoes, jars—from the museum's storage vaults and arranged them according to personal whim.

Like the modern art exhibition experiments of the 1920s and '30s, these shows met with critical acclaim and set the stage for new kinds of displays and installations and have influenced artists to this day. Avant-garde art, however, tended to attract small audiences, people who were already familiar with the art world. And sometimes curators paid the price for pushing museum culture farther than it was ready to go. In 1971, for example, the

Artist Andy Warhol turned the art museum's "white cube" gallery on its head with "Raiding the Icebox," on view in Providence, R.I., April 23-June 30, 1970. Courtesy of the Museum of Art, Rhode Island School of Design.

"Mathematica" was the first exhibit to use tangible objects and ideas to explain the abstractions of measurement, quantity and other mathematical concepts. Courtesy of California Science Center.

Guggenheim fired curator Edward Fry for commissioning Hans Haacke's piece, *Shalopsky et al. Manhattan Real Estate Holdings*, a social critique of museum trustees' real-estate dealings.

It was left to the educators at science centers and children's and neighborhood museums to introduce more exciting exhibition formats to the broader public. These staff members, concerned about the state of science and math education in the post-*Sputnik* era, sought to challenge traditional ways of teaching. They turned to educational psychologists and education reformers, whose research had found that people learn and retain more when they touch and manipulate objects. Maybe there was a way to convert this research into new kinds of museum exhibitions.

Los Angeles-based designers Ray and Charles Eames were among those who proposed a solution. The revolutionary wife-husband team already was famous for using modern design to bring sophisticated ideas to a mass audience. They had produced a best-selling reclining chair that graced both art museum exhibitions and middle-class homes, and films that communicated difficult scientific concepts in entertaining ways. At the California Museum of Science and Industry in Los Angeles (now the California Science Center) in 1961, the couple created "Mathematica: The World of Numbers and Beyond"—perhaps America's first participatory science exhibition. Hailed by critics as "a bold venture in exhibit communication," "Mathematica" combined the latest trends in industrial design, helped people make connections between ideas and tangible objects and aimed to make mathematics less intimidating. The Eameses' vision was to fill the museum with a "visual banquet" of lots of "beautiful things to

look at and fun things to do." Visitors were not meant to follow a strict linear pathway but to weave their way randomly through the infinite pleasures of mathematics.

In a shiny industrial space of stainless steel, fiberglass and blinking light bulbs, visitors could press buttons, pull levers and turn cranks that set various phenomena in motion. To discover the laws of probability, visitors could trigger a 12-foot-high machine to drop 30,000 plastic balls through a maze of pegs to form a bell curve. To learn how surfaces form, they could pull wires from a giant vat of detergent that stretched into bubbles. The beauty of mathematics was illustrated through natural phenomena: cracked mud, veins on a leaf, an egg. "'Mathematica' had a reassuring quality," recalls former California Science Center curator Jay Rounds, "communicating that, through mathematics—no matter how crazy things may seem—there is an underlying order to the world's chaos." A version of the exhibition can be seen today at the New York Hall of Science.

The Eameses were part of a wide circle of designers and educators interested in participatory experiences that made learning fun. One of their admirers was Frank Oppenheimer, a University of Colorado physics professor. Oppenheimer had achieved notoriety in the 1940s, when he and his brother J. Robert helped develop the atomic bomb in Los Alamos, N. Mex. Only a few years later, during the McCarthy era, the brothers were blacklisted for speaking out against nuclear weapons. Oppenheimer felt it was essential to appreciate rather than fear the power of science. He also worried that young people were avoiding science and retreating into a world of mysticism and drug use. He envisioned a "refreshing and stimulating" place that would connect them back into the concrete world of science and technology: "an exploration center [with a] laboratory atmosphere." This center would be filled with exhibits that had "aesthetic appeal, as well as pedagogical purpose . . . designed to make things clearer rather than to cultivate obscurantism or science fiction." Oppenheimer realized his dream in an abandoned airplane hangar near San Francisco's Golden Gate Bridge in 1969 when he opened the Exploratorium. Over the next two decades its staff would revolutionize science exhibits around the globe.

Starting with a few castaway exhibits from the National Aeronautics and Space Administration and a cadre of high school students, Oppenheimer dispensed with the formal trappings of museums, the polished exhibits, glass cases and discrete walled-off galleries. Instead he built his exhibits from scratch, using hardware store purchases and other cheap materials like scrap wood and dishwashing liquid. "He believed the audience would feel comforted by exhibitions that looked like they could be reproduced in a home workshop," recalled museum theorist Elaine Heumann Gurian.

Exploratorium exhibits sought to increase visitors' understanding of natural phenomena, like optics, waves and vibration. They transformed as visitors manipulated them. For example,

Left: A young visitor ponders the visual banquet that designers Charles and Ray Eames created for "Mathematica." © 2005 Eames Office LLC; www.eamesoffice.com.

one of Oppenheimer's first exhibits consisted of a rope separating two seemingly identical white rectangles. When visitors removed the rope, suddenly both sides appeared as different shades of grey. A handwritten label explained the science behind the optical illusion of "The Grey Steps." Throughout the Exploratorium, visitors were encouraged to create their own experiences, rather than simply absorb information through reading and looking. "People use it in many different ways," Oppenheimer wrote about an exhibit called "Relative Motion Pendulum." "Some just give the table a push as they walk by—but then, so do I. Others make everything move every which-way, producing a noisy, unintelligible relative motion pattern. I enjoy doing that, too. Many people . . . use the exhibit to instruct their friends and children—and I use it that way also. . . ."

Oppenheimer was more interested in what people *did* in an exhibition than in having them study objects and memorize facts about them. "Nobody flunks museum" was his famous mantra. To encourage visitors to learn by doing, he put the Exploratorium's carpentry shop in full public view. Staff fixed, built and tested things right in front of visitors. To encourage creativity, he founded an artists-in-residence program, where artists and scientists collaborated on pieces that featured prisms,

Above: *Frank W. Oppenheimer opened the Exploratorium in an abandoned airplane hangar—the ideal setting for his "exploration center with a laboratory atmosphere." The museum as it looked in the 1970s. © Exploratorium, www.exploratorium.org.*

Below: *Thirty years after it opened to the public, the Exploratorium is as loud, messy, exciting and joyous as ever. Photo by Lily Rodriguez, 2001. © Exploratorium, www.exploratorium.org.*

swirling mist, mirrors. The museum eventually produced more than 600 exhibits that traveled to museums around the world. Oppenheimer also imported an idea from the Palais de la Découverte in Paris and trained high-school students to conduct experiments, such as dissecting a cow's eye in the museum, then explain the science to visitors. The Exploratorium was loud, messy, confusing and joyous. Families and children of all ages were drawn to its rough and tumble space.

While Oppenheimer was building the Exploratorium in San Francisco, a museum director in Boston was redefining an institution half a century old. The Boston Children's Museum had been founded in 1913 by public school science teachers who wanted to use natural history specimens in their teaching. BCM's initial exhibitions consisted of cases of rocks, shells and stuffed birds. Fifty years later not much had changed.

Then in 1962 BCM hired the son of world-famous pediatrician Benjamin Spock to direct the museum. Michael Spock had much in common with Frank Oppenheimer. They had both grown up in New York, frequenting the city's museums and, coincidentally, attending the same private grammar school, which was based on John Dewey's philosophy of experiential learning. But unlike the academically precocious Oppenheimer, Spock was dyslexic and did poorly in school. He found himself drawn to museums as places of learning where teachers wouldn't judge his performance.

Spock joined BCM at an ideal time. First, there were lots of school-aged children around. Public schools were at peak capacity due to the post-war baby boom. Second, Congress was keenly interested in education reform, passing such legislation as Project Head Start (1964) and the Elementary and Secondary Education Act (1965). Third, with its plethora of universities and think tanks, Boston was a magnet for educational research and curriculum development.

Spock believed that the museum could aid education reform through a new approach to exhibitions. Thus began the hands-on exhibition movement, where children were encouraged not only to look at objects, but to manipulate them. Museums had long sponsored supervised "children's hours" where young visitors could touch specimens or partake in an art activity. Spock, on the other hand, believed that handling objects shouldn't be confined to occasional programs but rather an essential

Exhibits at the Boston Children's Museum encouraged children not just to look at objects but to handle them as well. "What's Inside" allowed young visitors to examine the insides of a variety of objects. "How Movies Move" invited them to create and view their own movie strips. "Before You Were Three" helped children recall their early years by simulating a baby's perspective. Courtesy of the Boston Children's Museum.

part of the museum visit. In fact, kids needed to create something related to an exhibition's theme, to join in, to interact, in effect to *become* scientists and artists.

In 1963 Spock hired Michael Sand, a young designer who had worked for the Eameses. For their first collaboration "What's Inside" (1964), Spock and Sand cut open a range of objects— a baseball, a car, a toilet—so children could examine the insides. Children could even crawl through a manhole and see the innards of a sewer system. BCM also asked a local undertaker to deliver leftover flowers to the museum daily so that children could take them apart to create art and science projects. "What's Inside" was an immediate success. For "How Movies Move," the museum's next hit, kids were encouraged to spin zoetropes made out of hatboxes to make their own mini-movies. "We had to coach the parents," recalls Sand, "and tell them— it's okay, your kids can touch and handle things even though we're a museum."

In 1969 BCM completely transformed its exhibition hall. Staff donated the wood and glass cases to museums around Boston. In their place arose an interactive exhibit center where collections were displayed creatively and supplemented with hands-on activities. Most of these activities used objects purchased from supermarkets and hardware stores, but BCM also experimented with hard-to-find technologies. Spock recalls one station where children could operate four Wang calculators, "which was a big deal at the time," and possibly the first use of computers in a public gallery space.

The museum's staff closely observed how children used the exhibit center. Those observations led to more innovations. In 1971 the museum built a carpeted Plexiglas® playpen to accommodate babies while parents and older siblings enjoyed the rest of the museum. Staff noticed that older kids were fascinated by the encased babies "on exhibit." In response they created a show called "Before You Were Three." When staff discovered that adults were sharing parenting experiences in the exhibit space, they added a parent resource center with books, bulletin boards and a private area for nursing and changing babies, a first in a museum.

Hands-on exhibitions and activity spaces soon made their way to mainstream museums. The Salt Lake City Art Center and North Carolina Museum of Art opened galleries of touchable work for blind audiences in the mid-1960s. A few years later the Bell Museum of Natural History in Minneapolis and the Florida State Museum in Tallahassee created rooms with touchable activities for children. In 1974 BCM educator Judith White and psychologist Caryl Marsh developed the Smithsonian Discovery Room, "an alternative space . . . halfway between the exhibits in glass cases and the actual collections." The cozy children's area had seating, touchable objects like mammoth molars and barnacles and a steady presence of staff and volunteers—all the more innovative because of its placement in an adult-oriented institution. Four years later BCM combined the discovery room and the parent resource room into "PlaySpace," a secure indoor exhibition with activities (including a play castle and slide) designed for very young children. One of the first exhibits in the country to serve both toddlers and their parents, it has been refined and replicated for museums, airports and other public destinations around the world.

To some curators the shift away from viewing masterpieces of art and toward making an emotional and physical connection with any kind of object questioned the very nature of what it meant to be a museum. Institutions that encouraged touching and playing, they argued, had no business calling themselves museums. According to Michael Spock, traditionalists in museums considered his experiments "a bunch of crap." Nonetheless, educators and social activists charged ahead, viewing museums as public spaces and exhibitions as vehicles for communicating important ideas.

Change was everywhere in a decade that has become synonymous with challenging the status quo. The Civil Rights movements of the 1960s raised questions about how exhibitions could resonate with a broader audience beyond the upper middle classes that comprised the majority of museum visitors. In 1967 the Smithsonian opened a branch museum in Anacostia, a low-income African-American neighborhood in Washington, D.C. According to its founding director John R. Kinard, the goal of the Anacostia Neighborhood Museum was to "restore a sense of place among [neighborhood] residents" and serve as "a catalyst for social change." Its initial exhibitions included a climb-in space capsule, displays about achievements by black Americans and a small petting zoo with two white rats. The museum buzzed with neighborhood kids. Noticing the children's terrified reaction to the rats, museum staff realized that vermin infestation was a serious health problem in Anacostia.

In response, the museum created an exhibition that later would inspire museum professionals interested in socially relevant issues. "The Rat: Man's Invited Affliction" (1969)

Organized by the Anacostia Museum in 1969, "The Rat" was one of the first exhibitions devoted to socially relevant issues—in this case, the health problems caused by rats in an urban neighborhood. Smithsonian Institution Archives, Record Unit 378, Box 6, #2004-63004.

featured a reconstructed, trashed-out backyard containing live urban rats. Visitors viewed the yard through peephole-windows as they learned about the history of rat infestation and obtained sociological, scientific and medical information on dealing with vermin.

The same year "The Rat" opened, the Metropolitan Museum of Art in New York decided that it too would reach out to African-American neighborhoods. It commissioned "Harlem on My Mind: The Cultural Capital of Black America," intended to "chronicle the creativity of the downtrodden blacks and, at the same time, encourage them to come to the museum." However well intentioned, the exhibition was a public relations disaster. "Reaching out to the black community was entirely new and unfamiliar for white cultural institutions," Allon Schoener, the show's curator, later recounted. "They had plenty of experience excluding blacks, but not many ground rules for inclusion."

"Harlem on my Mind" consisted of 15 rooms of enlarged black-and-white photographs that Harvard University professor Henry Louis Gates later called "one of the richest and most comprehensive records of the history of the African-American in the 20th century." Yet when it opened, many in the black community and elsewhere were aghast. Visitors expected to see paintings by black artists, long excluded from the museum, rather than historic photographs, many taken by white photographers. Some Harlem residents felt as though they had been "used" to make the Metropolitan look good.

Installation shot from "Harlem on My Mind: The Cultural Capital of Black America, 1900-1968." Image © The Metropolitan Museum of Art.

Then the show's catalogue rolled off the presses. Its first entry was an essay by the museum's director Thomas Hoving, who described his "privileged" white childhood, complete with a black maid of "sunny disposition" named Bessie, and confessed that as a child he believed that "Negroes were people. But they were happy, foot-twitching, smiling." Another essay by a Harlem high-school senior named Candice Van Ellison addressed the tensions between Jews and blacks in Harlem. "[P]sychologically, blacks may find that anti-Jewish sentiments place them, for once, within a majority," Ellison wrote. "Thus, our contempt for the Jew makes us feel more completely American in sharing a national prejudice."

Ellison's words made the *New York Times* and local television stations. Protesters from the Jewish Defense League and the black

"Drug Scene" aimed to present a realistic portrait of illegal drug use. The 1971 exhibit featured a photo cutout of a junkie shooting heroin and volunteers wearing "Ask Me" buttons to answer visitors' questions. Courtesy of the Museum of the City of New York.

community picketed the museum. Some protesters slashed eight paintings elsewhere in the museum and etched the letter "H" into a Rembrandt. The mayor threatened to slash the Met's funding. The museum was forced to withdraw the catalogue, close down the exhibition and increase security.

"Harlem on My Mind" was, if nothing else, revelatory for museums. It proved the power of an exhibition to galvanize a community, a lesson that would be applied in more positive ways in the future. It also revealed how much museums had to learn about the communities outside their walls. The Met was certainly guilty of naïveté at the very least, overestimating its own ability to understand and accurately present the experiences of people of color. It was lesson museums would not forget.

A few dozen blocks away, the Museum of the City of New York wanted to breathe new life into its 48-year-old institution. Director Joseph Veach Noble, a former executive at the Met, decided to confront the rising tide and impact of illegal drug use in the city, presenting as realistic a picture as possible. When "Drug Scene" opened in 1971 the exhibit entrance was framed by a photo cut-out of an addict shooting up heroin. As visitors proceeded, they encountered an LSD-laced sugar cube set into a photo of someone swallowing the drug. The museum's curators did not hire models to pose for photos; they sent a photographer out on the streets to find real addicts. They convinced the State Narcotic Addiction Control Commission that real drugs were needed. "[Getting genuine] heroin, LSD, marijuana, amphetamines and barbiturates became priority number one," Noble said. The show also included morgue pictures of DOAs and a soundtrack featuring popular singers who had died of overdoses. Ex-junkies were hired as staff, sporting "ask me" buttons and dialing a hotline to an Addiction Control Center for visitors who requested help. This happened about once a day, according to Noble.

"Drug Scene" broke all attendance records at the museum, then toured the state, breaking even more records. The museum followed with exhibitions about other hot issues, including alcoholism, sexually transmitted diseases and race relations. No matter how controversial a topic, if an exhibition was carefully researched and presented with sensitivity and authority, it could attract and educate visitors, not just stir up protestors.

■　■　■　■　■

Record-breaking attendance at museum exhibitions has a long history. In 1907 the American Museum of Natural History's instructional exhibit on tuberculosis drew huge crowds. So, too, the San Francisco Museum of Modern Art's (SFMOMA) 1940 showing of Pablo Picasso's *Guernica* and the National Gallery of Art's 1963 presentation of Leonardo da Vinci's *Mona Lisa*. But one event stands above all others in defining the museum blockbuster: "Treasures of Tutankhamun," known colloquially as "King Tut."

"Treasures of Tutankhamun," on view at the Metropolitan Museum of Art from December 1976 to April 1979, changed the focus from objects to crowds and money. Image © 1979 The Metropolitan Museum of Art.

From 1976 to 1979, more people lined up to see the ancient boy king, his solid gold funerary mask and 55 glittering treasures from his tomb than any other museum exhibition in history. "In Chicago the faithful queued up outside the Field Museum at ten o'clock the night before—rain or shine," noted *ARTnews*. In New Orleans they collapsed after a nine-hour wait in the blazing sun. In Los Angeles they camped outside for up to two days. Thousands were turned away. In venues around the country "King Tut" drew so many people—8.25 million to be exact—that it led to audience-control innovations such as timed tickets and advance sales that are standard in museums today.

The "King Tut" extravaganza was the result of a fortuitous confluence of events: diplomatic feats by U.S. and Egyptian government officials; the rise of corporate sponsorships; the 1974 Arts and Artifacts Indemnity Act through which the federal government guarantees insurance coverage of certain art objects; and the United States bicentennial celebration. Metropolitan Museum of Art Director Thomas Hoving also played a major role, negotiating with Egyptian authorities to make molds of the show's jewelry and sculpture, which were cast into merchandise and sold in an "official Tut Store" at the exhibition's exit. The Met spun-off even more products: scarves, posters, all the logo merchandise now commonly found in museum shops. Other "Tut" products—everything from towels to tote bags— appeared in department stores. Tut became such a celebrity that in 1978 comedian Steve Martin performed his "Funky Tut" routine on *Saturday Night Live*: "Now if I'd known/They'd line up just to see him/I'd've bought me a museum/King Tut. . . ." Meanwhile the term "blockbuster" had been coined in Hollywood after the success of the 1975 movie *Jaws*. For his marketing prowess, Hoving earned himself the unofficial title "King of the Museum Blockbuster."

Thanks to Tut's success Met director Thomas Hoving could add another title to his resume: "king of the museum blockbuster." Image © The Metropolitan Museum of Art.

Tut's success altered the course of museum exhibitions. As critic Herbert Muschamp wrote, "the collection of objects gave way to the collection of crowds." Seeing dollar signs, museums began to focus more attention on temporary spectacles rather than long-term shows. By the 1980s the number of temporary exhibitions at a typical urban art museum had jumped by more than 50 percent. Not all these shows had long lines of visitors, but critics began to complain about the "blockbuster mentality" and its resultant noise, lack of innovative scholarship, chintzy knock-off products and glossy advertisements.

Still, blockbusters have exposed millions of people, many of them first-time visitors, to museums and their most outstanding objects. And blockbusters can quickly erase a deficit, provide operating support or put a stop to budget cuts from local elected officials. In 1982 the Met ran a $2.1-million deficit. In 1983, after hosting the blockbuster "The Vatican Collection: the Papacy and Art," it was $263,000 in the black. In 1995 city officials pondered cuts to the Philadelphia Museum of Art. They changed their minds after the museum's exhibition of Cézanne paintings boosted city coffers with hotel and restaurant revenues. Three years later, the bottom line of the Museum of Fine Arts, Boston was buoyed by "Monet in the 20th Century." Cynics nicknamed the show "Money in the 20th Century." Yet in 2005 the Met turned down an opportunity to host "Tutankhamun and the Golden Age of the Pharaohs," billed in one museum's glossy promotional brochure as "King Tut Returns." The costs and expectations had simply grown too high.

Although successful at attracting large audiences, blockbusters rarely led to design innovation. Most of the mega shows that followed "King Tut" employed traditional designs, organizing spectacular objects in linear pathways, supplemented by lengthy text silkscreened onto labels and panels. History museums in particular drifted toward such shows as "Nation of Nations," the bicentennial celebration of American diversity organized by the Smithsonian. Filled with artifacts ranging from grandfather clocks to neon restaurant signs, such large-scale exhibitions have been called "aesthetic smorgasbords" of objects and information.

There were two major exceptions: children's museums and science centers. Without the responsibilities that came with exhibiting precious collections, these institutions had greater flexibility to innovate. They focused their exhibitions on people's educational needs, not on the need to highlight collections. This philosophy led to experimentation with new media, messages and methods that eventually spread to more traditional museums.

During the late 1970s and early '80s, exhibitions at the Exploratorium, Boston Children's Museum, Franklin Institute and Toronto's Ontario Science Center attracted attention from Junior League and parent groups. Frustrated with public schools, these groups wanted to create community learning environments by establishing hands-on museums that incorporated the theories of educational reformers like Maria Montessori, John Dewey and Jean Piaget. Suddenly it seemed like a youth museum was opening in nearly every city in America. In 1984 the Capital Children's Museum in Washington, D.C. (now the National Children's Museum), documented 531 requests from 47 states and 40 foreign countries on how to start a children's museum. Between 1976 and 2005, more than 180 new children's museums opened in the United States, with 65 more in the planning phases.

The Exploratorium assisted by creating low-tech traveling science exhibitions. The first of these efforts, its 1981 traveling show "Looking at the Light," consisted of easy-to-assemble materials and instructions for creating such intriguing exhibits as a pinhole camera and a walk-in kaleidoscope. With access to such packages and a series of publications called "Exploratorium Cookbooks," new children's museums and science centers were able to replicate mini-Exploratorium-type exhibitions.

Features at other children's museums, such as miniature grocery stores, doctors' offices, bubble-blowing vats and climbing areas for small children, were replicated around the country. Some museum professionals worried that the proliferation of museums with similar content was reducing the art of exhibition-making to a paint-by-numbers formula. They felt that all science centers and children's museums would start to look and feel alike, leading to what evaluator Randi Korn dubbed the "shopping-mallification" of hands-on museums. But parents and teachers didn't seem to care. They were delighted to have reliable hands-on exhibitions close by, especially on rainy weekends.

Furthermore, influenced by such shows as "The Rat" and "Drug Scene," some children's museums were now tackling topics that schools were afraid to touch, including death, disabilities, genocide, homelessness, prejudice. They explained those serious issues in ways that made sense to children. In 1983 the Boston Children's Museum opened "Endings: An Exhibit about Death and Loss." It included a diorama of a funeral parlor, a casket, bottles of embalming liquid and a time-lapsed video of a dead mouse being devoured by maggots. Recognizing the potency of its exhibition topics, BCM's staff added "talkback boards"—cork bulletin boards on which visitors could thumbtack opinions or questions written on small sheets of paper.

"Death and Loss" represented a visitor-oriented process of creating exhibitions. Janet Kamien, the show's developer, was neither an expert in the psychology of dying nor a curator in charge of a collection. She was an educator who worked with a team of experts and solicited visitors' opinions about what they wanted to learn. The exhibition and others across the country like it became dialogues between the museum and its audience.

"We are increasingly viewing youth museums as museums *with* children where we bring children in as colleagues," explained Peter Sterling, former director of the Indianapolis Children's Museum, "rather than museums *for* children where we make decisions for them and then present them with the results."

By the 1980s and '90s traditional museums were reexamining the social messages in their exhibitions. Few institutions, of course, were willing to throw away 60 years' worth of work perfecting dioramas, period rooms and art installations because of a few experiments in Boston and San Francisco. But they were ready to expand the often one-sided messages their exhibitions communicated about the state of the world. It became increasingly clear to museum directors, curators and educators that to be truly relevant and responsible in a multicultural society, exhibitions had to present multiple perspectives and interpretations. In the latter years of the 20th century, museums, along with American society in general, discovered that there was not one story but many, and those stories often had more than one side.

It was a time of considerable transformation, guided by several intersecting forces. Scholars urged natural history museums to talk about such social issues as global biodiversity, cultural diversity and the fragile relationship between people and the natural environment. Some attacked habitat dioramas for glorifying the trophies of the "great white hunter" or for inaccurate and misleading representations of animal behavior. Dioramas, said former Field Museum Director Willard Boyd, were "dead zoo[s] located in a dark tunnel—to be either avoided or used as a race track."

Meanwhile, anthropologists and Native American activists called attention to the stereotypes portrayed in life groups. Art historians argued that art museums largely ignored the works of women and artists of color. Social historians pointed out that period rooms depicted the idealized lives of the wealthy but ignored the lives of most other Americans. These discussions convinced many curators, especially those new to the field, that museums needed to change the stories their exhibitions were telling.

"Wolves and Humans" opened at the Science Museum of Minnesota in 1983, a time when the state's residents were debating the grey wolf's fate. The exhibition took visitors on a journey through many points of view. The central attraction—a diorama of a wolf pack spotlighting an alpha male killing a deer—was placed inside a series of concentric circles. A computer game allowed visitors to play the part of wolves on a deer hunt. Photos courtesy of the Science Museum of Minnesota.

WOLVES&
HUMANS
Coexistence Competition and Conflict

OPENS DECEMBER 10, 1983

The Denver Museum of Nature and Science's revamped dioramas feature fictional scientist-narrator C. Moore. Through field notes displayed as labels she tells the story of her ascent from prairie grasslands to alpine tundra. Image Archives, Denver Museum of Nature and Science.

More change came from the business world and social science research. Technology was becoming faster, louder and packaged to meet individual consumers' needs. In the 1980s products like personal computers, video games and the Walkman all hit the marketplace. Companies employed focus groups and customer surveys to market technological products to consumers. They also organized their creative workforces into cross-functional teams, composed of scientists, marketers and designers.

Children's museums and science centers already had used these tools. By the mid-1980s they were inching their way into more traditional museums. In the past, one or two people, usually curators, decided what would go on the gallery floor. Now museums were creating exhibitions that reflected the viewpoints of many people—inside and outside their walls. Surveys of museum visitors showed that many did not read labels or walk from object to object in the order curators intended. Designers moved away from the "book on a wall" approach and created exhibitions that presented compelling theatrical narratives.

The new ways of thinking helped bring the venerable diorama back into the museum field's good graces in the form of the Science Museum of Minnesota's "Wolves and Humans: Coexistence, Competition, and Conflict" (1983). Developed by biologist and taxidermist Curt Hadland and a design team that included former theater designer Dick Leerhoff, the exhibit opened at a time when the grey wolf's fate was hotly debated in Minnesota.

"Wolves and Humans" presented a diversity of human attitudes about wolves. The exhibit featured a diorama of a wolf pack, including an alpha wolf killing a deer; piped-in sounds of howling; a computer game that allowed visitors to play the part of wolves on a deer hunt; and a sound booth where people could imitate wolf sounds. A video loop presented different attitudes on reintroducing wolves to the wild, with a range of opinions from ranchers, trappers, hunters, environmentalists and biologists. The exhibit toured sites in 18 states, including Yellowstone National Park, and is now on permanent display at the International Wolf Center in Ely, Minn.

Other natural history museums transformed their dioramas from frozen vignettes into narrated adventure stories. In 1992 the Denver Museum of Nature and Science refashioned its 50-year-old dioramas into an organized presentation about Colorado's eco-systems. Visitors could join fictional scientist-narrator C. Moore as she ascended from prairie grasslands to alpine tundra and told her story through mock field notes, displayed as labels. The museum added video games and activities and also revealed the story behind the exhibition's creation, displaying photos of the old hall and the 1990s exhibition team, including a staff-member's dog.

The American Museum of Natural History had embarked on a project to bring Franz Boas's early-century Kwakiutl life groups into modern times and portray Native traditions and cultures with greater sensitivity. The resulting exhibition, "Chiefly Feasts: The Enduring Kwakiutl Potlatch" (1988), presented both historic and contemporary Kwakiutl objects. While in the past, anthropologist-curators had referred to field notes, this time they worked with teams that included Kwakiutl people, who identified important cultural themes, contributed personal stories, shared family picture albums and explained the

The Alcoa Hall of American Indians at the Carnegie Museum of Natural History depicts American Indian contributions to contemporary life, such as this mannequin of a Pittsburgh steel worker. Photo by Melinda McNaugher. Carnegie Museum of Natural History.

significance of different objects. In the mid-1990s, the Carnegie Museum of Natural History dismantled its 1901 "Hopi Snake Dance," sending the mannequins to the Custer Battlefield Museum in Garryowen, Mont., and reconfiguring its own exhibition hall to reflect American Indian contributions to contemporary society. The faces of the mannequins in the Carnegie's 1998 Alcoa Hall of American Indians were cast directly from Hopi, Lakota and Iroquois people. Some are dressed in traditional clothing, others in modern attire. To show American Indian contributions to industrial Pittsburgh, construction worker mannequins hang from models of skyscrapers.

Not content to let others interpret their history, Native Americans began to establish their own tribal museums across the country, developing dioramas, displays and narratives that reflected their own words and their own perspectives. The National Museum of the American Indian, which opened in 2004, near the U.S. Capitol in Washington, D.C., can be seen as a national forum for presenting American Indian perspectives to a wide audience.

Elsewhere a new kind of period room reflected scholarship in the field of social history. Developed with the input of former residents, community groups and educators, New York's Lower East Side Tenement Museum opened in a restored mid-19th-century tenement building in 1988. Cramped three-room apartments—complete with rumpled beds, shabby clothing, rickety furniture and rusty pots—reveal how various immigrant families eked out a living between the early years of the 20th century and the Great Depression. In one apartment, visitors can handle objects and even try on clothing. Labels, audio devices and well-scripted tours led by educators on staff provide fuller stories—where the families came from, how they made ends meet, what they did for entertainment. These period rooms were designed to provoke a dialogue among modern-day families by showing how immigrants formed an American identity in the face of prejudice and poverty.

The Lower East Side Tenement Museum inspired other institutions to exhibit stories of immigration. In 2004 the Wing Luke Asian Museum acquired the historic East Kong Yick Building, a former residence and social center for Seattle's Chinese, Filipino and Japanese laborers. The quarters are being refurbished into educational spaces supplemented with oral histories. Mining exhibitions also changed to reflect a heightened awareness of labor issues. When the Washington State Historical Society in Tacoma opened "Roslyn Coalmine" in 1996, it focused on the poor ventilation, long workdays and low paychecks miners endured. A mining shaft, for example, includes a mannequin of a worker trapped in rubble. The exhibition ends with display of union pamphlets.

Meanwhile, art museums were exhibiting more work by artists of diverse ethnic and cultural backgrounds and trying to create more inviting environments for art viewing. The Denver Art Museum was one of the first to add areas in the galleries with books, catalogues and comfortable couches for leisurely reading. DAM's educators started to rewrite labels in the 1980s, aiming to purge the obfuscated language of art historians. They hoped that different viewpoints in clear prose would help visitors make up their own minds about the artworks on display. Beginning in the late 1990s other art museums—notably those in the Bronx, Dallas and San Jose, Calif.—invited community members to write labels in their own words. The result was a fresher language that the public found more appealing than the starched language of the experts. These kinds of experiences, says Denver Art Museum Dean of Education Patterson Williams, make art museums less "academic and stuffy" and "more emotional, warmer, more embracing, more stimulating." Museums also began to experiment with bilingual labels, in English and Spanish, to better serve the nation's growing Latino population.

New digital technologies helped demystify the art world. In 1989 the Getty opened an Interactive Gallery for adults; among its many activities were art images loaded onto a compact disc, a first for a museum. Soon other art museums were featuring banks of computers with images, artists' biographies and historical atlases; the National Gallery of

Art's Micro Gallery opened in 1995. Staff at the University of California's Berkeley Art Museum went a step further, loading audio and video content onto portable computers that visitors then could tote to different works of art. As laptops became smaller and video imagery crisper, institutions—among them the Whitney, San Francisco Museum of Modern Art and American Museum of the Moving Image in Astoria, N.Y.—loaded information onto portable data assistants and handheld devices.

Audio guides, which had advanced considerably from their heavy, leather-strapped prototypes, remained the most popular handheld device. In the mid-1990s MP3 technology allowed museums to put vast bytes of sound onto a slim audio wand, which could be held to the ear like a cell phone. Visitors could set their own pace or follow a script, listen to descriptions of artworks in different languages and access different perspectives and ideas. At the Dayton Art Institute, which loaded seven different interpretations onto a single wand, visitors could stand in front of one painting and select commentary from a curator, an artist, a docent or information geared to children. By 2001, 60 percent of American art museums were using some kind of digital technology to enhance their exhibitions. Experiments with new kinds of audio-video technology, such as podcasting, continue to this day.

The Lower East Side Tenement Museum takes visitors back in time to the 1930s (above) through the kitchen of the Baldizzi family, Sicilian immigrants who weathered the Great Depression, and the Levine parlor (below), where a Polish family lived and operated a garment factory in the 1890s. Courtesy of the Lower East Side Tenement Museum.

At history museums the long, explanatory label and object-laden display gradually gave way to a new approach, a storyline that was more emotional and enhanced by personal, eyewitness accounts. Three successful examples could be seen in Washington, D.C.

"Field to Factory: Afro-American Migration" (National Museum of American History, 1987) invites visitors to walk through the story of the "Great Migration" of African Americans who, in search of a better future, moved from the rural South to the urban North between the two world wars. Visitors begin their journey at a recreated tenant farmhouse, learning about life in the South through artifacts ranging from agricultural tools to a Ku Klux Klan uniform; then view passengers in a segregated train car; and end up in the industrial

To continue their tour through "Field to Factory: Afro American Migration" visitors must choose between two Jim Crow-era passage ways: a door marked "colored" or a door marked "white." Smithsonian Institution, National Museum of American History, Behring Center, neg. #89-3890.

North with its factory time clocks and black businesses and churches. As visitors make their way through this story they confront an emotionally charged artifact: a Jim Crow-era passageway with one door marked "colored," the other marked "white." To continue visitors must choose a door. "Field to Factory," which later toured the nation, combined story with the power of authentic objects to evoke the realities of segregation.

"A More Perfect Union: Japanese Americans and U.S. Constitution," debuting at NMAH the same year, presents another difficult episode in American history: Japanese-American internment during World War II. The innovative exhibit incorporated oral histories, showing interviews with eight Japanese-American internees on two video monitors. "We wanted to create a document that was incontestable," says filmmaker Selma Thomas, who produced the oral histories, "so that even museum visitors who were strangers to the story would have to accept it as true. If you believe in the power of historical record, this is it. But the oral history also gives it a humanity that is often lacking in other kinds of documents."

In 1993 the U.S. Holocaust Memorial Museum went a step further, combining media and artifacts into a riveting theatrical experience. Designer Ralph Appelbaum used changing lighting and floor and wall coverings to set the mood as the story progresses from pre-Hitler Europe through the experience of the concentration camps. Visitors exit through a Hall of Remembrance, a hexagonal space lit by a domed skylight, intended to restore a sense of calm. Founding director Jeshajahu Weinberg, formerly of Tel Aviv's Cameri Theater, conceived of a "narrative museum" that would work "like the three acts of a drama. The mechanism is the same as with any good novel or film or play. You identify with the 'good guys,' you are anxious to see the outcome. The narrative has the potential of evoking psychological identification."

At the same time, the Minnesota Historical Society took history exhibitions in another direction, away from chronological narrative and toward a more impressionistic experience of the past. "Minnesota A to Z" (1992) arranged historical moments according to the alphabet, from A for Minnesota's animals, all the way to "Z," for zero-degree winter days. Next to each of the 26 letters were artifacts and stories of diverse Minnesotans supporting the themes. The "alphabet" technique spread to other history museums. A year later, influenced by firework festivals, rock concerts and science centers, MHS used a technique called "object theater" to develop its "Homeplace Minnesota" exhibition.

The term "object theater" was coined in the 1970s by Ontario Science Center designer Taiso Miyaki, who saw that a combination of light, objects and narrative provided a powerful theatrical medium for holding an audience's attention while illustrating complex information. In this spirit, "Homeplace" combines artifacts and narration to evoke a "feeling" for the state's history. Visitors enter a darkened space and sit in front of a stage that

rumbles with sound and light. Flashes of light illuminate different objects. Slides of historical photos click on and off. Recorded narration plays excerpts from famous Minnesota literature and oral histories from the museum's archives. "Homeplace" says MHS's former exhibitions director Paul Martin, creates an "emotional connection to the past through hearing and seeing people's stories."

"All the research we did indicated that people . . . didn't want [history] digested [for them]," says former MHS curator Barbara Franco. "They wanted the raw materials, the original voices. They wanted to hear all sides."

Object theater spread to other history museums, which applied it to such themes as culinary traditions (1998, Chippewa Valley Museum, Eau Claire, Wis.), the Boston Massacre (2001, Bostonian Society) and eyewitness accounts of World War II (2002, D-Day Museum, New Orleans). In 2004 the Mill City Museum, a branch of the Minnesota Historical Society, expanded the idea of object theater with "Flour Tower." The museum used workers' voices, flashes of sound and light, and a ride through a flour silo to tell the stories of retired flour millers. "Flour Tower," explains the exhibit's developer Dan Spock, is "a very conscious homage to the Museum of Science and Industry coalmine."

Rather than tell the story in chronological order, "Minnesota: A to Z" arranged the state's history according to the alphabet. Each letter represented an object that illustrated a theme, such as F for fire engine. The show closed in 2004. Photos by Eric Mortenson, courtesy of Minnesota Historical Society.

An homage to the "Coal Mine" exhibition at the Museum of Science and Industry in Chicago, "Flour Tower" features workers' voices, flashes of sound and light, and a ride through a flour silo. Courtesy of the Mill City Museum, Minnesota Historical Society.

The dramatic transformations in traditional museums in the 1980s and the years that followed were not without critics. Curators sometimes refused to accept new technologies, arguing that gadgets were more confusing than helpful to visitors. Audio guides, some believed, interfered with the enjoyment of art in an environment that was supposed to be peaceful and relaxing. Videos and computers turned museums into pachinko parlors. Object theater was sensationalist and manipulative. Visitors, however, overwhelmingly approved of new technologies that offered new perspectives and more information. "Some ask why audio-visual techniques should be used in a museum," wrote Joseph Veach Noble. "The answer is, for the same reason that Pope John XXIII changed the celebration of the mass from Latin to the vernaculars. In short, it is better for communication."

Another internal (and sometimes bitter) debate concerned the trend to create exhibitions through a team process rather than from a curator's singular vision. Many curators protested that a decision-by-committee model, even when informed by consumer research, would "dumb down" exhibition content and ultimately please no one. As John Killacky, former curator of the Walker Art Center, explains, "curators had to learn to not only share real estate, but to give it up to community groups." Nancy Villa Bryk, a curator at the Henry Ford Museum & Greenfield Village adds: "It was not about 'us'—the curators. It was about 'them'—our visitors. While the challenges curators faced at the museum seemed daunting and at times painful, those feelings diminished as we embraced new perspectives, learned new skills, and adjusted to new ways of working with others." Cross-disciplinary teams were creating almost 90 percent of museum exhibitions by the year 2000.

Exhibitions also faced increased criticism from the press and politicians. Using terms like "Disneyification," articles in the popular press accused natural history museums of compromising an illustrious past by abandoning the standard diorama for a theme-park atmosphere. Others claimed that the new exhibitions curated by ethnic groups were self-serving, "wrapped in layers of promotional and political gauze." Art and history museum curators were accused of succumbing to "political correctness," an argument that fueled the period's "culture wars," the often bitter debates about the right to exhibit potentially controversial perspectives.

In 1991 the Smithsonian's National Museum of American Art organized "The West As America: Reinterpreting Images of the Frontier, 1820-1920." Through provocative label text, this exhibition presented a "revisionist" perspective of the relationship between American western art, the "wild west" and the Manifest Destiny. "Wishful Thinking I: Doomed Indians," read one label, ". . . these grim artistic metaphors of death also convey a guilty longing that resilient Indians might really vanish. . . ." In comment books at the exhibition's exit, visitors praised the museum for its "eye-opening" and "courageous" labels. But some historians, like former Librarian of Congress Daniel Boorstin, condemned the art exhibition as "perverse, historically inaccurate, destructive."

At the same time, powerful conservative politicians accused other art and history museums of displaying sacrilegious art, pornography and anti-patriotic messages. They condemned exhibitions of allegedly anti-Christian photographs by Andres Serrano (1991), sexually explicit photographs by Robert Mapplethorpe (1992) and the National Air and Space Museum's proposal to include the Japanese perspective in an exhibition of the *Enola Gay*, the B-52 that dropped the atomic bomb over Hiroshima (1995). These exhibitions did not represent the nation's values, their detractors said, and as such should not receive federal funding. Repeated attempts failed to disband the National Endowment for the Arts, which had provided funds to museums hosting the Serrano and Mapplethorpe shows. But the NEA and its sister organization the National Endowment for the Humanities adopted a far more cautious approach to their funding of art and scholarship, and NASM scaled back its *Enola Gay* exhibition.

As educators and curators attempted to create more meaningful exhibitions, and politicians debated the ethics of funding controversial shows, artists poked fun at everyone. Dissecting and manipulating museums and exhibition techniques became a popular art form in itself, particularly during the 1990s. The Museum of Contemporary Art in La Jolla, Calif., exhibited a habitat diorama of urban raccoons preying on heaps of human garbage, created by artist Mark Dion. At the Gibbes Museum of Art in Charleston, S.C., Christian Boltanski deconstructed the period room, reassembling the furnishings of a middle-class kitchen and a college dorm room on museum pedestals, complete with labels identifying such objects as "mop" and "colander." Performance artist Andrea Fraser spoofed docent tours at the Philadelphia Museum of Art.

Janet Cardiff's version of the audio tour guided visitors into the stairwells and backrooms of the San Francisco Museum of Modern Art. The number of artists using museums as palettes was so large that in the late 1990s the Museum of Modern Art presented a collection of such works in "The Museum as Muse: Artists Reflect." Museum techniques had become so ubiquitous that it was now possible to create exhibitions about exhibitions.

Entire museums repackaged themselves as art installations. The Museum of Jurassic Technology, founded by performance artist David Wilson at an unspecified date and time, claims that it is "dedicated to the advancement of knowledge and the public appreciation of the lower Jurassic . . . through a hands-on experience of life in the Jurassic." A visitor to MJT's grungy commercial storefront in Culver City, Calif., is treated to a series of eclectic, possibly contrived, exhibits of scientific phenomena, seemingly historical events that may never have happened and works that may or may not be art. On display are such items as a solid piece of lead in which (supposedly) a South American bat is trapped and a microscopic portrait of Ernest Hemingway sketched onto an apple seed. Art critic Ralph Rugoff calls MJT a "modern meta-museum—a museum about museology. . . that uses falsehoods as a way of conveying a type of experiential truth that escapes analytical approaches."

Since 1992 artist Fred Wilson has manipulated collections to call attention to the sometimes racist subtext beneath an exhibition's surface. Photo by Jeff Ninztel. Courtesy of the Hood Museum of Art, Dartmouth College, Hanover, N.H.

History museums also found themselves the topic of their own exhibits. In 1992 Fred Wilson, a New York artist of Carib-African descent, took on the convention of museum display as well as museums' attitudes toward people of color. At the Maryland Historical Society in Baltimore, he manipulated what he called the "the language of a museum," that is, its collections, to call attention to the silent and sometimes racist codes of exhibitions. He called his installation "Mining the Museum," a triple pun on the word "mining:" digging something up, blowing something up and making something mine.

Wilson juxtaposed items from the collections in rooms that he painted gray and titled "grim historical truths." He arranged finely carved dining-room chairs around a crude wooden whipping post from the Baltimore City Jail and altered the

spotlighting on an antebellum painting to reveal a black slave hovering behind his young white master. One display featured fancy silver juxtaposed with slave shackles. "Actually they had a lot to do with one another," the artist said. "The production of one was made possible by the subjugation enforced by the other." Wilson went on to mine other museums from Seattle to Chicago, exposing their collections and critiquing their practices. "Mining the Museum" changed museum practice, reminding collectors and curators about the unintentional messages they sometimes communicate to visitors.

*In search of "grim historical truths," Wilson created groupings of objects such as the fancy silver items and slave shackles **(above)** and finely carved chairs next to a crude wooden whipping post from the Baltimore City Jail **(top)**. From "Mining the Museum," courtesy of the Maryland Historical Society, Baltimore.*

■　■　■　■　■

In the early years of the 21st century marketing experts called on museums to create exhibitions that "delivered an experience," taking visitors beyond viewing objects and acquiring information and toward "active engagement, immediacy, individuality and intense, memorable or unusual encounters." Museums gave visitors backpacks filled with activities to tote around the institution, as well as puzzles, treasure hunts, inventing labs, whodunits, high-tech computer games, low-tech smell boxes and portable laminated placards and labels (often in different languages). They added more content to handheld devices, video kiosks and websites. Visitors were encouraged to relax and socialize. Depending on the museum, a variety of experiences became available in a single visit.

In the midst of this continuous stream of activity, a major change took place. The terrorist attacks in New York and Washington, D.C., on Sept. 11, 2001 took museums by surprise, just as they did the rest of American society. Overnight the conversation changed to topics that were deeper, more personal and spiritual. Among the American public there was a new sense of vulnerability, a new appreciation for community. In the days and weeks following the attacks, people frequently turned to museums as places where they could find solace and a sense of tradition and community. Museums across the country responded by opening their doors and inviting people to come together for comfort and reassurance. From the South Street Seaport Museum in New York City to the Oklahoma City National Memorial, institutions developed exhibitions that captured the nation's outpouring of grief over the events of Sept. 11.

Above: 78th floor elevator plaque, South Tower, World Trade Center. The 78th floor was the one hit by the plane on Sept. 11, 2001. Collection, New York State Museum.

Below: The 9/11 Room at the New York City Fire Museum pays tribute to the firefighters who died on that terrible day. Courtesy of the New York City Fire Museum.

■　■　■　■　■

Over the past century museum exhibitions have told countless stories in many different ways. Some of the transformations, such as inviting community input to create exhibitions, are far from obvious to most visitors. Others—new technologies, interactive exhibits and new social perspectives—are readily apparent. But both these internal and external changes are part of the same impulse: the transformation of American museums into more complex, pluralistic and responsive organizations. Using the growing repertoire of exhibition techniques and energetic research about how visitors learn and enjoy, museums continue to fashion experiences that matter to contemporary audiences. Whatever the medium, message or method, the American exhibition remains, at its heart, what it has always been: a space where, as former Exploratorium exhibits director Kathleen McLean puts it, "objects, ideas, and people are brought together and transformed."

PEOPLE & MONEY

Museums should "begin with people first...."

—ARTHUR C. **PARKER**, FOUNDING DIRECTOR,
ROCHESTER MUSEUM OF ARTS AND SCIENCES

Members of the Charleston, S.C., city council could relax at last. They'd just appointed the Charleston Museum's new director, a "bluestocking New England spinster" named Laura Bragg (1881-1978), the museum's former curator of public instruction. The date was Aug. 6, 1920, and the council was optimistic about the institution's future. It was, after all, the oldest museum in the country—an important feature of a city that was undergoing a dramatic cultural renaissance. But the new director's five-and-a-half-year tenure would give Charleston society more grief than joy.

Despite her museum experience, Laura Bragg was an unusual choice for the director's post. Unlike most women working in museums in the 1920s, she had few personal financial resources. She suffered a disability—severe hearing loss. And to the dismay of Charleston's upper crust, she bravely stood up to the city's Jim Crow laws, opening the museum's doors to African Americans at a time when South Carolina schools had two sets of textbooks, one for whites, the other for blacks.

Aghast, the city fathers overturned her efforts, passing a statute decreeing that the "Museum and its use is for white citizens of Charleston." But Bragg was not deterred. Determined to introduce the wonders of the museum to everyone, she developed traveling kits, later called "Bragg Boxes," which contained lessons on history, geography, nature study, home economics and conservation. These she continued to circulate to

Laura Bragg, director of the Charleston Museum, with "Clipper Ships," an exhibit designed to tour local schools, c. 1920s. Courtesy of the Berkshire Museum, Pittsfield, Mass.

both black and white schools. Bragg's goal was "to end the apathy and ignorance of schoolchildren. She hoped that they would become educated adults who would visit the museum and bring their [own] children."

That Laura Bragg could be such a social activist when women had little influence in other spheres says much about the museum's status in the early 20th-century. The field was largely disorganized, with each institution marching to the beat of its own drum. Museums could be used to advocate for social reform because, in truth, they had little political power and virtually no collective influence on society. Very different from other organizations in the cutthroat and masculine business world, most museums were quirky places, run more like private clubs than public institutions.

For one, "museum" was not yet a profession. Few publications described how museums could become more efficient, organize artifacts and exhibitions or serve the public better. Facilities were often grimy and poorly lit. Public amenities were scarce. Displays of collections often overwhelmed the average visitor. Lectures, tours and even children's story hours could be dreadfully dull.

Yet the people came—individually and by the dozens. Children flocked to the free lantern slide shows at the Toledo Art Museum. Adults went to public lectures on civics offered by the Georgia Historical Society and exhibitions of foreign postage stamps at the State Historical Museum of Wisconsin. Teachers took students to the Brooklyn Children's Museum, where they could learn to use a butterfly net. Professors sent their students to the galleries on the campuses of Smith College, Cornell University and Michigan State, where they learned about the Old Masters by copying their works into sketchbooks.

"The public response has justified the experience," wrote one director about a 1913 exhibition of locally produced clay products. "The attendance, 25,000 visitors during the six weeks, included manufacturers and builders . . . men interested in South American trade, art potters . . . teachers of ceramics and china . . . [w]omen's clubs, groups of saleswomen from the department stores, and classes of schoolchildren. . . ."

Schoolchildren line up to see an exhibition about tuberculosis organized by the American Museum of Natural History in 1907.

From their earliest days, American museums have bustled with activity, serving as places of education and encounter, enlightenment and entertainment, and "intensely human institutions, dedicated to serving the broad-ranging interests of a diverse audience." Whether known today for its buildings, collections or exhibitions, every American museum also is a reflection of the people—the founders, workers, supporters, politicians and visitors—who shaped its journey through the 20th century.

Curators at work, c. 1910. Courtesy of the Public Museum of Grand Rapids.

■   ■   ■   ■   ■

In those early years, as the field tried to find its footing, men and women with any sort of museum experience were in short supply. News journals published letters to the editor beseeching industrialists to stop founding new museums until they could adequately train a workforce. In that way, wrote one correspondent, "the public will find that museums accomplish something more than the mere storing of private collections." A few visionary workers tried to define a national "museum sense" by founding the American Association of Museums in 1906. And responding to what he called museums' "slipshod and haphazard business methods," in 1910 librarian Henry Watson Kent developed filing systems for organizing and keeping track of collection records. But what visitors might encounter or experience in a museum on any given day depended largely on the idiosyncratic whims of individuals, especially the people who were footing the bills.

Many 19th-century museums had been established to educate the masses, but by the early years of the 20th century "service to the public" was a distant goal. Focused as they were on their own legacies and social stature, wealthy founders didn't always look for or try to train qualified workers. To staff their fledgling institutions many resorted to the time-honored hiring methods of nepotism, intuition and luck. At some museums "wayward" nephews and "spinster" daughters suddenly found themselves with the title of "director," charged with tasks like uncrating collections, dusting them off, fitting them into cases and turning on the lights when visitors arrived.

Other institutions managed to hire more talented personnel. Perhaps it was a combination of luck and intuition, for example, that led the Brooklyn Children's Museum to recruit Anna

Anna Billings Gallup and other staff at the Brooklyn Children's Museum in 1913. Left to right: George P. Engelhardt, assistant curator; Miriam S. Draper, librarian; Gallup; Agnes E. Bowen, special assistant; Marguerite Carmichael, assistant to the curator; Mary Day Lee, assistant curator. Courtesy of the Brooklyn Children's Museum.

Billings Gallup (1872-1956) as a curator in 1903. Or maybe it was just good business sense. A Mayflower descendant, Gallup held a degree from the Massachusetts Institute of Technology, a rarity for a woman at that time. Due to her skills as a science teacher as well as her dedication, she soon ascended to the director's seat. She spent the next 35 years charting the direction of children's museums nationwide and advocating for the needs of young people in all museums.

Even without training or experience, early museum staff—both men and women—embraced their work. Some even doubled as benefactors, donating their own collections or money to keep their institutions afloat or doing without a salary, content simply to participate in a world of beautiful things. They understood that they were running unique organizations. Exhibitions and collections had to change continuously if they were to keep up with the aspirations of the growing nation.

Smithsonian curator George Brown Goode (1851-96) expressed their feelings succinctly. "A finished museum is a dead museum," he wrote. These unique institutions were living breathing organisms that required workers who possessed a "museum sense" to arrange constantly changing exhibitions and collections in ways that could expose more and more people to the world of culture and knowledge.

Gradually the concept of a museum workplace started to develop, though it was a concept that reflected the standards of the day. The ideal museum director or curator needed what financier and art collector J. P. Morgan called "gentlemanly qualities," which included a charming European accent and a burning desire to build an empire of collections. One such gentleman was a German-born, former Civil War lieutenant named Carl Doerflinger (1843-1909). As the first director of the Milwaukee Public Museum, he coaxed a well-known but financially strapped dealer from upstate New York into selling the museum an extraordinary natural

Carl Doerflinger, the first director of the Milwaukee Public Museum, had the "gentlemanly qualities" expected of a museum director at the turn of the century. Courtesy of the Milwaukee Public Museum.

Enoch G. Bourne of the Trenton School of Industrial Arts demonstrates pottery-making techniques to a group of schoolchildren during the exhibition, "New Jersey Clay Products," 1915. The Newark Museum Archives.

history collection for a pittance. Eventually the dealer's son, Henry L. Ward, moved to Milwaukee to direct the museum that held his father's beloved collections—the only way he could get close to them.

Other directors eliminated the middle man and doubled as private dealers themselves. The first director of the Metropolitan Museum of Art was Col. Emanuele Pietro Paolo Maria Luigi Palma di Cesnola (1831-1904), an antiquities dealer born in Italy. He sold the Met his own collection of Greek antiquities, many at a profit, some allegedly fake. "In those times," explains Thomas W. Leavitt, first director of the museum division, National Endowment for the Arts, "directors were riding high, hobnobbing with the very rich, seldom challenged by scholars, much less by a public which never felt completely at home in [museum] palaces."

Through the years, however, increasing numbers of directors began to use their "museum sense" to move their institutions toward the higher ideal of public service and education. Arthur C. Parker (1881-1955), the founding director of the Rochester Museum of Arts and Sciences, didn't mince words when he described his vision for museums. Most museums in the years between the world wars were collections of "relics and rubbish . . . monument[s] of confusion and mosaic[s] of conceit," he said. They should "begin with people first and by showing an interest in human beings bring a more appreciative interest in what the museum does and has to show."

The galleries of the Portland Art Museum, c. 1915. Courtesy of the Portland Art Museum, Portland, Oreg.

Display of articles costing no more than 10 cents from the Newark Museum's "Beauty Has No Relation To Price, Rarity, or Age," 1928. The Newark Museum Archives.

Putting people first was also the mantra of the outspoken and irascible John Cotton Dana (1856-1929), founder of New Jersey's Newark Museum. Described by his colleagues as pungent, provocative, mischievous, mordant, kind, critical and then some, Dana came from an established Vermont family. His interest in public service began when as a recent college graduate he ventured westward and took a job at the Denver Public Library, where he developed the nation's first children's reading room.

Moving to Newark, he pioneered the open-stack system at the city's public library and in 1909 persuaded local collectors to display their art and specimens in its halls. Dana then talked city officials into turning part of the library into a community museum, with exhibitions and programs for the growing population of factory workers, African Americans, Catholics and Jews, who often did not feel welcome in other museums. Like Laura Bragg in South Carolina, he believed profoundly that museums should open their doors to everyone, and the Newark Museum became a beacon in the field. There, visitors could find "attendants ready to guide groups and explain collections" and show school teachers how to use museum resources in their classrooms. Dana believed in a museum that "arous[ed] in casual visitors more than a casual interest in the objects they see."

Female museum directors at the 1923 meeting of the American Association of Museums in Charleston, S.C. Courtesy of the Charleston Museum, Charleston, S.C.

He also believed that women were the key to providing better services to the public. While most outside the field viewed the museum merely as an acceptable hobby for the genteel lady, Dana encouraged women to think in terms of a career. Women were less likely to embroil themselves in collecting showmanship and more likely to care about educating people, he said: "A director should have common sense, enthusiasm for education in all its forms, and an eagerness to learn of the good work a museum can do for a community. . . . In almost every community, large or small today, it will be easier to find a woman than a man who is fitted to the director's task and is willing to take it."

Ellen Schulz Quillin, founder of the Witte Museum. Courtesy of the Witte Museum, San Antonio, Tex.

Since the mid-19th century, hundreds of women had played key roles in the historic preservation movement and organized period room and colonial kitchen displays at world's fairs. In fact, decades before they had the right to vote, women like Anna Billings Gallup were running museums. Their influence extended well beyond the obvious purview of children's education. Many women were accomplished naturalists, especially in the areas of botany and ornithology, and led some of the nation's first natural science museums, including the Worcester Natural History Society (now EcoTarium) in Massachusetts, Fairbanks Museum (and Planetarium) in St. Johnsbury, Vt., and the Museum of Vertebrate Paleontology at the University of California, Berkeley. In Texas, Ellen Shulz Quillin (1892-1970)—a high-school teacher, avid birder and expert in wildflowers and cacti—helped organize San Antonio's Witte Museum in 1927. She later established the Reptile Garden, one of the museum's most endearing attractions and a certified crowd pleaser—the perfect combination of serious scholarship and public entertainment.

True to Dana's words, women used their museum positions to help the underprivileged. Several considered themselves social reformers. Nobel Peace Prize winner Jane Addams (1860-1935) founded Chicago's Hull House Labor Museum, which offered immigrant women cooking and shopping classes that taught them to be "more American." At the Burke Museum on the campus of Seattle's University of Washington, anthropologist Erna Gunther (1896-1982) used her director's pulpit to call attention to the injustices waged upon Native Americans at a time when it was impolitic to bring such issues to light. Women also helped launch museums that exposed Americans to modern art and ideas, including the Whitney, Guggenheim and Museum of Modern Art in New York, Cincinnati Contemporary Art Center and San Francisco Museum of Modern Art.

Not possessing "gentlemanly qualities" was a professional handicap that was difficult for most women to overcome. The Guggenheim's first director, artist Hilla Rebay von Ehrenwiesen (1890-1967), claimed to be of Alsatian nobility and used the title "Baroness." A "close confidante" of founder Solomon Guggenheim, Rebay had a profound influence on the museum's collecting practices and architecture. Yet she frequently was derided in the press and described as "a prima donna . . . and buxom hausfrau."

A notable battle of the sexes took place between Alfred Barr, Jr., MoMA's first director, and the inimitable Adelyn Breeskin (1896-1986), director of the Baltimore Art Museum and a divorced mother raising three children. During the 1930s Barr made frequent trips to Baltimore to court a collection of works owned by two wealthy sisters, Dr. Claribel and Miss Etta Cone. The masterpieces included canvases by Matisse and Picasso and, Barr claimed, were too exquisite to remain in the dull backwater of Baltimore. But Breeskin held tough and scored the donation for the people of her city. The Cone Collection can be seen at the Baltimore Art Museum today.

■　　■　　■　　■　　■

In the roaring 1920s new economic forces began to break the control wealthy collectors had over museums. Middle-class citizens who lacked vast sources of cash to purchase their own collections banded into "friends" groups, pooling their money to purchase objects and collectively influence the direction of museums such as the Cleveland Museum of Art. Reaping the benefits were curatorial departments with lesser prestige (those focused on American or decorative arts, for example) than those concentrating on European Old Masters. By supporting displays of Americana, the middle class now had a modicum of influence in what the public could see in museums.

At the same time, a new form of the philanthropic organization was starting to exert its own influence. The charitable foundation was a funding source established by wealthy families to support civic projects, benefit society and, by the way, reduce their tax burden. The first one in the United States was the Carnegie Corporation (1911); the second, the Rockefeller Foundation, was founded in 1913, the same year Congress passed the federal income tax act. Although they pledged to do good, charitable foundations were not without their critics. Skeptics accused the foundations of manipulating the country's educational and social structure and wealthy people of dodging taxes by financing ventures—i.e., libraries, parks and museums—that the government eventually would have to maintain. Museums were especially vulnerable to this criticism, since municipalities already had donated buildings, land and, in some cases, local tax revenues to what some people considered extravagant private playpens.

In face of such doubts, those in charge of foundations realized that museums needed to do a better job of promoting their societal value. The best way to accomplish this was to develop an independent network of trained museum workers who clearly were dedicated to working on the public's behalf.

The foundations turned to the American Association of Museums, which in 1923 received its first grant from the Laura Spellman Rockefeller Foundation, a branch of the organization founded in 1913. The grant allowed the association to establish a permanent office in Washington, D.C., launch a four-page national journal for museum workers and write the field's first professional code of ethics (1925). This two-page document promoted a standard of professional behavior and, among other things, encouraged museum staff to refrain from "jealous acts, gossip, inquisitiveness, sarcasm [and] practical jokes."

In 1922 Frederick Keppel, formerly dean at Columbia University and assistant secretary of war, became head of the Carnegie Corporation. No doubt influenced by his Columbia colleague, educational philosopher John Dewey, Keppel believed foundations could help museums and universities create formal training programs that would expand the pool of qualified curators and directors. He steered Carnegie funds to the first serious museum training course in the country, established by Paul Sachs at Harvard University in 1922. Sachs, son of a founder of the financial firm Goldman/Sachs, joined up with Edward Waldo Forbes (1873-1969), grandson of poet Ralph Waldo Emerson. At Harvard they trained art connoisseurs and restorers through the 1940s, developing a rigorous curriculum that covered

By the 1920s and '30s art museums were designing exhibitions to appeal to large numbers of people. Courtesy of the Philadelphia Museum of Art.

museum history, philosophy and management. The program's illustrious students eventually would direct some of America's most prestigious art museums, including the Museum of Fine Arts, Boston, Saint Louis Art Museum and Museum of Modern Art in New York.

Museums also started apprenticeship programs in the more community-oriented aspects of their work: teaching children, providing materials for researchers and designing appealing shows for the masses. In 1923 the Newark Museum launched a course in museum education that attracted young women from wealthy East Coast families; some of its graduates later established the curatorial and registration departments at the Museum of Modern Art. Starting in 1929, with funds from the Rockefeller Foundation, the Buffalo Museum of Science trained budding designers and builders of dioramas, which were gaining in popularity in science and nature museums around the country. Graduates of Buffalo's program later influenced the development of museums in the national parks and elsewhere.

These newly trained men and women shared practices with one another and organized regional support groups, beginning in 1927 with the Association of Midwest Museums. Until this point the field's professional literature had featured such inspiring topics as "how to mount an African Warthog" and "how to fluff a vulture's feathers." Now museum pamphlets began to talk about civic value, urging staff to abandon the "insidious decadence" of collectors and instead bridge the worlds of "high" and "low" culture for the public. Furthermore, the first psychological studies of museums showed how visitors *really* behaved in the galleries. Between 1924 and 1928 Yale University professors Edward Stevens Robinson and Arthur Melton and their students documented the insidious

condition known as "museum fatigue"—the exhaustion felt after even a few minutes of navigating interminable rows of displays, galleries and flights of stairs.

The combination of training and research led to action. Museum workers uncluttered exhibitions and created more attractive habitat dioramas and period rooms. They fought with architects to minimize the number of stairs people had to climb and ensure there were fewer confusing spaces. They invented such devices as "portable museum stools" to help visitors combat their fatigue. They developed public courses to promote art appreciation.

In the 1930s, with funds from the Carnegie Foundation, large urban museums established branches in suburbs, designed to be more intimate and less intimidating than the marble palaces in the cities. Philadelphians, for example, could venture to a storefront branch of the Philadelphia Museum of Art in Upper Darby, Pa. With window displays opening out to the street, the museum produced 17 exhibits in its first 12 months and stayed open until 10 p.m. every night, including Sunday. Supported by the Carnegie, Rockefeller and other foundations, museums also sent exhibitions to the nation's black colleges, reaching out to students who had restricted access to traditional urban art museums. Though these short-lived experiments ended when the Great Depression set in, they set the stage for later experimental practices that aimed to introduce museums to a broader part of the population.

Old-style directors, however, were appalled by the crowds of people who came to educational programs. Watching large groups of boisterous children arrive for the popular 1920s Saturday classes at the Public Museum of Grand Rapids, Director Henry

L. Ward exclaimed, "The whole thing is wrong; unbecoming a city department; inimical to gentlemanly and ladylike deportment; dangerous to health and to life and limb." But museums had never been more popular.

■　■　■　■　■

With the stock market crash of 1929 and the onset of the Great Depression, the nation seemingly had little time to worry about museums. People were "hungry, desperate and angry"; by 1933 the nationwide unemployment rate had skyrocketed to its all-time high of 25 percent.

Yet museums did play a large public service role during those grim years. Due to cuts in school funding, they experienced a sharp demand for children's classes. Adults, too, were drawn to free cultural events and visited museums in larger numbers than ever before; attendance numbers climbed by 50 percent. Most surprising, benefactors who lost large fortunes in the crash actually donated *more* money to museums in the 1930s than they had in the roaring 1920s.

An important boost to museums came from President Franklin Delano Roosevelt's job creation program, the Works Progress Administration (WPA), established in 1935. WPA funds led to a huge expansion of the National Park Service (NPS), including new museums along park trails around the country. At a centralized design studio in Berkeley, Calif., NPS artists created

Holger Cahill with Georgia O'Keeffe and Maria Chabot, 1942. Under Cahill's leadership the Federal Arts Project employed thousands of artists—many in museums—during the worst years of the Depression. Courtesy of Palace of the Governors, Museum of New Mexico. Negative no. 165669.

relief maps and other exhibits for these museums. In 1937 its exhibit-building activities were so widespread that NPS inaugurated a museum division; its first chief, Ned J. Burns (1899-1953), was a master diorama maker and exhibition designer. Create exciting displays that looked "lived-in, not died-in," Burns urged the hundreds of illustrators and artisans under his supervision. "Exhibits should be dynamic and fresh as today's newspaper."

Another WPA program, the Federal Art Project (FAP), represented the largest infusion of federal cash the arts community had ever seen, and the first federal monies to go directly to the nation's museums. In 1935 Holger Cahill, who built the Newark Museum's American art collection in the 1920s, was called to Washington, D.C., to head the FAP. "It'll be terrible, with a dead cat coming your way every few minutes," warned Cahill's friend Francis Henry Taylor, director of the Worcester Art Museum. "Congressmen will have you up on the carpet every other minute, but of course you've got to take the job!"

Under Cahill's leadership FAP employed almost 40,000 artists, many in museums. They excavated and documented historic sites, organized and catalogued paintings and sculptures, repaired and cleaned specimens, and designed and installed exhibits, dioramas and period rooms. Thousands of artists participated in this dynamic work program, including Jacob Lawrence, Lee Krasner, Wilhelm de Kooning and Jackson Pollock.

The general public benefited immensely from the FAP. During this period residents of small Midwestern towns could visit local history museums spruced up with new cases and furniture built by FAP artists. City dwellers flocked to see new exhibits such as the wildlife dioramas at what is now the Denver Museum of Nature and Science and the meticulously restored Chinese Buddhist shrine at the Milwaukee Public Museum. In Boise, Idaho, they watched workers construct a new building for the local art museum and attended exhibitions organized by the WPA-sponsored Indian Arts and Crafts Board. Other people enrolled in painting and sculpture classes at community centers in Roswell, N.Mex., and Raleigh, N.C., which later were turned into permanent museums. The exuberant activity of the FAP years, notes historian Howard Zinn was "an exciting flowering of arts for the people, such as had never happened before in American history, and which has not been duplicated since."

FAP was dismissed as "radical," however, mainly because its participants included New York-based artists and African Americans, Native Americans, Jews and other minorities. Red-baiting politicians claimed that a photography exhibition documenting housing squalor in Oklahoma City and similar projects were "tools of the Communist party designed to breed class hatred in the United States." Others disapproved of the program's racially integrated classes. Still others felt that with a war on the horizon, there would be plenty of work for everyone and the job-creation program no longer would be necessary.

Unable to withstand the political pressure, WPA folded in 1943. However, it had a lasting museum legacy, contributing almost $20 million to projects across the country and proving that museums were much more than just playgrounds for the rich. Most important, many Americans entered museums for the first time in their lives and discovered that art and culture can nurture the spirit during difficult times.

As the nation prepared for war, museums vanished from the federal radar. In this era of patriotic sacrifice, the U.S. government classified museums as recreational, not educational—that is, non-essential. That meant that museums did not merit special rations, such as gasoline or tires. Some were forced to suspend operations and shut their doors. A few were converted into temporary hospital wards or bomb shelters, with their collections stored off site.

The government's approach was exactly right, agreed one progressive educator. Museums didn't deserve special treatment. In neglecting their obligations to the "common man" while their institutions received "tax privileges," the men and women who controlled museums were as guilty as "the dictators in Europe and Asia" of betraying "democratic ideals." Theodore Low of the Walters Art Gallery in Baltimore reminded his colleagues that government officials would not "support a cultural Fort Knox."

But others understood that museums could be essential gathering places for their communities, especially during wartime. The staff at the Bishop Museum in Honolulu exemplified this commitment. In December 1941, as "dense columns of black smoke continued to rise from Pearl Harbor," the shell-shocked staff was in high gear, securing the museum. Within days they had arranged new exhibits and developed creative art classes for children unable to attend school. "I believe the museum is going to play a more important

Left: *During World War II many museums supported the war effort with such patriotic exhibitions as "From the Halls of Montezuma" at the Walker Art Center. Photo by Rolphe Dauphin, Walker Art Center, Minneapolis.*

Right: *Some museums planted victory gardens, such as this one at the Cleveland Museum of Art, c. 1943. Courtesy of The Cleveland Museum of Art.*

part than ever as a morale builder for the community," wrote the Bishop's director, Peter H. Buck. The can-do attitude carried over to the mainland. Two weeks after the attack several museum directors gathered at the Metropolitan Museum of Art and resolved "to do their utmost in the service of the people in this country during the present conflict." Museums should strive to "be sources of inspiration illuminating the past and vivifying the present [so] that they will fortify the spirit on which Victory depends." Within months hundreds of museums had launched programs to help people cope with the stresses of wartime.

During the World War II years, visitors viewed exhibitions about military strategy and civil defense, such as the Walker Art Center's "Halls of Montezuma," "Airways to Peace" at the Museum of Modern Art and the Franklin Institute's large-scale exhibition about the art and science of camouflage. They visited museums at night, as institutions like the San Francisco Museum of Modern Art adjusted their hours to consider wartime work schedules, blacking out windows to guard against the possibility of enemy attack.

Soldiers listened to lectures about the values of democracy, a required part of their military training, at Colonial Williamsburg in Virginia. Navy and Army recruits learned about celestial navigation at the Hayden Planetarium in New York. G.I.'s stationed at Florida's Morrison Field Airbase gave public band concerts at the Norton Gallery of Art in West Palm Beach. Military personnel on leave could spend time at art museums across the nation, in special "smoking rooms" that invited them to learn how to paint, see a film or sample refreshments—all free of charge.

Saturday craft classes at the Public Museum of Grand Rapids, 1950s. Courtesy of the Public Museum of Grand Rapids.

Women enrolled in Red Cross sewing classes at the Philbrook Art Center in Oklahoma, learned how to plant victory gardens at the Berkshire Museum in Massachusetts and prepared surgical dressings for the armed forces at the New-York Historical Society. Children sometimes spent entire days at the local museum, enrolled in free programs such as the Syracuse Museum of Fine Art's "Playschool."

Offering these services was both patriotic and practical. "Museums had to convince politicians and those who controlled the purse strings that they were contributing to economic recovery, to the fight against totalitarianism, and to winning the war," explains historian Terry Zeller. The strategy worked. During the 1940s two-thirds of museums reported increased financial support from their municipalities; a few were even able to construct new facilities to accommodate expanded public use.

Michigan's Public Museum of Grand Rapids was one of several institutions that transformed itself during the war years. In 1939 its visionary new director, science teacher Frank "Dewey" DuMond (1898-1989) launched a campaign for a new building for the crumbling 84-year-old institution. "We do not wish to stand aloof," DuMond declared. "Our aim is . . . to give the taxpayers a lot for the little they invest. . . ." The museum produced flyers that showed citizens how to spot enemy planes and donated a Spanish-American war cannon to be

Adding this suit of armor to the collections of the Public Museum of Grand Rapids in 1951 so thrilled Director Frank DuMond, he had to try it on—something that no museum professional would dare attempt today. Courtesy of the Public Museum of Grand Rapids.

melted down for the "Salvage of Victory Clean-up." After the war, the museum created a brochure titled "Servicemen: What of Those Souvenirs?" that encouraged the donation of war-related artifacts for the benefit of future generations. By 1947 the building project was a rousing success. The museum had expanded services, reached new audiences and doubled its budget through "legitimate promotional stunts and publicity." It was, DuMond said with pride, "accessible as a dime store and friendly as your next door neighbor."

Other directors realized that their institutions could serve as valuable public relations tools—and not just for wartime concerns. Exhibitions, for example, could help businesses sell products by showing how appliances worked or goods were designed. During the 1940s Lennox Lohr, director of the Museum of Science and Industry in Chicago, brokered deals with companies to create exhibits about consumer goods, including "Electric Theater" with Commonwealth Edison and a B. F. Goodrich display on the wonders of rubber and latex. At the same time, the Museum of Modern Art and other contemporary art museums worked with department stores to promote modern designs of home furnishings, appliances and utensils.

As the Cold War loomed politicians saw that museums could help them present certain messages to the public, and the government commissioned exhibitions that aimed to soothe people's fears about atomic testing and Soviet nuclear attack. The federal government opened the American Museum of Atomic Energy in Oak Ridge, Tenn., in 1949—the year it revealed that the city was a site of the atomic-bomb-producing Manhattan Project. There, an exhibition called "Atoms for Peace" contained a diorama

Staff member Alfred Lee Rowell installing a miniature diorama at the Field Museum. A90412, © The Field Museum.

about mining uranium and bombastic prose about the promise of atomic energy. The show traveled around the country. In the early 1950s, to further put the nation at ease and promote the country's technological and military superiority, the Smithsonian opened several exhibitions about U.S. military history and triumphs.

Behind the scenes curators and scientists focused on their research and paid little attention to the public. Museum directors sank back into a comfortable "old boys" network. "Museums are the last places where Captains of Industry can act with no government meddling," proclaimed an editorial in *Art News*. "This is the last area where Big Money, and in the older cities, Old Money, has its nineteenth-century prerogatives." But the postwar political and economic climate was about to change.

■　■　■　■　■

America in the 1950s was "the affluent society," wrote economist John Kenneth Galbraith, a time of booming educational opportunities and material wealth for all. One result of middle-class prosperity was a new labor force for museums: white female volunteers. With their husbands at work, their children enrolled in high-quality public schools and their leisure time increased due to labor-saving appliances, more and more women lent their energies to museums as volunteers. During the 1950s women's committees were indispensable to day-to-day operations. At a time when exhibition improvements lagged due to curatorial indifference, energetic volunteers kept the museum connected to its public.

The volunteer transformed the American museum and became the antidote to the stereotypical stern-faced uniformed guard. She greeted visitors at the front door, cheerfully answered questions at the information desk, guided people through exhibitions, ran rental galleries and invited middle-class patrons to afternoon teas, special concerts and glittering galas organized by the women's committee. Finally the museum had a friendly face, and a rather fashionable one at that. Volunteers were considered so glamorous that the July 1952 issue of *Vogue* featured two of them, the chic Mrs. C. Matthews Dick, Jr., and Mrs. Edward B. Smith, posing in front of a painting at the Art Institute of Chicago. That same year a young doctor's wife named Mary Naquin Sharp wandered into the Baltimore Art Museum because "it was what everyone I knew was doing at the time." She remained an indispensable docent for more than 50 years. "We were doing everything," she recalls, "including lots of things that paid staff do now."

At many museums women volunteers outnumbered paid male staff two-to-one. In 1952 their numbers were so great that Sharp and others organized the American Association of Museum Volunteers, which was based at the Saint Louis Museum of Art. Soon volunteers founded their own museums. Thirteen volunteers in southern California founded a new institution in 1962: the Newport Harbor Art Museum, now part of the Orange County Museum of Art. Children's museums also benefited enormously from women's service organizations, most notably Junior Leagues whose members launched scores of youth-oriented institutions during the latter part of the century.

With growing attendance and backed up by their volunteer corps, directors renewed calls for federal dollars. A government agency would become an important player in this regard, though museums were the furthest things from President Harry S Truman's mind when he signed legislation creating the National Science Foundation (NSF) in 1950. Truman saw NSF as a way to support scientific research for national defense during the Cold War. Within the next few years, however, the agency would fund more than 200 biology research projects in natural history museums and botanical gardens. By the 1957 launching of *Sputnik*, the foundation and museums were sharing a mutual interest educating the public about careers in science.

The government also took a few small steps toward supporting arts and culture museums. In 1954 President Dwight D. Eisenhower signed the Excise Tax Reduction Act, which exempted museums from paying taxes on admissions charges. Ike was an amateur painter; his secretary of the treasury, Douglas Dillon, was a collector and trustee of the Metropolitan Museum of Art. But though the president professed an interest in museums, he did not push for more systematic funding. Direct federal support was politically unfeasible, due to Cold War paranoia about communism. In 1949 Michigan Rep. George Dondero delivered a speech on the House floor titled "Communist Conspiracy in Art Threatening American Museums," accusing museums of displaying "dangerous" abstract art created by artists with "foreign names" as a "rich source for hidden conspiracy." Sen. Joseph McCarthy of Wisconsin took up the cause and blacklisted artists he believed were "un-American."

Even though the U.S. Senate condemned McCarthy's tactics in 1954, the ripples of McCarthyism were strong. In 1955 a local women's luncheon club presented trustees of the Dallas Museum of Fine Arts (now the Dallas Museum of Art) with a list of "suspected communist sympathizers" and asked that their works be removed from display. The trustees refused. The museum's director, noted Texas artist Jerry Bywaters (1906-89), later received a special commendation from the American Association of Art Museum Directors for "withstanding the assault."

The next year an even-larger group, the Dallas County Patriotic Council, pressured the city to withdraw the museum's maintenance funds. The reason: a traveling exhibition called "Sport in Art," sponsored by *Sports Illustrated*, contained works by artists who allegedly were affiliated with "communist-front activities"; images included paintings of a fisherman and an ice skater. "The Reds are moving in upon us," warned the council. "Let those who would plant a red picture supplant it with the red, white, and blue. White for purity, blue for fidelity, as blue as our Texas bluebonnets."

Again, the trustees and the exhibit's local sponsor, department store magnate Stanley Marcus, held fast. "Museum says Reds can stay," announced the *Dallas Morning News*. "Sport in Art" opened as planned, its galleries flanked by armed guards. It drew larger than usual crowds and resulted in dozens of new memberships to the museum. Yet city officials acknowledged that the "main issue was far from being settled for good."

Fears of communism dominated the Cold War years and led to increased international showmanship. To highlight American ingenuity and democratic values, the United States Information Agency (USIA) toured exhibitions like the Museum of Modern Art's immensely popular "Family of Man" to Europe and the USSR. (The USIA tour of "Sport in Art," was cancelled, however, because of its association with "subversive" elements.) In 1959 congressmen and senators began to advocate for funding the arts at home. The next year the nation elected John F. Kennedy, who promised to advance the values of progress, education and social equity.

Strictly speaking, the arts and culture funding boom that followed JFK's election was the result of a confluence of astute lobbying, Cold War politics, economic good times and complex negotiations regarding tax laws. American hearts, however, were won over through a major public relations event.

In December 1962 French Minister of Cultural Affairs André Malraux flew from Paris to Washington, D.C. His traveling companion was a small canvas with a big appeal—Leonardo da Vinci's *Mona Lisa*—which came to the United States on a two-and-a-half-month loan orchestrated by the Kennedy White House. Amid great fanfare President and Mrs. Kennedy attended the opening at *Mona Lisa*'s first stop, the National Gallery of Art. For the next 26 days, 518,000 people waited in line to glimpse the famous canvas, installed on a baffle draped in red velvet and guarded by Marines around the clock. Even with extended evening hours the museum could barely manage the crowds; sometimes the wait in line was over two hours—in freezing winter temperatures. The painting then traveled to the Metropolitan Museum of Art, where more than a million people paid homage to the woman with the enigmatic smile. *Mona Lisa*'s triumphant tour helped the White House garner popular support for a federal arts and culture policy.

On the morning of Nov. 22, 1963, the *New York Times* featured two long articles detailing JFK's plan to create an arts council to "bolster the cultural resources of the nation." This goal was so important to Kennedy that he planned to appoint several prominent members of his cabinet as well as artists and arts leaders to the council. The elaborate scheme would never come to pass. That afternoon, in Dallas, the president was assassinated.

MONA LISA, *on loan from the government of France to the president and people of the United States, was a guest of the National Gallery of Art from Jan. 9 to Feb. 3, 1963. Courtesy of the National Gallery of Art, Washington, D.C., Gallery Archives.*

Vice President Lyndon Baines Johnson inherited a grieving nation on the brink of unrest. Civil rights issues loomed; there was a strong sense that the old order had to go. It was time to create, as LBJ called it, "A Great Society that . . . rests on abundance and liberty for all, where the city of man serves not only the needs of the body and the demands for commerce, but the desire for beauty and the hunger for community." His vision included federal programs and reform intended to bring the nation's arts and culture to all of its citizens.

■　　■　　■　　■　　■

"Sometime around 1965," sociologist Victoria Alexander tells us, "a rumble was heard in the museum world. It was the sound of an old funding system cracking as a new one emerged to displace it." The momentous system was a combination of brand-new federal agencies, foundation reform and changing corporate interests.

On the federal side, working closely with Rhode Island Sen. Clairborne Pell, President Johnson invited the directors of the Museum of Modern Art, Houston Museum of Fine Arts and Toledo Art Museum to join arts luminaries like singer Marian Anderson, composer Leonard Bernstein and author John Steinbeck on a National Council of Arts and Humanities. In 1965 LBJ signed the National Endowment for the Arts (NEA) and National Endowment for the Humanities (NEH) into existence. A year later, he signed the

The reading room at the Fogg Art Museum library, c. 1962. HUV 155 (5-9), courtesy of the Harvard University Archives.

National Museum Act, whose funds for training and research would be administered by the Smithsonian Institution. Foundations soon were required to make their records public and donate a certain percentage of their annual earnings to bona fide charities, thanks to the 1969 Tax Reform Act. Businesses were making changes, too. In response to accusations that corporations abused labor, the environment and consumers, corporate managers introduced the concept of "social responsibility." It made good business sense. A logical way to contribute to the welfare of communities and present the corporation's human side was to support that most human of activities, the arts.

"The emergence of the corporation as the controller of an enormous new medium of world-wide communications," said George Weissman, chairman of Philip Morris, "the growing awareness of the corporation's potential and responsibility for enlightenment, the ever-widening scope of the corporation's horizons—these are the factors that will cement lasting relationships to the arts." In 1967 David Rockefeller, chairman of Chase Manhattan Bank, founded the Business Committee for the Arts. Rockefeller's goal was to encourage more business leaders to give money to cultural organizations.

The opening of federal, foundation and corporate coffers was the equivalent of a Texas-size oil gusher for museums. High-society museum patrons were glad to have others step up to the plate, and many testified before Congress in support of the NEA. But first there was another hurdle to clear. The Internal Revenue Service (IRS) still clung to its World War II classification, designating museums as recreational, not educational. As a result, they were denied the tax benefits and grants enjoyed by other nonprofits. Museums needed to organize if they hoped to truly benefit from the new funding opportunities and expand their reach.

And organize they did. In 1967, 12 directors from art and science museums, large and small, gathered at a country estate in Belmont, Md., at a meeting convened by the American Association of Museums (AAM). Led by E. Leland Webber, director of Chicago's Field Museum, they were joined by a rising star, Nancy Hanks, executive secretary for the Rockefeller Brothers Fund. The outcome was a landmark document known as *The Belmont Report*, essentially a pitch for "substantial national aid" in the form of tax benefits and direct federal dollars. It opened by reminding its readers of the field's educational and research impact on the American people: groundbreaking scientific discoveries, life-altering moments for children and adults, the power of collections objects to inspire.

The Belmont Report also documented the poor condition of museum buildings and collections, the lack of staffing, sharply rising costs and scant government and foundation support. Then came the message to Congress: "The Federal Government has an obligation, as yet unmet, to assist in preserving, maintaining and wisely utilizing the national treasure in museums on behalf of all the American people."

Thanks in part to *The Belmont Report,* Congress was convinced that museums were educational organizations. With the 1969 Tax Reform Act, they qualified for an avalanche of financial support.

To bolster the report's claims AAM strived to help museum workers do their jobs better. Beginning in 1970 it launched programs that encouraged museums to aim toward the highest standards and helped staff elevate their professional practice. To the typical museum visitor, however, the legislative victories and structural systems were barely noticeable. With few exceptions, museums looked and felt much the same as they had a decade earlier. Outside on the streets, Americans were marching for civil rights, free speech and peace. But inside, museums remained ivory towers removed from the nation's turmoil. Docents retained their matronly styles. Art museum directors focused on upholding the upper-class values of their trustees, 60 percent of whom were over the age of 60.

Exhibits also did not reflect the public's mood. The Field Museum's "Races of Mankind" had remained unchanged since the 1930s, unapologetically presenting the idea of racial hierarchy. Chicago's Museum of Science and Industry developed an exhibition supporting the country's escalating military presence in Vietnam. It displayed a Huey helicopter with a machine gun pointing at a diorama of a Vietnamese village. Visitors could sit in the copter and electronically aim the gun at a thatched hut, which presumably hid members of the Viet Cong. In the language of the times, it is fair to say that at the close of the 1960s, museums were the "establishment" and bastions of "square" values.

But the field could not remain immune to the country's growing concerns about the Vietnam War, bigotry, sexism and poor conditions in the workplace. Idealistic young activists and artists began to take on museums. In 1968 civil rights activists conducted a letter-writing campaign that persuaded the Field to dismantle "Races of Mankind." That same year, war protesters swarmed MSI and forced the removal of the Huey helicopter. New York artists marched on the city's major art institutions. Forming groups like the Artists and Workers' Coalition and Women Artists in Revolution, they staged such unruly actions as unleashing cockroaches at a white-glove event at the Metropolitan Museum of Art and bursting bags of cow blood on the floor of the Museum of Modern Art (MoMA) while they shouted "rape."

Inside museums, staff began to voice their concerns. "We were passionate about the Great Society and all the new possibilities that were opening up around us," recalls Bonnie Pitman, deputy director at the Dallas Museum of Art, who began her museum career in 1968. "And we were not afraid of standing up and saying that things have to change."

On June 1, 1970, the museum "establishment" and young political activists faced off at the Waldorf Astoria Hotel in New York, where luminaries in the federal funding world had gathered to address the American Association of Museums' annual convention. Suddenly, 30 protesters stormed the halls with signs bearing the words "Art Strike Against Racism, Sexism, Repression and War." Rafael Montanez Ortiz, director of New York's El Museo del Barrio, a museum founded by Puerto Rican activists, grabbed the mike and spoke to the shocked audience. He accused museums of "complicity with the atrocities of the times." The dialogue became loud and contentious. Half of the audience began to pour out their frustrations about museums failing to confront the larger political issues of the day, especially the Vietnam War. The other half was furious, painting the protesters as "abrasive extremists." Was it right to lash out at the government just as it was about to open its coffers to museums?

The discussions continued into the next day, evolving from the war overseas to workplace conditions at home, especially hiring practices in museums. "[Discrimination in the museum field] certainly is prevalent," John Hightower, MoMA's director, admitted to the delegates. "Someone recently objected to a museum being referred to as racist. I replied that I knew the particular museum was not consciously anti-black or anti-Puerto Rican, only anti-Semitic. As far as the exploitation of women is concerned, the museum profession is notorious . . . museums hire bright, well-educated and talented women for extremely responsible jobs because it does not cost as much. This attitude is true throughout the country."

In the weeks and months that followed museum professionals continued to raise similar issues. In an editorial in *ArtNews*, Thomas B. Hess, a former curator at MoMA, laid bare the field's anti-Semitism, what he called "the most widely known, unspoken fact in the field." According to Hess, trustees were having a hard enough time dealing with American Jews

Pro-military exhibitions at the Museum of Science and Industry and other museums were taken down during the anti-war years of the 1960s. Courtesy of the Museum of Science and Industry, Chicago.

inching their way onto boards and "brushing aside Jockey Club protocols." Hess's conclusion: "No Jew need apply" for a director job, "unless he has changed his name and religion." In the grassroots journal *Ramparts*, critic Barry Schwartz launched an even more scathing exposé. No African American or Hispanic need apply for *any* museum job, other than guard or janitor. Schwartz took on the Oakland Museum, based in a California city that was 45-percent black and birthplace of the 1960s radical group, the Black Panthers. The "lily-white museum commission" (most of whom did not even reside in Oakland) recently had fired the museum's director for hiring the wife of

Workers at the Museum of Modern Art went on strike in 1971, arguing that their low wages were subsidizing the social status of wealthy art patrons. The Museum of Modern Art/licensed by SCALA/Art Resource, New York.

a local black militant in a professional position. Schwartz noted that there was hope through activism; the Oakland Black Caucus had called for a boycott of the museum.

Women, too, fought for their rights to equal pay and advancement opportunities, an outgrowth of the feminist movement. In 1971, 20 female employees at the Metropolitan Museum of Art filed complaints of sex discrimination with the State of New York Civil Rights Bureau, with dozens more supporting their claims about a glass ceiling. The double standard could be seen throughout the field. In 1975 Susan Stitt, later the first female director of the 150-year old Historical Society of Pennsylvania, published the first data on the economic status of women museum workers. She documented a salary gap of 30 percent, as well as at least one case where a museum (illegally) offered pensions to men but not to women.

One issue that all museum workers had in common, no matter their race or gender, was their low paychecks. In 1971, PASTA/MOMA—the Professional and Administrative Staff of MoMA—organized a strike at the Museum of Modern Art, demanding fair wages and arguing that poorly paid workers were subsidizing the social status of wealthy patrons. The Teamsters took their side, refusing to cross PASTA's picket line to deliver food to MoMA's restaurant, leaving that task to volunteer "matrons in station wagons." MoMA unionized and workers at museums around the nation began to organize. But strikes and worker dissent would continue to flare up for years as livable wages and the gender pay gap remained major challenges for the museum field.

Throughout the 1970s the "change in museums occurred so quickly . . . that it was hard to grasp," wrote art critic Sophy Burnam in *The Art Crowd*, her 1973 tell-all book about those radical years. The combination of idealistic, energetic workers and a new influx of funds launched museums into an era of unprecedented idealism and growth, both inside and out.

■ ■ ■ ■ ■

If a museum visitor had fallen into a decade-long Rip Van Winkle-style nap circa 1968, waking up at the end of the decade, she would have found herself in a radically changed environment. At a large urban art museum she would have witnessed crowds of tourists lining up to see great treasures from abroad assembled into blockbuster shows. She could visit an array of historical sites newly renovated for the 1976 bicentennial celebration or one of the many new ethnic museums like the Mexican Museum in San Francisco (1975) or the Afro-American Historical and Cultural Museum (now African American Museum) in Philadelphia (1976). She might have been shocked by the freewheeling atmosphere of a new kind of museum called the "hands-on science center," a far cry from the rows of specimens laid out in glass cases that she'd seen in the late 1960s.

NEA head Nancy Hanks was ideally qualified to get things done in Washington. Photo courtesy of the National Endowment for the Arts.

Inside all of these institutions she could read signs with words like "funded by the National Endowment for the Arts" or "made possible by the Mobil Oil Foundation." She would have picked up a free map and a glossy calendar filled with notices of educational events: papermaking workshops, yoga classes, a foreign film series. Peeking inside offices she would have spied workers frantically typing out grant proposals to fund new educational programs. She might have met a graduate student completing a summer internship as part of a new kind of curriculum called "museum studies." She might even have seen the museum's director heading to the airport, on his way to a meeting at a funding agency in Washington, D.C., part of his plan for keeping the whole enterprise afloat.

All over the country museums were exerting their influence on Capitol Hill. They were aided in their efforts by the first chair of the National Endowment for the Arts. Nancy Hanks (1927-83) had no museum experience to speak of, other than her participation in *The Belmont Report*. But she turned out to possess a remarkable "museum sense" and the impeccable political credentials needed to advocate in the corridors of power. Hanks was from a conservative Southern family, a distant relation of Abraham Lincoln and once was a close confidante of Nelson Rockefeller, then governor of New York. She was, by all accounts, charismatic, gracious and a workaholic, making her a perfect candidate to get things done in Washington.

Funds from the National Endowment for the Arts allowed the Grand Rapids Art Museum to commission an outdoor sculpture for its plaza—LA GRANDE VITESSE, 1969, a stabile by Alexander Calder. Courtesy of Grand Rapids Art Museum.

One of her first actions was to allocate NEA money in equal amounts to state arts councils (regardless of the state's population) to encourage the spread of arts and culture across the nation; that won her almost 100 friends in the Senate. Hanks then appointed as her deputy Michael Whitney Straight, a collector with family ties to the Whitney Museum of Art. That won her friends among the East Coast cognoscenti. (In an intriguing historical footnote, Straight later would admit that he was a former Communist spy who had passed classified materials to the Soviets.)

Hanks ensured that arts and humanities experts—rather than bureaucrats or politicians—reviewed funding requests from artists and cultural organizations. That befriended her to the arts community. She also supported the idea that every federal dollar needed to be matched from another funding source, which encouraged corporations and foundations to donate more money to the arts. With Nancy Hanks at the helm, the great era of cultural democracy had begun.

The funding edifice in the nation's capital grew vigorously. In 1971, with a budget of just under $1 million. NEA distributed its first round of museum grants—103 in all, averaging about $3,000 each—to organizations ranging from the tiny Pacific Grove Natural History Museum in California to the huge Cleveland Museum of Art. That same year Rep. John Brademas of Indiana introduced the Museum Services Act, a bill to establish a separate federal agency devoted to shoring up museums' internal operations. By 1972 NEA's budget for museum projects had swelled from $927,000 to $4.4 million and allowed museum workers to create a vast array of new educational programs not only for their institutions but for hospitals, prisons, rural elementary schools and senior centers. Likewise, the National Endowment for the Humanities (NEH) began to fund art and history museum exhibitions, community education and training of museum personnel.

The funds each museum received may have been small but the hopes the money engendered were large: programs for children, senior citizens, low-income citizens and minorities. But directors still faced severe staffing shortages, astronomical insurance premiums and the rising costs of day-to-day operations.

In 1973 Congress held a series of special hearings about the financial stresses museums were facing. In testimony that transcribed into almost 800 single-spaced pages, director upon director informed Congress of their continued woes. "It was as if a great release valve had opened," noted one observer.

Congress responded with a new program to reduce the costs of insuring international exhibitions. As the Nixon administration brokered diplomatic relations with the People's Republic of China, the government underwrote insurance for a traveling exhibition of ancient Chinese jade, porcelain and statuary, meant to create good will between the two nations. It was so successful that in 1974 NEA inaugurated its Arts and Artifacts Indemnity Program, which reduced museums' insurance costs (some say by as much as $400,000 per show) for many of the international blockbusters of the 1970s, including "Treasures of Tutankhamun," "The Splendors of Dresden" and "Dead Sea Scrolls." Blockbuster shows also benefited from an emerging and promising method of funding called "corporate sponsorship."

A native of Grand Rapids, Mich., Nixon's successor Gerald Ford had warm memories of courting his wife Betty on dates at the Public Museum. His vice president was Nelson Rockefeller, son of the founders of Colonial Williamsburg and the Museum of Modern Art. Under Presidents Nixon and Ford federal budgets for arts and culture soared, sometimes doubling in one year, sometimes "only" increasing by 25 percent, but always growing. As Jimmy Carter entered office in 1977, Nancy Hanks ended her dynamic tenure at the NEA. Under her watch the number of applications for funding increased by a factor of nine and the agency's total budget grew at an even faster rate, from an initial $2 million to $115 million.

Exploratorium founder Frank Oppenheimer— pictured here with a young museum visitor in 1982—helped persuade Congress that science centers could inspire children to become scientists. Photo by Nancy Rogers. © Exploratorium, www. exploratorium.org.

During the Carter administration support for museums continued to flourish. Joan Mondale, wife of Carter's Vice President Walter Mondale, became a leading spokesperson for all things cultural and artistic, earning the nickname "Joan of Art." Before becoming a political spouse Mrs. Mondale had worked at Boston's Museum of Fine Arts and the Minnesota Institute of the Arts. In 1977 she helped launch the Institute of Museum Services—whose legislation had been signed by Ford—at the Brooklyn Children's Museum. For the first time in history museums had an agency devoted solely to them, run by a vivacious Washington socialite, Lee Kimche McGrath (1934-2002).

An engineer by training, President Carter was committed to developing a more competitive workforce in the science professions and increased funding for the National Science Foundation (NSF). Science-center leaders like Frank Oppenheimer of the Exploratorium and Joel Bloom of the Franklin Institute traveled to Washington, D.C., to make the case that hands-on science centers could inspire young people to become scientists. By 1978 NSF money was supporting interactive exhibitions and curriculum development at science centers.

By the end of the decade museums of all disciplines and sizes had become part of a vast public process. Grants spilled forth from state and federal agencies. Still federal money represented only a small part of museums' overall budgets—an average of 3 percent— particularly when compared to the sums European governments devoted to their cultural institutions. At its peak in the late 1970s NEA spent about $1.10 per American, whereas Great Britain spent $4 and France $10 per citizen in their respective nations. But federal funds were an important catalyst for broad cultural development whose reverberations still are felt today. Museums now were able to fill "multiple responsibilities," said Nancy Hanks, "to the public, to their collections, to their staffs, to artists, scientists, and historians, and to the past, as well as the present and future."

Along with federal dollars came federal reporting requirements that forced museums to clean up their sloppy business practices. Administrators had to implement financial audits, pay attention to employment laws, keep accurate records and straighten out filing systems. The National Endowment for the Humanities required museums to consult with outside academic experts to enhance the content of their exhibitions. As relationships with universities increased, museum scholarship became more rigorous. Curators and educators were exposed to the postmodernism and social history that was sweeping college campuses and began to incorporate these perspectives in their exhibitions and programs.

Museum workers began to share ideas with each other more freely, forming or revamping specialized professional committees and organizations devoted to their specific job functions, disciplines and regions. These groups included the Association of Art Museum Directors, Association of Science and Technology Centers and Association of Children's Museums. Like the American Association of Museums, all of these organizations continue to thrive today, advocating for museums and helping their staff and trustees deliver programs for the public.

Current and future museum professionals benefited from a fledgling discipline called "museum studies" that focused on museum work as a career and not as an afterthought. People without specialized degrees benefited from workshops and books that explained the intricacies of collections care, legal issues and nonprofit administration.

Trained staff were joined by long-time volunteers and people who wandered into museums through the proverbial back door. They came from the worlds of theater, journalism and political activism, among other areas. Museums were becoming filled with bright, enthusiastic staff. In the 1890s George Brown Goode had called on workers to possess a "museum sense." By 1980 Milwaukee Public Museum Director Kenneth Starr

Stephen E. Weil taught, wrote and thought constantly and insightfully about museums, art and the law, noting in particular how the field had changed "from being about something to being for somebody." Courtesy of the Hirshhorn Museum and Sculpture Garden, Smithsonian Institution.

could report that workers had "'a sense of profession,' an ever heightening awareness of our common character and purposes, and an ever greater understanding of who we are and what we are about."

Growing professionalism led to a deeper concern about ethical issues. The code of ethics issued by the American Association of Museums in 1925 sat forgotten in many a file drawer. Yet museums were under scrutiny for all kinds of dubious activities—deaccessioning, acquiring looted objects, partaking in insider transactions, tampering with wills, violating copyright law—which sometimes landed them in court. "In my first years as a [museum] director," stated E. Leland Webber, former head of the Field Museum, "I consulted a lawyer only a few times a year; by 1981 it seemed daily." Understanding the letter of the law was becoming essential to leading a museum. Trials not only drained financial and staff resources, they threatened to erode public confidence at a time when museums were rising in popularity and visibility.

Two lawyers led the way for reform. In 1971 Marie Malaro became associate general counsel to the Smithsonian. She would go on to head the museum studies graduate program at George Washington University and write the standard legal primer for managing museum collections. In 1974 Stephen E. Weil (1928-2005) joined the Hirshhorn Museum and Sculpture Garden as deputy director. A prolific author on legal, ethical and philosophical challenges facing museums, Weil would serve as councilor-at-large, vice president and treasurer of the American Association of Museums as well as scholar emeritus at the Smithsonian Institution. Lawyers such as Weil and Malaro joined registrars, conservators and other museum leaders in instituting firmer ethical and legal guidelines for museums.

In 1978, after much haggling, the field finally agreed to a more substantial ethical code. The stakes were high. Even though "on matters of both substance and wording, [museums] were in total accord on few if any issues," the new code meant business. It called museum workers "professionals" and sought their loyalty not only to their place of work but to the larger goal of preserving humankind's culture and heritage. Adherence to ethical principles would help determine whether a museum could receive accreditation from the American Association of Museums, i.e., assurance that the institution was meeting the highest standards of public service. Loyalty to the museum's mission was now more important than loyalty to a donor, a trustee or even one's boss.

In less than two years the new code of ethics was put to the test. In the mid-1960s Jack Morris had been hired to direct the Greenville County Museum of Art in South Carolina, then a sleepy organization located in an old house on the edge of town. By all accounts Morris was adept at charming donors, collectors and art dealers. By 1979 the Greenville museum was scarcely recognizable. Under Morris's leadership it had moved into a state-of-the-art building. Its display of Andrew Wyeth paintings drew crowds. It had professional staff and proudly displayed the coveted AAM accreditation decal.

But it turned out that Morris had pocketed kickbacks from dealers—$200,000, in fact—in return for helping the museum's leading patrons purchase the Wyeth works. In 1980 two employees questioned Morris's financial dealings, calling them a violation of the professional ethics that forbade museum employees from profiting on collections dealings. They further alleged that they had suffered harassment and reprisals for attempting to confront Morris directly. Distraught, they asked the museum's board to intervene and also turned to AAM for help. Under the field's new ethical guidelines all museums were responsible for ensuring that their peer institutions operated solely to benefit the public trust.

Testifying in South Carolina before an investigative panel organized by the museum's board was H. J. Swinney, director of Rochester's Strong Museum and a member of AAM's own board of directors. By accepting accreditation, Swinney said, the Greenville board was "obligated to resolve the situation, to do something." Morris resigned, and the museum's board adopted a code of professional conduct. It was becoming increasingly hard to do business the old way, particularly after the code of ethics was tightened in 1991 and again in 1994.

Questions also were raised about a growing trend in museums: the increased presence of corporate logos and names in exhibition galleries. With museum visitorship growing, corporations saw the benefits of associating their products with museums. They hired public relations firms to create exhibitions that then were packaged and offered to museums. From 1971 to 1977, for example, the Campbell Soup Company arranged a touring exhibition of antique soup tureens and other soup-related paraphernalia, picking up all expenses for any museum that agreed to host the show. Around the same time cigarette manufacturer Philip Morris circulated a show called "Two Hundred Years of American Indian Art," tying the topic to its core product, tobacco. "At Philip Morris," noted the exhibition catalogue, "we have a great debt to repay to the North American Indians . . . who first cultivated tobacco and helped to found the oldest industry in the West."

Some curators questioned the ethics of these arrangements. They worried that museums were giving up too much control, that corporate managers were more concerned with product placement than scholarship and artistic integrity. To make matters more complicated, industries with tarnished images—tobacco, chemical and oil—and even some corporations doing business with South Africa during apartheid began to sponsor exhibitions, to the tune of millions of dollars. An example is the Metropolitan Museum of Art's "Gold Show," sponsored by South African mining company Engelhard Minerals & Chemicals in 1973.

Artists continued to hammer museums for their growing willingness to "sell out." In the mid-1970s Hans Haacke created a series of political artworks about corporate funding that had titles like *The Road to Profits is Paved with Culture* (1976). One thing was clear: museums no longer sat on the sidelines of American society. As more and more groups of people worked to establish their role in the nation's story, museums found themselves at the heart of the debate over cultural politics. This public role would only grow in the decades to come.

■ ■ ■ ■ ■

The country's priorities changed in the 1980s as the public pulled away from the seemingly freewheeling years of the previous decade and started to worry about gas shortages, high inflation and government integrity, thanks to the Watergate scandal. Promising to restore America's traditional values and make the country strong and prosperous again, Ronald Reagan was elected president in 1980. Intent on streamlining the government and cutting most non-military federal spending, the former actor saw federal support of the arts as unnecessary and even harmful. "The arts should do what they do best," Reagan said, "and leave the politics to the government."

Reagan set about dismantling government programs and appointed a Taskforce on Arts and Humanities to recommend ways the private sector could make up for his proposed cuts. In 1981 the president announced 50-percent cutbacks to the National Endowments for the Arts and Humanities, with the goal of phasing out both agencies. Citing an earlier controversy over the theory of evolution, Reagan eliminated the science education division of the National Science Foundation.

Within a year more than half of the museums in the country were reporting cuts in personnel and programs. As the age of entrepreneurship and "enlightened self interest" dawned, museums sought ways to stay afloat. Many began to charge admissions fees and market themselves through paid advertising for the first time. In 1979 no U.S. museum had allocated a budget for advertising. By the mid-1980s more than half of the nation's museums were purchasing ads.

Politicians began to battle over the fate of the federal cultural agencies. To run the Institute for Museum Services (IMS), which provided valuable financial support for museum operations, Reagan appointed Lilla Tower, an attorney and wife of a Texas senator. Tower got to work immediately, spending the next three years trying to shut the agency down. But museums were protected by Rep. Sidney Yates of Illinois, who repeatedly took their side.

Performing "minor miracles of political maneuvering," Yates saved the agency.

To head the National Endowment for the Humanities, Reagan chose William Bennett, director of the North Carolina Humanities Council. In 1986 when Bennett was promoted to secretary of education, Lynne Cheney, wife of the future vice president, took the helm at NEH. As articulate, well-educated neoconservatives, Bennett and Cheney believed that museums' newfound interest in multiculturalism and social history diluted the intellectual and aesthetic standards of Western history. Both later testified in favor of eliminating the NEH.

A young visitor learns how to make candles at Old Sturbridge Village. Courtesy of Old Sturbridge Village Visual Resource Library.

Appointed as director of the National Endowment for the Arts was Frank Hodsoll, a career foreign service officer. Although he professed to know nothing about the arts, Hodsoll proved to be a skillful negotiator who withstood attempts to cut the agency's budget. During his eight years as NEA chief he funded studies that showed how much museums contributed—in dollars and jobs—to their local regions and finessed new programs focused on conservation, outreach and job training for minorities. He also approved a grant for an exhibition that would later launch a thousand hate letters and several lawsuits: a show that included sexually explicit photographs taken by Robert Mapplethorpe.

Science and children's museums fared better than their counterparts in art, culture and history largely due to an alarm sounded by the National Science Board about the quality of science education. Research showed that schools in the United States were failing to motivate students to pursue careers in science. Faced with a shortage of trained scientists and engineers, 1980s America was losing its competitive edge to Japan.

In response Congress not only reinstated the science education funds to the National Science Foundation but quadrupled them, from about $50 million in 1984 to $200 million in 1989. Many of the funds went to science centers and children's museums, whose leaders made a convincing case that their hands-on exhibits and teaching techniques inspired large audiences.

Residents of small communities now could visit their local science centers and view exhibits created from easy-to-assemble traveling kits from major institutions like the Boston Children's Museum and Exploratorium. High school students' understanding of science was enhanced through programs like the one at the Center of Science and Industry (COSI) in Columbus, Ohio, which trained youths to explain scientific principles to the public. Public school science teachers attended summer teaching institutes at places like the Pacific Science Center in Seattle and used the hands-on curriculum written by staff at the Lawrence Hall of Science in Berkeley. The additional NSF funds made all of these activities, and more, possible.

Carefully navigating the political waters, science centers justified their funds with attendance figures and evaluation reports. As former NSF division head George Tressel explains, "You can have the best exhibit or educational program in the world, but if there's no audience for it, as far as NSF was concerned, we hadn't bought anything." The practice of measuring a program's success with its audience dovetailed with museums' shift toward customer service.

Corporations stepped up to help art and culture museums. "With the government giving less for art and education, somebody's got to give," explained an advertisement for Chase Manhattan Bank. "And that somebody is America's corporations." Throughout the 1980s the art of corporate sponsorship matured. When David Rockefeller founded Business Committee for the Arts in 1967, private companies were donating about $22 million to the arts annually. By the mid-1980s that number had climbed to $700 million. Museum exhibitions were the top beneficiaries on the list. Businesses made it clear, however, that they wanted their names prominently displayed on credit panels and in advertising campaigns—sometimes as large or even larger than the institution they were supporting. "There's not much P.R. potential in funding a shelter for abused women," admitted one executive, "You get the best visibility from art [exhibitions]."

Some exhibitions directly supported a company's advertising campaign. The 1985 traveling exhibition "India!" was linked to products at Bloomingdale's; a series of 1988 shows of gems, silver and jewelry was tied to Tiffany & Company's 150th anniversary. Within a decade museum walls were adorned permanently with corporate names, such as the Omaha Steaks Room at the Joslyn Art Museum, the Altoids Curiously Strong collection at the New Museum of Contemporary Art in New York, the Coca-Cola Café at the Atlanta History Center and the Taco Bell Discovery Science Center in Santa Ana, Calif.

Consumers could participate in a new advertising technique called "cause-related

"Tiffany: 150 Years of Gems and Jewelry" helped mark the company's 150th anniversary in 1987. The show was on view at the American Museum of Natural History, Metropolitan Museum of Art, Museum of Fine Arts, Boston and the Field Museum, pictured here. GN85037c. © The Field Museum.

marketing." Each time they purchased a certain product or used a designated credit card, the company made a donation to a museum. Other schemes seemed over the top; one example—placing a new car in a museum lobby in exchange for a donation from an auto manufacturer. Soon museum professionals and the press began to question the fine line between corporate sponsorships and blatant advertising. Shouldn't museums be respites from corporate logos and advertising messages? "He who would ride the tiger may end up inside," warned J. Carter Brown (1934-2002), director of the National Gallery of Art.

Meanwhile, art and history museums found themselves battling a fiercer tiger. Conservative politicians and citizen's groups once again began to question the museum's role in American society. Who determined whether an artist's creation was art, blasphemy or pornography? How should museums present American history? The central issue at stake was the appropriate use of federal funds. Elected officials argued that federally funded exhibitions and artworks should reflect traditional values, including those of rising conservative watchdog groups like the Moral Majority and the American Family Association (AFA), a membership organization whose mission is to "motivate and equip citizens to change the culture to reflect Biblical Truth." Cultural historians and artists, on the other hand, believed that museums had an obligation to all Americans and operated in a gray area where objects have multiple and complex meanings. In the late 1980s two defining episodes placed museums squarely on the front lines of these culture wars.

The first episode nearly destroyed the National Endowment for the Arts and almost landed a museum director in prison. In 1987, the Southeastern Center for Contemporary Art in Winston Salem, N.C., received a $15,000 NEA grant for a traveling exhibition that included a work called *Piss Christ* by photographer Andres Serrano. *Piss Christ* was an image of a plastic crucifix submerged in urine, symbolizing the artist's ambivalence toward religion. It traveled with the show to various sites with little notice, until it reached the Virginia Museum of Fine Arts in 1989. There, a visitor outraged by the photograph wrote a letter to the local paper, attracting the attention of Rev. Donald Wildmon, head of the AFA.

Declaring that "the bias and bigotry against Christians which has dominated television and the movies has now moved over to art museums," Wildmon launched a mail campaign to stop federal support of "anti-Christian" art. He soon gained the support of an influential senator. Jesse Helms of North Carolina, who had long opposed the NEA, spoke out against Serrano on the Senate floor. Within days, 107 congressmen and 39 senators had signed a letter protesting the exhibit.

Around the same time another NEA grantee, the University of Pennsylvania's Institute of Contemporary Arts, was organizing "The Perfect Moment," a retrospective of 175 photographs by Robert Mapplethorpe. The show featured formal compositions of flowers, portraits of children and adults, and what the photographer dubbed his "sex photos," which included graphic images of sadomasochism. Like the Serrano photo, the Mapplethorpe works were displayed without incident in their first venues.

That is, until another AFA mass mailing dubbed the show "child pornography" and Robert Dornan, a California congressman, denounced the show on the floor of the House. Wary of the political fallout, the show's next venue, the Corcoran Gallery of Art in Washington, D.C., cancelled it. Artists and gay rights activists protested, attracting national attention to Mapplethorpe (who died from AIDS in 1989 at the age of 43), museums and the NEA. The night before the show was to have opened at the Corcoran, protesters held a vigil outside and projected several Mapplethorpe photos, including one of a threadbare American flag, onto the building's façade. "The projection indicted the Corcoran's cancellation of 'The Perfect Moment,'" says art historian Richard Meyer, "by ironically simulating the museum's official function—the public display of art." The protest made national headlines. The Corcoran's director and other staff members resigned and the museum's membership plummeted.

Under congressional pressure NEA withdrew two new grants from the Institute of Contemporary Art, the museum that organized "The Perfect Moment." During the 1990 Senate appropriation hearings Helms introduced an amendment to withhold federal funds from "obscene or indecent materials . . . including but not limited to depictions of sadomasochism, homoeroticism, the exploitation of children, or individuals engaged in sex acts." After much debate the amendment passed; all organizations receiving NEA grants would have to comply. President George H. W. Bush supported the actions and, in deference to proponents of "family values," fired the NEA's chief, John Frohnmayer.

One museum director refused to comply. The Mapplethorpe show was scheduled to open in April 1990 at the Contemporary Arts Center (CAC) in Cincinnati, a city that had banned adult bookstores, X-rated theatres and nude dancing parlors. A group called Citizens for Community Values demanded its cancellation, calling it "the kind of thing you expect to find in a porno shop in somebody else's town." CAC's director Dennis Barrie decided that the show must go on, a position that subjected his family to death threats and his museum to economic blackmail. Even before the show arrived "the groups began a campaign of economic intimidation against our board," Barrie recalled. "The chairman eventually resigned from the board because the bank of which he was an officer was under tremendous pressure. . . ." On opening day, police evacuated the museum, shut it down and led Barrie away in handcuffs as several hundred of his supporters chanted "Gestapo go home." He was indicted on charges of pandering obscenity and child pornography, the first museum director prosecuted because of an exhibition's content.

The controversy revealed, however, that the American public was not ready to censor museums or artists in this way. As Barrie's colleagues spoke out on his behalf, public sentiment came out on the side of the museum. CAC's membership nearly doubled, Mapplethorpe's estate tripled

Emanuel Gottlieb Leutze (1816-68), **WESTWARD THE COURSE OF EMPIRE TAKES ITS WAY** *(mural study, U.S. Capitol), 1861— one of the paintings featured in the Smithsonian's controversial "The West as America." Smithsonian American Art Museum, Washington, D.C./Art Resource, New York.*

in value and a jury acquitted Barrie, who went on to direct the Rock and Roll Hall of Fame in Cleveland and the International Spy Museum in Washington, D.C.

Still, despite the legal victory in Cincinnati, Helms's obscenity clause went into effect and most organizations receiving NEA funds complied. Fifteen grantees refused to sign the oath; of these, only two were museums—the Lehman College Art Gallery at the City University of New York and the Newport Harbor Art Museum (now Orange County Museum of Art) in southern California, which took the strongest action of all. Located in the district of Robert Dornan, the congressman who had railed against Mapplethorpe, the museum sued the NEA for violating the First and Fifth Amendments. The judge ruled in the museum's favor, citing the obscenity clause's vagueness as well as its "chilling effect" on artistic expression.

The culture wars raged on. Museums remained front and center in the larger national debate about the interpretation of history that was taking place across the country—on college campuses, among veterans' groups, in churches and in the media. In 1991 Native American activists made headlines with a 16-day, 24-hour encampment at the Florida Museum of Natural History in Gainesville. They were protesting the absence of Native American perspectives in an exhibition designed to celebrate the quincentennial of Christopher Columbus's voyage and funded by the National Endowment for the

Humanities. When "First Encounters: Spanish Exploration in the Caribbean and U.S.: 1492-1570" traveled to the Science Museum of Minnesota, protesters threw a vial of blood on it to symbolize the legacy of Columbus's conquest. The museum responded by augmenting the exhibition with labels, a video and a separate show about Native American resistance to colonial rule. Reacting to such controversies, former NEH chair Lynne Cheney would go on to accuse museums of being "in the business of debunking greatness, Western society and even history itself" and advancing politically correct "anti-culture" values.

That same year senators and former Librarian of Congress Daniel Boorstein challenged "The West As America: Reinterpreting Images of the Frontier, 1820-1920," an exhibition of paintings at the Smithsonian's National Museum of American Art in Washington, D.C. Curators were accused of using Marxist terminology, popular in art-historical discourse at the time, in the wall text. Writing in the show's comment book, Boorstein called the labels "perverse, historically inaccurate, destructive." Reacting to these remarks, Alaska Sen. Ted Stevens vowed to battle the museum's funding.

Veterans groups also took issue with museum displays. In 1992 at Anchorage Alaska's Visual Arts Center, they complained to city officials about an installation by artist Dread Scott. The veterans said that "What Is the Proper Way to Display a U.S. Flag?' was unpatriotic because it featured an American flag spread out on the floor. An even larger group of veterans, the 180,000-member Air Force Association, went head-to-head with the Smithsonian Institution over the display of one of the most profound military icons of the 20th century—the *Enola Gay*, the B-29 aircraft that dropped the world's first atomic bomb over Hiroshima, Japan. The controversy that ensued marked the second defining episode of the culture wars.

WWII veterans had raised funds to restore the plane, which sat disassembled in a storage facility. Looking ahead to the 50th anniversary commemoration of the war's end, the vets envisioned a mint-condition aircraft proudly on display at the Smithsonian's National Air and Space Museum (NASM). But NASM Director Martin Harwit, a WWII veteran, and his curators saw a different

Above: *Constructing a balanced exhibition about the* **ENOLA GAY** *proved to be impossible during the culture wars of the 1990s. Photo by Eric Long/OIPP, National Air and Space Museum; image # SI2003-29268-5, © Smithsonian Institution.*

Left: *Dread Scott,* **WHAT IS THE PROPER WAY TO DISPLAY A U.S. FLAG**, *1992. Reproduced with permission of the artist.*

role for the exhibition, which was to be called "The Last Act: The Atomic Bomb and the End of World War II." "[We] worried that a massive, gleaming *Enola Gay* would give the impression that the museum was celebrating raw power," Harwit recalled. "To avoid this perception we needed to show that the bomb had caused unimaginable damage and suffering."

For five years the exhibition's curators wrestled with the daunting task of constructing a balanced story about the *Enola Gay* that described the events of 1945 but also questioned the decision to drop the bomb. The Air Force Association accused the Smithsonian of political-bias and political-correctness. *Air Force Magazine* declared the proposed exhibit "unpatriotic" and "designed for shock value" rather than objective education. Eight thousand veterans signed a petition denouncing the show.

Because at the time the Smithsonian received 70 percent of its budget from federal appropriations, the veterans took their concerns directly to Congress. Taking up their cause was Sen. Stevens, who was joined by 80 members of the House. When the veterans and the curators were unable to reach a compromise, the Smithsonian aborted the show and Harwit resigned. The fuselage of the *Enola Gay* went on exhibit, on a smaller scale than had been envisioned, remaining on view until 1998. In 2003 the Smithsonian moved the restored plane to NASM's Udvar-Hazy annex in Virginia in an exhibition that focused on the technology of the B-29.

Politicians and historians used the *Enola Gay* controversy to voice their own points of view. "You are seeing . . . a renewal of American civilization," said then Speaker of the House Newt Gingrich. "The *Enola Gay* was a fight, in effect, over the reassertion by most Americans that they're sick and tired of being told by some cultural elite that they ought to be ashamed of their country." Hiroshima's mayor, on the other hand, called the cancellation "extremely regrettable" and noted that the people of Hiroshima and Nagasaki "simply hoped to heighten public opinions toward the building of a world free of nuclear weapons." University of North Carolina historian Richard Kohn said the Smithsonian's decision was "the worst tragedy to befall the public presentation of history in the United States in this generation. In displaying the *Enola Gay* without analysis of the event that gave the airplane its significance, the Smithsonian Institution forfeited . . . an opportunity to educate a worldwide audience in the millions about one of this century's defining experiences." Newspapers around the country ran political cartoons and editorials that reflected all three perspectives.

Although the public was visiting museums in higher numbers than ever, the *Enola Gay* and "Perfect Moment" controversies hurt the field's ability to garner outside support for educational programs. Politicians were questioning museum professional standards and, in some cases, threatening jobs and institutional budgets. Funding agencies survived, but in a weakened state.

When President Bill Clinton took office in 1992, his administration focused on reducing the federal deficit and balancing the budget rather than on restoring cultural funding. In 1997 the administration merged Institute of Museum Services with the Institute of Library Services, to become "one efficient, centrally managed" agency: the Institute of Museum and Library Services (IMLS). During the 1990s IMLS slowly rebuilt itself, distributing over 40,000 grants for museum operations and collections conservation, conducting two nationwide surveys of museums' work with schools and jumpstarting several digitization projects that helped make collection objects accessible online. Likewise, the National Endowments for the Arts and Humanities reshuffled their priorities. NEH funded exhibitions on "safe" topics like German Expressionist Art and Japanese teenage life, two exhibitions that would have been controversial during the World War II years. NEA concentrated on multicultural projects; during the late 1990s over three-quarters of its grants went to exhibitions or conservation projects involving Asian, African-American, Native American, Latino or female artists. In 2003 the agency gave $3.6 million—equivalent to the annual operating budget of a medium-sized museum—to 91 museum projects. Its 2005 priority, under the administration of President George W. Bush, was "American Masterpieces: Three Centuries of Genius."

Opponents of federal funding for arts and culture won a key battle of the culture wars: lower budget appropriations. Yet in a larger sense, they lost the war. The troubles in Cincinnati became a lightning rod for activism over the next decade, especially gay rights, civil liberties and freedom of expression. Museum professionals resolved to present multiple viewpoints in exhibitions and tell fuller stories of the human condition. They developed new exhibition presentation methods that incorporated community perspectives through advisory boards and focus groups, and enlisted the help of public relations experts to anticipate and diffuse controversy.

■ ■ ■ ■ ■

Even before the culture wars, museums saw that the safety net of old money donors and generous federal grants was dissolving. Only 25 percent of museums, mostly art institutions, had an endowment. Most existed year to year, with the ever-present possibility that one natural disaster could put them out of business. Money, always an issue, became a top concern. Once again, the professional literature shifted its tone. Articles in *Museum News* offered strategies for fund raising, often in a business-like jargon, previously unseen on the magazine's pages.

An obvious solution was to spend less and earn more. To cut costs some institutions banded together, forming consortia. National organizations like the Science Museum Exhibition Collaborative (1988) and the Youth Museum Exhibition Consortium (1991) allowed organizations to divide the costs of creating high-quality shows, such as a traveling

A mother and daughter examine ceramics from ancient South America at the Art Institute of Chicago, one of the
11 institutions that participated in the Pew Charitable Trusts' "Art Museums and Communities" initiative. © The
Art Institute of Chicago.

exhibition about AIDS prevention that went to many science museums and the popular
Magic School Bus exhibitions that toured children's museums.

As in the rest of the nonprofit world, the marketing and development departments in
museums grew in size and sophistication, hiring more staff with business and fund-
raising skills. Donors also became more sophisticated and generous, making gifts that were
more targeted to specific programs. Computer technologies opened up the world of mass
mailings, databases and other techniques that turned fund raising from a social art into
a social science. Membership—a money-losing service that museums had offered since
the late 19th century—now was viewed as a way to "capture" names and build a base of
"supporters" who could be "cultivated" to give larger donations in the future. Museum
members found themselves the targets of increasingly clever fund-raising drives; their
support was rewarded with perks like special events and hours, gift-shop savings and
preference on tickets for blockbusters.

Like the rest of Reagan-era America, museums embraced the spirit of entrepreneurship.
Directors increasingly used words like "product development" and "leveraged assets"
instead of "masterpiece" and "NEA grant." Museums used their largest physical asset, the
building, to generate revenue. There were new shopping and dining opportunities. Capital
campaigns were centered on bold iconic buildings that would attract attention, large
audiences and large donations. And as they functioned more and more like businesses,
museums leveraged their most intangible and valuable quality: their allure, their
trustworthiness, their reputation—the very word "museum."

Though museums seemed increasingly commercial, a far more profound revolution was simultaneously taking place. Professionals who had come of age during LBJ's Great Society were now in leadership positions. With a grander vision for museums than mere economic survival, these leaders called on museums to respond to societal change by opening their doors wider. Led by task forces of directors, curators and educators, the American Association of Museums published two seminal reports—*Museums for a New Century* (1984) and *Excellence and Equity: Education and the Public Dimension of Museums* (1992)—that reasserted the museum's public role. These publications, widely circulated within the profession, argued that museums should "help to create a sense of inclusive community that is often missing in our society [and] be a welcoming place for all people."

To find innovative ways to reach out to a changing population, museums turned to their long-time partners, philanthropic foundations, whose bank accounts were swelling due to the bullish stock market of the 1980s and '90s. As the president of the Wallace Foundation M. Christine DeVita put it, foundations could be "non-ideological 'honest brokers' of solutions" to the nation's problems. A host of multi-million dollar initiatives from foundations like W. K. Kellogg, Ford, Howard Hughes Medical Institute and the J. Paul Getty Trust underwrote new research, staff training, exhibitions and educational programs.

Through an initiative called "Art Museums and Communities," the Pew Charitable Trusts helped 11 art museums study their visitors' needs and develop programs that served ethnically diverse audiences. The DeWitt and Lila Wallace Reader's Digest Funds (now the Wallace Foundation) created the "Museum Collections Accessibility Initiative," donating nearly $330 million to 29 art museums to help them attract new audiences by creating clearer labels and more appealing arrangements of their permanent collections. Wallace also financed Youth Achievement through Learning, Involvement, Volunteering and Employment (Youth ALIVE!), which trained hundreds of young people, mostly from low-income families of color, to work in 52 science centers and children's museums around the country. Some participants advanced to full-time staff positions.

Many of the foundation-sponsored programs aimed not only to impart knowledge but also to break down racial stereotypes. In communities around the nation audiences and staff slowly began to reflect the growing diversity of the American population. Not everyone, however, looked kindly on this transformation. Conservatives accused foundation officers of "philanthropical correctness"—that is, having a "liberal and multiculturalist agenda." Inside museums, skeptics said that foundations had too much power and too little knowledge of how museums really worked. Moreover, most of the projects folded when funds ran dry, especially when foundation endowments shrank during the stock market tumble of the early 2000s. Still educators agreed that the foundation projects pointed their organizations toward a future of "truly collaborating with audiences, partner organizations, artists and colleagues alike."

Dancers entertain guests at "Our Fringe Swings," an evening event organized by the Walker Art Center in 2001.
Photo by Dan Dennehy, Walker Art Center, Minneapolis.

All the while museums were increasing their public visibility in ways that would have astonished their 19th-century founders. They courted cab drivers and hotel concierges, who could encourage cultural tourists and conventioneers to visit nearby museums. They placed promotional exhibitions in airport lobbies and restaurants. They hosted radio giveaways and purchased Internet pop-up ads. They advertised on supermarket bags, coffee cups, anywhere and everywhere.

To appeal to America's growing population of single, educated adults, art museums began to sponsor evening events such as the Asian Art Museum's 1999 "Sex, Sushi and Sake" and the Walker Art Center's "Mix, Mingle and Muse" the following year. By 2000, 80 percent of art museums were offering programming targeted to young single adults; about half were billed as "mixers," featuring after-hours cocktails and live music. Others, like the Dallas Museum of Art, appealed to the all-night crowd, sponsoring a 33-hour marathon exhibition party, with a midnight jazz concert, 2 a.m. tours for insomniacs and sunrise events for early risers. Historical house museums capitalized on the seasonal allure of ghost stories, the occult and 19th-century culture, sponsoring "haunted house" tours during Halloween season and "authentic" Victorian candlelight tours during the winter holidays.

Museums worked especially hard to appeal to inveterate shoppers, hiring buyers and retailing experts to develop specially targeted merchandise. Art museums sold trendy accessories, refashioning bits of old exhibition banners into fashionable purses and producing lines of artful jewelry. Botanical gardens sold unusual and hard-to-find plants. Children's museums repackaged discarded industrial materials as recycled supplies for art and science projects. Planetaria did a hot business in space food sticks and astronaut ice cream, science museums in polished rocks and beanie babies. Even elephants generously contributed to the zoo's bottom line: their dung was repackaged and sold as garden fertilizer.

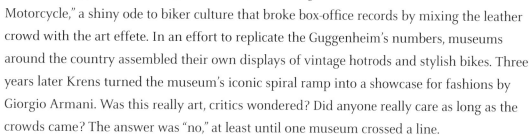

By the late 1990s the museum had become a diversified economy with a formula for success: "great collections, great architecture, a great special exhibition, a great second exhibition, two shopping opportunities, two eating opportunities, a high-tech interface via the Internet, and economies of scale via a global network." So stated the Solomon R. Guggenheim Museum's Thomas Krens, poster child for the new entrepreneurial director. In 1998, with funding from BMW, Krens staged "The Art of the Motorcycle," a shiny ode to biker culture that broke box-office records by mixing the leather crowd with the art effete. In an effort to replicate the Guggenheim's numbers, museums around the country assembled their own displays of vintage hotrods and stylish bikes. Three years later Krens turned the museum's iconic spiral ramp into a showcase for fashions by Giorgio Armani. Was this really art, critics wondered? Did anyone really care as long as the crowds came? The answer was "no," at least until one museum crossed a line.

In 1999 the decades-old ethical debates about insider dealing, censorship and blasphemy resurfaced at the Brooklyn Museum of Art, where entrepreneurial director Arnold Lehman presented an exhibition called "Sensation: Young British Artists from the Saatchi Collection." Some critics accused Charles Saatchi, a private dealer who helped finance the show, of having an implicit goal: to associate his collection with prestigious museums and increase the market value of the artworks he owned. But "Sensation" garnered more attention than the Brooklyn Museum had bargained for due to a painting on display: Chris Ofili's *The Holy Virgin Mary* (1996), which was embellished with elephant dung. Many Roman Catholics were offended by the

100 YEARS OF MUSEUMS IN AMERICA

work, including then Mayor Rudolph Giuliani who threatened to cut $7.2 million from the museum's budget and evict it from its city-leased space. In the end, the museum stayed, attendance boomed and the art increased in value. It was a stunning example of how museums now occupied a high-profile position in American society. They were, more than ever before, both destinations and targets for criticism.

Museums now needed leaders who were not only scholars and educators but could deftly navigate financial and political waters. Universities introduced new training programs in arts administration and museum studies, but the gap was almost too large to fill. Newspaper headlines about blowups between directors and boards replaced stories about controversial buildings and exhibitions; dismissals of directors became commonplace. Like museums, directors had to be all things to all people: scholars, educators, fund raisers, pillars of the community, social butterflies, political animals. With such an impossible set of demands, they were burning out. Once a museum directorship had been seen as a lifelong post; now the average tenure shrank to four years. Many directors were so frustrated that they gave only two weeks notice; half said they never wanted the job again. But when some museums sought out directors from the corporate world, that fueled even more discontent. It seemed that boards were abandoning decades of hard-fought gains in professional practice.

The post-Sept. 11 economy brought additional worries. Like everything else in the country, museums struggled to recover from the disaster. Attendance dropped when tourism plummeted. Foundation grants dropped due to plummeting stock portfolios. Corporate grants dropped due to mergers and weakening profits. State funding for the arts dropped by more than 10 percent, city funding by even more. Layoffs were rampant, even at Krens's flashy Guggenheim. In 2004 a Johns Hopkins University study found that 91 percent of the museums surveyed were in fiscal trouble, with over one-quarter describing their situation as very severe.

Still, the public sought solace in museums, and the field reacted with its characteristic generosity and humanity. Within minutes of the crashes on Sept. 11, 2001, staff at the New York City Fire Museum, located only one mile north of the World Trade Center, rushed to help in the rescue effort. Within hours, staff at other nearby museums were providing water and shelter. Within days, museums around the country were opening their doors free of charge to grief-stricken citizens seeking a respite in their own community. "As we gaze on the symbols of our shattered world we seek assurance in those things and values that bond us as members of the human family," Robert R. Macdonald, then director of the Museum of the City of New York, wrote only a few days after the tragedy. "Museums have provided this confirmation throughout their history."

Indeed it was confirmed almost four years later to the day, in September 2005, as Louisiana and Mississippi experienced the worst days of Hurricane Katrina. In New Orleans, staff at the Museum of Art and other museums remained on duty, heroically protecting the city's beloved collections from the ravaging floods. Within days of the natural disaster, museum workers nationwide were organizing fund-raising drives and expert assistance so that institutions in the devastated areas could reopen their doors as quickly as possible.

As the 21st century unfolds it is clear that museums in the United States have undergone enormous change in the past century. It is a transformation as profound and far reaching as the one experienced by American society in the same period. And how could it be otherwise? Museums at their best have come to reflect society, not stand above it or aloof from it. In the words of the museum scholar Stephen E. Weil, the successful museum has gone from being about something to being for someone, a human place filled not primarily with things but more importantly with our memories, our stories and our emotions. The American public has at last developed a profound "museum sense" that goes well beyond the riches, rivals and radicals that shaped museums in the previous century. We demand more of our museums. We treasure them as public forums that allow us to acknowledge our differences, feed our curiosity and nourish our souls. We aspire for museums to be trusted, transparent and flexible institutions that reflect a nation, and indeed a world, that transforms itself constantly, often taking us by surprise.

A sign of hope and optimism about the future outside what remained of Beauvoir after Hurricane Katrina. The Biloxi, Miss., estate was once the home of Confederate President Jefferson Davis. Courtesy of the Beauvoir staff.

NOTES

INTRODUCTION

Notes to pages 1–28

1 Henry James, *The Golden Bowl*, 1909 edition, 146.

3 Other examples of public service during the First World War gleaned from early issues of *Museum News* include: sending museum newsletters for the reading pleasure of soldiers stationed in Europe; plans to establish a museum in Norfolk, Va., for the use of sailors and marines; and recommendations that historical museums display Red Cross posters and war maps on bulletin boards.

6 In 1928 the American Association of Museums (AAM) reported that 32 million people attended museums. The U.S. population was 123,203,000. In 1997 AAM estimated that the number of museum visits was 865 million. The U.S. population was 272,912,000.

9 Neil Harris, "A Historical Perspective on Museum Advocacy," *Museum News*, Nove mber/December 1980, 75.

The founding of the Brooklyn Children's Museum is described in *The Twelfth Year Book of the Brooklyn Institute of Arts and Sciences* (Brooklyn: Brooklyn Institute of Arts and Sciences, 1900), 417-418. Cited in Vanessa Van Orden, Blazing New Trails: Community, Cultural, and Age Issues in Children's Museums, unpublished honors thesis, Wellesley College, 2000.

John Dewey, *Experience and Education: The Sixtieth Anniversary Edition* (West Lafayette, Ind.: Kappa Delta Pi, 1998), and George E. Hein, "John Dewey and Museum Education," *Curator* 47, no. 4 (October 2004), 413-427.

10 Henry James, "The Sense of Glory: A Memory of Paris in Youth: The Louvre and the Galerie D'Apollon" in *The Portable Henry James*, Morton Dauwen Zabel, ed. (New York: Viking Press, 1960), 561.

Charles Eliot Norton, quoted in Steve Conn, *Museums and American Intellectual Life, 1876-1926* (Chicago: University of Chicago Press, 1998), 43.

Initially, Sunday openings were controversial. Museums did not seem too concerned that they were infringing on church-going. Rather, they feared an influx of "the laboring classes" and immigrants. In 1891 a group called the "Working People's Petition Committee" presented 80,000 signatures to the Metropolitan Museum of Art, requesting Sunday hours. Although the experiment worked, the Sunday opening "offended some the Museum's best friends and supporters" and resulted in the loss of a $50,000 bequest. See Lillian D. Wald, *The House on Henry Street* (1915, reprint, New York: Dover Publications, 1971), 79-81.

11 Carol Duncan analyzes the ritual of the museum visit in *Civilizing Rituals: Inside Public Art Museums* (New York: Routledge, 1995).

Calvin Tompkins, *Merchants and Masterpieces: The Story of the Metropolitan Museum of Art* (New York: E. P. Dutton & Co., Inc., 1970), 85.

Examples of museums that worked with boards of education to lend specimens include the Educational Museum of St. Louis, the American Museum of Natural History, and the Detroit Children's Museum.

12 Geraldine Santoro, "'To Stamp Out the Plague Consumption': 1908-1909," *Curator* 36, no. 1 (1993), 13-28.

13 Benjamin Ives Gilman, *Museum Ideals* (Cambridge, Mass.: Harvard University Press, 1923), 51.

Gilman quoted in *From Knowledge to Narrative: Educators and the Changing Museum* by Lisa Roberts (Washington, D.C.: Smithsonian Institution Press, 1997), 22.

"School Classes Help the Museum," *Newark Museum Association Monthly Journal*, January 1927, 124.

14 "New museums also were founded. . . ." See Laurence Vail Coleman, *Handbook of American Museums* (Washington, D.C.: American Association of Museums, 1932), and Ellen C. Hicks, "AAM after 72 Years," *Museum News*, May/June 1978, 47.

Arthur C. Parker, quoted in "Arthur C. Parker: A Pioneer in American Museums" by Terry Zeller, *Curator* 30, no. 1 (1987), 46.

"During the 1920s. . . ." *A Statistical Survey of Museums in the United States and Canada* (Washington, D.C.: American Association of Museums, 1965), 15.

"Today a museum is found in every city. . . ." Paul J. DiMaggio, "Constructing an Organizational Field," in *The New Institutionalism in Organizational Analysis*, Paul J. DiMaggio and Walter W. Powell, eds. (University of Chicago Press, 1991), 272.

Philip Youtz, quoted in DiMaggio, 285.

Franklin D. Roosevelt at the 1932 inauguration of the Museum of Modern Art's new building, quoted in *Art in Our Time: A Chronicle of the Museum of Modern Art*, Harriet S. Bee and Michele Eliot, eds. (New York: Museum of Modern Art, 2004).

15   John Franklin White, ed., *Art in Action: American Art Centers and the New Deal* (Metuchen N.J.: The Scarecrow Press, Inc, 1987).

"Eastern Museums Circuit Saint Paul National Security Exhibit," *The Museum News*, Dec. 1 1941, 1.

"Art Museum Directors Hold New York Meeting on War Emergency," *The Museum News*, Jan. 1, 1942.

16   "Museums of Honolulu Go Through Japanese Air Raids Unharmed," *The Museum News*, Jan. 15 1942., 1.

"Wartime Activities in Two NYC Museums," *Museum News*, March 1, 1944, 1.

Details on "Road to Victory" from Mary Anne Staniszewski, *The Power of Display: A History of Exhibition Installations at the Museum of Modern Art*, (Cambridge, Mass.: MIT Press, 1998), 212-221.

Attendance in 1952 was 83 million; attendance in 1962 was 200 million. *A Statistical Survey of Museums*, 16.

18   "Schools now widely discredited John Dewey. . . ." Myra Pollack Sadker and David Miller Sadker, "The History of American Education," in *Teachers, Schools and Society* (New York: McGraw-Hill, Inc, 1991), 291.

Working with Dewey in the 1920s, Barnes had created a series of classes about his prized Impressionist paintings. Open only to those without formal education, including "Negroes," the classes focused on a viewer's feelings (rather than intellectual knowledge) about a picture. As MoMA educator Carol Morgan explains, "Barnes's unique application of Dewey's theories became legendary in the art world, and perhaps has done more to undermine a serious reading of the uses of progressive educational theories in art education in the first half of the twentieth century than any other single factor." See Carol Morgan, "From Modernist Utopia to Cold War Reality: A Critical Moment in Museum Education," in *The Museum of Modern Art at MidCentury: Continuity and Change*, John Elderfield, ed. (New York: Museum of Modern Art, 1995), 172-173. Morgan cites Howard Greenfield's *The Devil and Dr. Barnes: Portrait of an American Art Collector* (New York: Viking Press, 1989).

19   "The seven original *Mercury* astronauts. . . ." Rose Bennett Gilbert, "Space Age Education," *Museum News*, November 1965, 25.

W. Eugene Smith, *Popular Photography*, 1959, n.p.

Sherman Lee, "The Art Museum as Wilderness Act, "reprinted in *Museum News*, February 1984, 59.

20   June Jordan quoted in Barry Schwartz, "Museums: Art for Who's Sake," *Ramparts* 9, no. 11 (1971), 38.

21   John R. Kinard, "The Neighborhood Museum as a Catalyst for Social Change," *Museum* 37, no. 4 (1985), 217-222.

For more on federally funded community outreach projects, see articles by Ildiko Herrernan, Sandra Schnee and Linda Graetz on "Art Museums and Older Adults" in *Museum News*, March/April 1981, 30-36.

22   *Attracting Older Visitors to Museums* (Washington, D.C.: American Association of Retired Persons, 1985), 1. This report cites a 1981 Louis Harris poll published by the American Council for the Arts.

". . . nearly 2 million acres was . . . added to the museum landscape . . ." from *Museums Count* (Washington, D.C.: American Association of Museums, 1994), 35, 78.

23   For more on the typical museumgoer, see Paul DiMaggio and Francie Ostrower, "Participation in the Arts by Black and White Americans," *Social Forces*, March 1990, 753-778.

24   Donna Haraway, "Teddy Bear Patriarchy: Taxidermy in the Garden of Eden, 1908-1936," *Social Text* 11 (winter 1984).

Excellence and Equity: Education and the Public Dimension of Museums (Washington, D.C.: American Association of Museums, 1992), 8.

25 One of the earliest museum theatre programs began in 1971 at the Science Museum of Minnesota. See *Theatre in Museums*, Tessa Bridal, guest editor (Washington, D.C.: American Association of Museums Technical Information Service, 1993).

See Janice Majewski, *Part of Your General Public Is Disabled: A Handbook for Guides in Museums, Zoos, and Historic Houses* (Washington, D.C.: Smithsonian Institution Press, 1987); *The Accessible Museum: Model Programs of Accessibility for Disabled and Older People* (Washington, D.C.: American Association of Museums, 1993); and Elana Kalisher, "Reexamining Diversity: A Look at the Deaf Community in Museums," *Curator* 41, no. 1 (March 1998), 13 – 35.

26 "They also went on another building frenzy. . . ." Jane Lusaka and John Strand, "The Boom—And What to Do about It," *Museum News*, November/December 1998, 55-60.

Helen and Brice Marden quoted in Michael Kimmelman, "The Solace in Sharing the Beauty of Great Art and Music," *New York Times*, Sept. 17, 2001.

For more on museums after Sept. 11, 2001, see Vanessa Van Orden, Exhibiting Tragedy, unpublished master's project, John F. Kennedy University, Berkeley, Calif., 2004.

Lonnie Bunch, "In the Shadow of Uncertainty: Museums in the Aftermath," *Museum News*, January/ February 2002, 41; quoted in Van Orden, 149.

27 Robert R. Archibald, *The New Town Square: Museums and Communities in Transition* (Walnut Creek, Calif.: AltaMira Press, 2004), 212.

THE BUILDING

Notes to pages 29–66

29 James Renwick quoted in *Guide to the Architecture of Washington, D.C.* (Washington, D.C.: American Institute of Architects, 1965), 42.

In the early 19th century, the Massachusetts Historical Society was located for a short while near the butcher stalls at Faneuil Hall Marketplace in Boston. See Walter Muir Whitehill, *Independent Historical Societies* (Boston: Harvard University Press, 1962), 11.

30 Ada Louise Huxtable, "Review of Towards a New Museum," *New York Review of Books* 46 (April 22, 1999), 10.

Douglas Crimp discusses Schinkel's influence on museum architecture at length in *On the Museum's Ruins* (Cambridge, Mass.: MIT Press, 1993), 285-318 and "The End of Art and the Origin of the Museum," *Art Journal* (winter 1987), 261-266.

32 "Land was cheap and available . . ." from Daniel M. Fox, *Engines of Culture: Philanthropy and Art Museums* (Madison, Wis.: The State Historical Society of Wisconsin, 1963), 79.

For an account of the politics behind the Met's decision, see Calvin Tompkins, *Merchants and Masterpieces: The Story of the Metropolitan Museum of Art* (New York: E. P. Dutton & Co., Inc.), 39-42. The New-York Historical Society was to occupy this parcel of land, as discussed in Kevin M. Guthrie, *The New-York Historical Society: Lessons from One Nonprofit's Long Struggle for Survival* (San Francisco: Jossey Bass, 1996). The NYHS could not raise the funds to move to Central Park in the 1860s, but did purchase a building in there in 1904.

Geoffrey Hellman, *Bankers, Bones and Beetles: The First Century of the American Museum of Natural History* (Garden City, N.Y.: The Natural History Press, 1969), 77.

Tompkins, 50.

33 For an interesting account of the impact of the 1893 Chicago Exposition on American society, see Erik Larson, *The Devil in the White City* (New York: Vintage Books, 2004). For a scholarly analysis of the fair's influence on museum architecture, see Linda S. Phipps, "The 1893 Art Institute Building and the 'Paris of America': Aspirations of Patrons and Architects in Late Nineteenth Century Chicago," *The Art Institute of Chicago Museum Studies* 14, no. 1 (1988), 28-45.

Henry James, "New York Revisited," (1906) in *The Portable Henry James*, Morton Dauwen Zabel, ed. (New York: The Viking Press, 1960), 547.

James N. Wood, "Preface," *The Art Institute of Chicago Museum Studies* 14, no. 1 (1988), 5.

34 ". . . Beaux-Arts museums had little place for visitor amenities." Neil Kotler and Philip Kotler, *Museum Strategy and Marketing: Designing Missions; Building Audiences; Generating Revenue and Resources* (San Francisco: Jossey Bass, 1998), 279.

John Cotton Dana, *The New Museum* (Woodstock, Vt.: The Elm Tree Press, 1917), 12.
William A. Peniston, ed. *The New Museum: Selected Writings by John Cotton Dana* (American Association of Museums and The Newark Museum, 1999). Bamberger was a prominent Jewish philanthropist, notable for his role in bringing Albert Einstein to Princeton University.

35 For more on the goals of early museum founders, see Ingrid A. Steffensen-Bruce, *Marble Palaces, Temples of Art: Art Museums, Architecture, and American Culture, 1890-1930* (Lewisburg, Pa.: Bucknell University Press, 1998).

Kenneth Donahue, "The Ringling Museums—Baroque Art and Circus History," *Museum News*, October 1960, 14-21. For a more complete history of this fascinating museum, see Mitchell Merling, *Ringling: The Art Museum* (Sarasota, Fla.: The John and Mable Ringling Museum of Art, 2002).

36 Edward Stevens Robinson, *The Behavior of the Museum Visitor* (Washington, D.C.: American Association of Museums, 1928), 31. The term "museum fatigue" was coined by Benjamin Ives Gilman in 1916. Horace H. F. Jayne, "A Preliminary Report from the Pennsylvania Museum," in *The Behavior of the Museum Visitor* by Edward Stevens Robinson (Washington, D.C.: American Association of Museums, 1928), 68-72.

Fiske Kimball, "The Modern Museum of Art," *The Architectural Record* 66 (December 1929),174.

37 George and Mary Roberts, *Triumph on Fairmont: Fiske Kimball and the Philadelphia Museum of Art* (Philadelphia and New York: J. B. Lippincott Company, 1959), 82-87.

For more on early visitor studies, see Ross J. Loomis's discussion in *Museum Visitor Evaluation: A New Tool for Management* (Nashville: American Association for State and Local History, 1987), 21-25.

Rocky Balboa's relationship to the Philadelphia Museum of Art is discussed in two articles by Danielle Rice: "The 'Rocky' Dilemma: Museums, Monuments and Popular Culture in the Postmodern Era," in *Critical Issues in Public Art: Content, Context and Controversy* (New York: HarperCollins, 1992), 228-236; and "Rocky Too: The Saga of an Outdoor Sculpture," in *Cultural Resources Management* 18, no. 1 (1995), 9-11. In 1982, Thomas Schomberg's bronze statue of Sylvester Stallone as the muscular boxer was installed by United Artists at the front of the building for the filming of *Rocky V*. Elitists balked. Tourists came in droves. After much controversy (including Sylvester Stallone's claim that he had done more for the city of Philadelphia than had Benjamin Franklin), the statue was removed to a sports arena in 1990.

38 Anders Greenspan, *Creating Colonial Williamsburg* (Washington, D.C.: Smithsonian Institution Press, 2002). Greenspan uses archival research to document the history of Colonial Williamsburg and its transformation from the original nostalgic vision of John D. Rockefeller, Jr., to a vibrant contemporary educational and tourism center. Rockefeller's interest in the architecture of the past extended to his sponsorship of the preservation of Mesa Verde and his 1930s involvement in purchasing French medieval architectural elements, which were assembled meticulously into the Cloisters in New York.

39 Henry Ford, quoted in *The Chicago Tribune*, 1916. See also Neil Baldwin, *Henry Ford and the Jews: The Mass Production of Hate* (New York: PublicAffairs, 2001), and Margaret Sterne, *The Passionate Eye* (Detroit: Wayne State University, 1980), which discuss Ford's anti-semitism.

Steven Conn offers a thorough account of Ford's and Mercer's visions and explains why they were significant to the dissemination of knowledge at that time in his book, *Museums and American Intellectual Life*, 151-191.

40 Harold Stark, "Painting," in *Art in America: A Complete Survey*, Holger Cahill and Alfred H. Barr, eds. (New York, Halcyon House, 1934), 3.

"Directors began to see. . . ." Philip Youtz, December 1937, quoted in Migs Grove, "The Monuments of Half a Century," *Museum News*, February 1984, 31.

Graham W. J. Beal, *Joslyn Art Museum: A Building History* (Omaha, Nebr.: Joslyn Art Museum, 1997).

The Nelson Gallery was founded in 1929 from a bequest left by William Rockhill Nelson, editor of the *Kansas City Star*. By 1933, it had amassed a collection, constructed a building, and was open for business.

For an amusing discussion on the choice of marble for the National Gallery of Art, see S. H. Behrman, *Duveen* (New York: Random House, 1952), 272-276. Mellon wanted to build in limestone, a less expensive material. According to Behrman, Mellon's art dealer, the infamous Joseph Duveen, talked him into spending an extra $5 million on marble so Duveen could impress other potential clients.

41   Lewis Mumford, *Sticks and Stones: A Study of American Architecture and Civilization*, 2d. ed. (New York, Dover, 1955), 68-69.

One director who referred to the "'me too' Louvres" was Alexander Dorner, then head of the Museum of the Rhode Island School of Design. Quoted in Samuel Cauman, *The Living Museum: Experience of an Art Historian and Museum Director—Alexander Dorner* (New York: New York University Press, 1958), 79.

Modern architecture was in some respects a reaction to fascist and Nazi neoclassical monuments. Ironically the man who introduced this alternative style of design to America, Philip Johnson, was himself a Nazi sympathizer. See Kazys Varnelis, "'We Cannot Not Know History: 'Philip Johnson's Politics and Cynical Survival," *Journal of Architectural Education*, November 1995.

For more information on the life of this remarkable visionary, see Sybil Gordon Kantor, *Alfred H. Barr, Jr., and the Intellectual Origins of the Museum of Modern Art* (Cambridge, Mass.: MIT Press, 2001), and Alice Goldfarb Marquis, *Alfred H. Barr, Jr.: Missionary for the Modern* (Chicago: Contemporary Books, 1989).

Alfred Barr quoted in *Abby Aldrich Rockefeller* by Bernice Katz (New York: Random House, 1993), 382.

42   Tom Wolfe, *From Bauhaus to Our House* (New York: Washington Square Press, 1982), 38-39.

43   Frank Lloyd Wright quoted in *Seed Money: The Guggenheim Story* by Milton Lomask (New York: Farrar, Straus and Company, 1964), 183.

See Spiro Kostof, *A History of Architecture: Settings and Rituals*, 2d. ed., rev. by Greg Castillo (New York: Oxford University Press, 1995), 732. On the other hand, artists ranging from Milton Avery to Robert Motherwell signed letters of protest about the building. The January 1960 issue of *Museum News* devotes 10 pages of discussion to the pros and cons of Wright's building.

44   Gregory Wittkopp, "The Evolving Mission of the Cranbrook Art Museum," in *Cranbrook Art Museum: 100 Treasures* (Bloomfield Hills, Mich.: Cranbrook Art Museum, 2004), 17-18.

Carolyn Harrison, "Boston Builds a Science Museum," *Museum News*, May 1960, page 15.

45   Robert W. Rydell, John E. Findling and Kimberly Pelle, *Fair America: World's Fairs in the United States* (Washington, D.C.: Smithsonian Institution Press, 2000), 100-105.

The December 1959 issue of *Museum News* is devoted to modern planetaria and includes an article extolling their virtues by the great modern architect Richard J. Neutra.

Rose Bennett Gilbert, "Space Age Education," *Museum News*, November 1965, 25.

David Hancocks, *A Different Nature: The Paradoxical World of Zoos and Their Uncertain Future* (Berkeley: University of California Press, 2001), 105. See also Jean Wineman and Yoon Kyung Choi, "Spacial/Visual Properties of Zoo Exhibition," *Curator* 34, no. 4 (1991), 304-315.

"Frank Lloyd Wright . . . proposed a suction mat system. . . ." Laurence Vail Coleman, *Museum Buildings* (Washington, D.C.: American Association of Museums,1950), 121.

46   Nancy Kriplen, *Keep An Eye on that Mummy: A History of the Children's Museum of Indianapolis* (1982: The Children's Museum of Indianapolis), 89-90.

Robert Bruegmann, "The Art Institute Expands. Challenges of Mid-Century," in *The Art Institute of Chicago Museum Studies* 14, no. 1, p. 73.

"Edward Ruscha's mid-1960s painting *The Los Angeles County Museum on Fire . . .*" discussed in Kynaston McShine, "The Museum as Muse: Artists Reflect," reprinted in *Museum Studies: An Anthology of Contexts*, Bettina Messias Carbonell, ed. (Malden, Mass.: Blackwell Publishing, Ltd., 2004), 516-517.

A Statistical Survey of Museums, 16. The report documents annual museum attendance of 83,188,831 in 1952; 121,869,646 in 1957 and 184,766,678 in 1962. Since 1975 Michigan's Kresge Foundation has played a large role in awarding "bricks-and-mortar" grants. *Museums Count* documents that 3,279 museums were founded over the 20-year period, 1970-90. (Washington, D.C.: American Association of Museums, 1994), 35, 78.

Paul Goldberger, "The Museum as Design Laboratory," *Museum News*, April 1987, 7.

47   ". . . painters were asked to work on larger canvases . . ." from Karl E. Meyer, *The Art Museum: Power, Money, Ethics* (New York: William Morrow and Company, 1979), 131.

Betty J. Blum, "Oral History of Gordon Bunschaft," 1990. Compiled under the auspices of the Chicago Architects Oral History Project, Art Institute of Chicago, 100.

"... critics called it a 'defensive pillbox'..." from Steve Connor, *Postmodernist Culture* (Cambridge, Mass.: Blackwell Press, 1997), 79.

48   Philip C. Johnson, "Letter to the Museum Director," *Museum News* (January 1960), 23.

For more on MoMA's 1984 expansion, see Alan Wallach, "The Museum of Modern Art: The Past's Future," in *Exhibiting Contradictions* (Amherst: University of Massachusetts Press, 1998), 82-87.

For an analysis of community building through mixed-use space, see Elaine Heumann Gurian, "Function Follows Form: How Mixed-Use Spaces in Museums Build Community," *Curator* 44, no. 1 (January 2001), 97–113.

49   Harry Parker, quoted in *New American Art Museums* by Helen Searing (New York: Whitney Museum of American Art in association with University of California Press, 1982), 87.

National Trust for Historic Preservation, "Railroad Depot Acquisition and Development," Information Series Pamphlet No. 44, 1989. By 1989, "Historically and architecturally significant depots [were] prime opportunities for preservation and adaptive use ... to restaurants, shops, offices, transit centers and museums."

50   Somerset R. Walters, "Museums and Tourism," *Museum News*, January 1966, 32-37.

51   For more information on the Baltimore revival as it went forward in the 1990s, see Jane Lusaka, "Bluecrabs and Biotechnology: Baltimore's Museum-based Revival," in *Museum News*, March/April 1997, 42-49.

"... 116 cities developed cultural districts ..." from Hilary Anne Frost-Kumpf, Cultural Districts: Arts Management and Urban Redevelopment, unpublished doctoral dissertation, Pennsylvania State University, 2001.

See Victor J. Danilov, "Imax/Omnimax: Fad or Trend?" in *Museum News* (August 1987), 32-39.

52   The High Museum of Art is discussed in Searing, 106-113.

Robert Venturi, *Complexity and Contradiction in Architecture* (New York: Museum of Modern Art, 1966), 23.

53   Douglas Crimp, "The Postmodern Museum," in *On the Museum's Ruins* (Cambridge, Mass.: MIT Press, 1993), 285-318.

See Mitchell Schwarzer, *Zoomscape* (New York: Princeton Architectural Press, 2004) for a discussion on the architectural messages in signs.

Glenn Weiss, "In Praise of SAM," *Seattle Magazine*, December 1999.

Robert Venturi, quoted in Susan Kahn, "The Seattle Art Museum: A Post-modernist Architecture of Ironic Self Denial," in *Museum Architecture and Changing Civic Identity* (Los Angeles: University of Southern California Architectural Guild Press, 1999), 42.

54   "The building sits uncomfortably at the very point that the grids of 'town and gown' intersect. ..." Herbert Muschamp, "Who's That Peering Out Of the Grid?," *New York Times*, March 18, 2001, 2, 38.

Ellen Posner refers to the Wexner's "teensy, narrow stairways" in "A $43 Million Arts Center Opens—Minus the Art," *Wall Street Journal*, Dec. 14, 1989, n.p.

Peter Eisenman quoted in Leon Whiteson, "The Gap Between Use and Users of Buildings," *Los Angeles Times*, Dec. 5, 1989, 2.

Marilyn Hood, "Staying Away: Why People Choose Not to Visit Museums," *Museum News*, 1983, 50-57.

55   "I felt like was a rat in a maze. ..." Glenn Zorpette, "What Do Museum Visitors Want?" *ARTnews*, December 1992, 94.

Frank Gehry quoted in Gerhard Mack, *Art Museums into the 21st Century* (Basel, Switzerland, and Boston: Birkhauser, 1999).

"A new museum building ... opened roughly every 15 days ..." from Jane Lusaka and John Strand, "The Boom—And What to Do about It," *Museum News*, November/December 1998, 55-60.

"The pristine white High Museum. ..." See Roger K. Lewis, "High Expectations," *Museum News*, March/April 1993, 37.

The relationship between architecture and elaborate fund-raising schemes is argued persuasively by economist Karl E. Meyer in *The Art Museum: Power, Money, Ethics*.

56   "... museums were becoming cities unto themselves...." Marjorie Schwarzer, "Schizophrenic Agora: Mission, Market and the Multi-tasking Museum," *Museum News*, November/December 1999, 40.

Homer Simpson quoted in Diana Cohen Altman, "Exhibition Criticism: A Pretty Okay Idea," *Exhibitionist* 19, no. 1 (spring 2000), 24.

Nancy Oestreich Lurie, *A Special Style: The Milwaukee Public Museum, 1882-1992* (Milwaukee: Milwaukee Public Museum, 1983), 115.

Laura Doty: "The National Gallery: Artful Renovations Bring Foodservice into the 21st Century," *the consultant*, third quarter, 2001, 54-62.

57   "America's favorite leisure time activity...." Betsy Morris, "Big Spenders: As a Favored Pastime Shopping Ranks High with Most Americans," *Wall Street Journal*, July 30, 1987.

"... spaces accessible to non-museum customers...." Mary Miley Theobald, *Museum Store Management* (Walnut Creek, Calif.: AltaMira Press, 2000), 1. Theobald discusses stores that reflect their museum's collections or architectural style on page 25.

According to the Association of Science and Technology Centers, as of 2004, 66 percent of science centers offered camp-ins.

Victoria Newhouse, "Is the 'Idea of a Museum' Possible Today?" *Daedalus: America's Museums*, summer 1999, 323.

59   Herbert Muschamp quoted in Mark W. Rectanus, *Culture Incorporated: Museums, Artists and Corporate Sponsorships* (Minneapolis: University of Minnesota Press, 2002), 181-185.

Frank Gehry's designs for Guggenheim Bilbao and the Experience Music Project are discussed in Witold Rybczynski, "The Bilbao Effect," *The Atlantic Monthly*, September 2002, 138-142.

60   Franz Schulze, "Disclosing Santiago Calatrava's Milwaukee Masterpiece," in *Milwaukee Art Museum* (New York: Hudson Hills Press, 2001).

The Nov. 24, 2003, issue of *The New Yorker* features the ad with a Solara whizzing by the Milwaukee Art Museum at dusk; see pages 11 and 12.

61   "They battled Richard Meier and the Getty...." Nicolai Ouroussoff, "Cuture? Not in Our Backyard," *Los Angeles Times*, November 5, 2000.

Franklin W. Robinson, "No More Buildings!" *Museum News*, November/December 2002, 28-29.

Sheila Farr, Cheryl Phillips, and Warren Cornwall, "Trail of Miscalculations, Missteps Led to Bellevue Art Museum's Closure," *Seattle Times*, Nov. 16, 2003, n.p.

62   Guggenheim flyer, 2002.

63   Stastny & Burke: Architecture, "The Warm Springs Tribal Museum," *Museum News*, March/April 1993, 38.

"The museum won a Merit Award...." Alice Parman, "A Joint Effort: Planning Exhibit for the Museum at Warm Springs," *History News* 54, no. 3 (summer 1998), 23.

64   Michael Hammond in a personal conversation with the author, October 2003. The original source of this oft-repeated quote is attributed to Lisa Watt.

The Madison Children's Museum designed 'First Feats'...." Brenda Baker and John Robinson, "The Sustainable Museum: It's Not Easy Being Green," *Hand to Hand*, winter 2000, 4-5, 7.

65   "Daniel Libeskind: Designing Soul," *Museum News*, March/April 2005, 44-51

66   Karen R. Miller, "Whose History, Whose Culture? The Museum of African American History, the Detroit Institute of Arts and Urban Politics at the End of the 20th Century," *Michigan Quarterly Review* 41, no. 1 (winter 2002), 136-154, and Jeffrey Abt, *A Museum on the Verge: A Socioeconomic History of the Detroit Institute of Arts, 1882-2000* (Detroit: Wayne State University Press, 2001).

69   Walt Whitman, "Song of the Exposition" in *Leaves of Grass*, 5th printing (New York: Signet, 1962), 172. John Cotton Dana, *The New Museum* (Woodstock, Vt.: Elm Street Press, 1917).

70   Theodore Henry Hittell, *The California Academy of Sciences (1853-1906)*, (San Francisco: California Academy of Sciences, 1997), ed. and rev. by Alan E. Leviton and Michele Aldrich, 467-482, 500-506. See also "Alice Eastwood," in Marcia Myers Bonta, *Women in the Field: America's Pioneering Woman Naturalists* (College Station, Tex.: Texas A&M Press, 1991), 93-102.

      H. G. Dwight of the Frick Collection, quoted in S. N. Behrman, *Duveen* (New York: Random House, 1952), 243.

      S. Dillon Ripley, *The Sacred Grove* (Washington, D.C.: Smithsonian Institution Press, 1969), 23.

71   *Museums Count* (Washington, D.C.: American Association of Museums, 1994) defines collections in the following way: "Objects/specimens are discrete items such as a painting, a mounted bald eagle or a locomotive. Lots/taxa are groups of small objects counted as a group, e.g., insects. Archival materials are documentary materials such as a correspondence found in a historic house or a scientist's field notes. Books are different from archival materials. They are defined as printed, bound materials that are part of a collection. Finally, sites, structures and acres of land that are used for educational purposes, such as a historic farmstead, a house designed by a famous architect or a botanical garden." This author's own unscientific estimate of holdings, derived from totaling the collections of the large U.S. museums as reported on their websites, comes to over 2 billion objects.

      Aggregate rate of collection growth discussed in Stephen E. Weil, ed., *A Deaccession Reader* (Washington, D.C.: American Association of Museums, 1997), 2-3.

72   Richard Wollheim, "Berenson," *The Spectator*, March 25, 1960, 435. Ernest Samuels, *Bernard Berenson: The Making of a Legend* (Cambridge, Mass.: Belknap Press, 1987), 195.

      Behrman, *Duveen*. Meryle Secrest, *Duveen: A Life in Art* (New York: Knopf, 2004).

      Nathaniel Burt, *Palaces for the People: A Social History of the American Art Museum* (Boston: Little, Brown and Company, 1977), 364. See also Philipp Blom, *To Have and to Hold: An Intimate History of Collectors and Collecting* (Woodstock, N.Y.: Overlook Press, 2002), 124-136.

      Aline B. Saarinen, *The Proud Possessors* (New York: Conde Nast Publications, Inc., 1958), 26.

      "To many people the making of a great collection. . . ." David Edward Finley, *A Standard of Excellence: Andrew W. Mellon Founds the National Gallery of Art At Washington DC* (Washington, D.C.: Smithsonian Institution Press, 1973), 21. Finley was director of the National Gallery of Art from 1938 to 1956.

73   John Anderson, *Art Held Hostage: The Battle Over the Barnes Collection* (New York: W.W. Norton & Company, 2003). Grayson Harris Lane, Duncan Phillips and the Phillips Memorial Gallery: A Patron and Museum in Formation, 1918-1940 (unpublished doctoral dissertation, Boston University, 2002).

      Douglas and Elizabeth Rigby, *Lock, Stock and Barrel: The Story of Collecting* (Philadelphia: J. B. Lippincott Company, 1944), 286-287.

      Deborah Franklin, "When One Man's Castle Was His Home," *Via*, January/February 2003, 39. See also Blom, *To Have and to Hold*, 133, and Victoria Kastner, *Castle: The Biography of a Country House* (New York: Harry N. Abrams, 2000).

74   David Goodrich, *Art Fakes in America* (New York: Viking Press, 1973), 81. Saarinen, *The Proud Possessors*, 61.

      For an analysis of early art tariff laws and their impact on art collecting, see Kimberly Orcutt, "Buy American? The Debate Over the Art Tariff," *American Art* 16, no. 3 (fall 2002).

75   Calvin Tompkins, *Merchants and Masterpieces: The Story of the Metropolitan Museum of Art.* (New York: E. P. Dutton & Co., 1970), 296.

      Wilhelm von Bode quoted in Samuels, *Bernard Berenson*, 195.

76   Behrman, *Duveen*, 28. "Mellon & Madonna," *Time*, March 4, 1935, 32.

      Andrew Mellon, letter to Franklin D. Roosevelt dated Dec. 22, 1936, in Finley, *A Standard of Excellence*, 47.

77   There are many versions of the story behind Mellon's collecting and tax scandals. The most sympathetic one is relayed by his son Paul in *Reflections in a Silver Spoon* (New York: William Morrow & Co., 1992).

Valentiner described Rivera as "a strange looking and heavy set man, wearing a black serape and a large Mexican hat" and Kahlo as wearing "a large reboso, a white veil over her forehead, a red rose in her hair." Quoted in Margaret Sterne, *The Passionate Eye*, (Detroit: Wayne State University Press, 1980), 189.

78   Prominent collectors of Native American art included: Milford Chandler, considered to the first person to collect Indian artifacts based solely on their aesthetic merits; David T. Vernon (Colter Bay Visitor Center in Grand Teton National Park, Wyo.); Adolph Spohr (Buffalo Bill Historical Center, Cody, Wyo.); Charles Fletcher Lummis (Southwest Museum, Los Angeles, now under the auspices of the Autry National Center); Mary Cabot Wheelwright (Santa Fe, N.Mex.) and George Gustav Heye (National Museum of the American Indian, New York). This research was conducted by Adam Lovell during a graduate internship at John F. Kennedy University in winter 2003. See also E. Shepard Krech III and Barbara A. Hall, *Collecting Native America 1870-1960* (Washington, D.C.: Smithsonian Institution Press, 1999).

79   Mary Lea Bandy, "Nothing Sacred: 'Jock Whitney Snares Antiques for Museum,'" *The Museum of Modern Art at Mid-Century* (New York: Museum of Modern Art, 1995), 75-103.

"Texacana": Texas wasn't alone in this regard; records at the de Young Museum suggest that in the 1920s Californian collectors coined the word "Californiana" for objects associated with the state's missions and pioneers. Information on Bayou Bend accessed April 1, 2003, from www.fn.coe.uh.edu.

80   Shirley Moskow, "Henry Francis du Pont: Brief Life of a Passionate Connoisseur: 1880-1969," *Harvard Magazine*, July-August 2003, 40.

Louis C. Jones, *The Farmers' Museum* (Cooperstown, N.Y.: New York State Historical Association, 1948). Wendy Moonan, "A Discoverer of Folk Art [Electra Havemeyer Webb]," *New York Times*, Jan. 3, 2003, B43.

81   Carnegie discussed in Charlotte M. Porter, "Natural History in the 20th Century: An Oxymoron?" in Paisley S. Cato and Clyde Jones, eds., *Natural History Museums* (Lubbock, Tex.: Texas Tech University Press, 1991), and Charles Gallenkamp, *Dragon Hunter: Roy Chapman Andrews and the Central Asiatic Expeditions* (New York: Viking, 2001), 38-39. M. Graham Netting, "The Carnegie Museum," *Museum News* (April 1959), 10.

84   Roy Chapman Andrews quoted in Gallenkamp, *Dragon Hunter*, 184. James L. Clark, *Good Hunting: Fifty Years of Collecting and Preparing Habitat Groups for the American Museum* (Norman: University of Oklahoma Press, 1966), 89-95. Andrews's handwritten journals, available at the library of the American Museum of Natural History, begin with his rules for his crew members: "No cussing the weather. No insinuations if there is sand in the soup. No profanity unless of picturesque variety. All male members must share in the pumping of tires."

Edward P. Alexander, *The Museum in America: Innovators and Pioneers* (Walnut Creek, Calif.: AltaMira Press, 1997), 27. For a fuller discussion of Osborn's views, see Charlotte M. Porter, "The Rise of Parnassus: Henry Fairfield Osborn and the Hall of the Age of Man," *Museum Studies Journal*, spring 1983, 26-34, and Claudia Roth Pierpont, "The Measure of America," *The New Yorker*, March 8, 2004, 48-63.

85   Kim Masters, "Smithsonian to Charge Fee for Animated Dinosaur Show," *Washington Post*, April 4, 1990, A1, A18.

See Steve Fiffer, *Tyrannosaurus Sue: The Extraordinary Saga of the Largest, Most Fought over T. Rex Ever* (New York: W. H. Freeman & Co., 2000), and Lauren Grant and Marie Malaro, "Disputed Bones: The Case of a Dinosaur Named Sue," ALI-ABA Course of Study Materials, (Philadelphia: March 1993), 121-157. Tessa Gunawan-Gonzalez, research paper on the Sue controversy, written for the Museum History and Theory graduate seminar at John F. Kennedy University, fall 2002.

See Catherine Donnelly, "Dinosphere: Now You're in Their World," *Exhibitionist*, spring 2004, 10-3, and Elizabeth Schwinn, "Coming of Age," *Chronicle of Philanthropy*, March 4, 2004, 25-27.

Warren D. Allmon, *Evolution and Creationism: A Guide for Docents* (Ithaca, N.Y.: Museum of the Earth, 2005). Cornelia Dean, "Challenged by Creationists, Museums Answer Back," *New York Times*, Sept. 20, 2005, n.p.

86   Franz Boas, quoted in www.nceds.ucsb.edu, accessed Dec. 29, 2002.

James Nason, quoted in "Heading Home: The Burke Museum Returns Artifacts to Northwest Tribes," *Arts and Sciences Perspectives* (University of Washington, Seattle) , autumn 2001.

87   David Hancocks, *A Different Nature: The Paradoxical World of Zoos and Their Uncertain Future* (Berkeley: University of California, Press, 2001), 92. "Take the Child Outdoors," *Museum News Letter* (American Association of Museums), November 1917, 1-2.

Stephen E. Nash and Gary M. Feinman, eds., "Curators, Collections and Contexts: Anthropology at the Field Museum, 1893-2002," *Anthropology*, no. 36 (Field Museum, Chicago, September 2003), 89.

88 "In other cases, tribal elders. . . ." Allyson Lazar, Repatriating More Than You May Know: The Problem of Native American Objects and Past Museum Conservation Practices (unpublished master's project, John F. Kennedy University, 2000), 39. Laurence Vail Coleman, *The Museum in America* (Washington, D.C.: American Association of Museums, 1939), 60.

Francis P. McManamon, "The Antiquities Act: Setting Basic Preservation Policies," *Cultural Resources Management* (National Park Service, 1996); http://crm.cr.nps.gov.

Nason, "Heading Home."

Kenn Harper, *Give Me My Father's Body* (South Royalton, Vt.: Steerforth Press, 2000.) See also Geoffrey Hellman, *Bankers, Bones & Beetles: The First Century of the American Museum of Natural History* (New York: The Natural History Press, 1968), 89.

89 Stephen E. Weil, "From Being about Something to Being for Somebody: The Ongoing Transformation of the American Museum," *Daedalus*, summer 1999, 229.

Lynn H. Nicholas, *The Rape of Europa* (New York: Alfred A. Knopf, 1994), 3-5.

90 The commission was named for Owen Roberts, U.S. Supreme Court Justice. Appointed museum specialists included David Edward Finley, director, National Gallery of Art; Horace Jayne, curator, Metropolitan Museum of Art; George L. Stout, director of conservation, Fogg Art Museum; Paul Sachs, educator, Harvard University; Francis Henry Taylor, director, Metropolitan Museum of Art; and John Walker, chief curator, National Gallery of Art.

A. Noblecourt, *Protection of Cultural Property in the Event of Armed Conflict* (Paris: UNESCO, 1956), 125, 211. Hermann Warner Williams, Jr., director, Corcoran Gallery of Art, "The Museums' New Dilemma," *The Museum News*, March 1, 1951, 7.

91 Carl Wittke, *The First Fifty Years: The Cleveland Museum of Art 1916-1966* (Cleveland: Cleveland Museum of Art, 1966), 114.

Francine du Plessix, "Collectors: Mary and Leigh Block," *Art in America* 54 (September 1966), 64-65. See Pamela G. Smart, Sacred Modern: An Ethnography of an Art Museum (unpublished doctoral dissertation, Rice University, 1997) for the history of the de Menil collection. "Lydia Winston Malbin: A Futurist Eye," *ARTnews*, April 1988, 91.

Homegrown artists discussed in Sophy Burnham, *The Art Crowd* (New York: David McKay Company, Inc., 1973). Daniel M. Fox, *Engines of Culture: Philanthropy and Art Museums* (Madison, Wis.: The State Historical Society of Wisconsin, 1963), 29. See also Peter B. Trippi, *Association of Art Museum Directors: A Review of its First 75 Years, 1916-1991* (New York: Association of Art Museum Directors, 1992), 10-11.

92 Art collecting discussed in Terry Teachout, "The Price Is Right," *Wall Street Journal*, Aug. 23, 2005.

Victor D'Amico quoted in Carol Morgan, "From Modernist Utopia to Cold War Reality," in John Elderfield, ed., *The Museum of Modern Art at Mid-Century: Continuity and Change* (New York: Museum of Modern Art, 1995), 158.

Sheldon Keck, *Museum News*, September 1964, 13.

91 "Ethics and Professionalism," *Museum News*, November/December 1988, 41. Marjorie Cohn, curator of prints at the Fogg Art Museum, shares Paul Sachs's "phone a director-pal" story in Janet Tassel, "Reverence for the Object," *Harvard Magazine*, September/October 2002, 54.

Caroline K. Keck, *A Handbook on the Care of Paintings* (Nashville, Tenn.: American Association for State and Local History, 1965), 27. "Solving the Problems of Art by X-ray," *American Magazine of Art* 17 (November 1926), 578-580.

The lab at Oberlin College, founded by conservator Richard D. Buck, was preceded by one at the University of Delaware, founded in 1951 by historian Charles Montgomery. During the 1950s Oberlin College was the site of the Intermuseum Conservation Association, jointly sponsored by art museums in Buffalo, N.Y.; Columbus and Toledo, Ohio; Indianapolis; and Davenport, Iowa. As stated on pages 29-31 of the college's fall 1952 Bulletin, the lab's goal was to 1) embrace the idea of conservation, a long-term plan for the maintenance of the structure and artistic integrity of museum objects, and 2) provide these services as a professional rather than a commercial enterprise."

Stephan De Borhegyi, "Curatorial Neglect of Collections," *Museum News*, January 1965, 35.

93 Arthur Beale, "A National Strategy for the Conservation of Collections," *Collections* 2, no. 1 (August 2005), 11-28. Dorothy H. Dudley and Irma Bezold, *Museum Registration Methods* (Washington, D.C.: American Association of Museums, 1958). A. L. Freundlich, "Museum Registration by Computer," *Museum News*, February 1966.

Jonathan Walters, "Tracking Advances: As Technological Advances in Conservation Occur, Conservators Are Developing a New Approach to Their Museum Role," *Museum News*, January/February 1989.

As Stephen E. Weil explains in "Deaccession Practices in American Museums" (*Museum News*, February 1987, 44-50), "the only alternatives to deaccessioning are to accept the expense of continually increasing storage facilities, maintenance budgets, and staff, or else to cease collecting entirely."

Martha Morris, "Deaccessioning," in Rebecca Buck and Jean Gilmore, eds., *The New Museum Registration Methods* (Washington, D.C.: American Association of Museums, 1998), 167.

The Museum News, June 15, 1942, 4.

94 Tompkins, 332. Thomas Hoving, *Making the Mummies Dance: Inside the Metropolitan Museum of Art* (New York: Simon & Schuster, 1994), 290-306.

96 John Rewald, "Should Hoving Be De-accessioned," reprinted in Weil, *A Deaccession Reader*, 34.

97 "Funds obtained. . . ." Trippi, *Association of Art Museum Directors*, 62. See also Marie Malaro, "Deaccessioning—The American Perspective," in Weil, *A Deaccession Reader*, 49, and Steven Miller, "The Pitfalls and Promises of Deaccessioning," in AAM 1991 Conference Sourcebook (Washington, D.C.: American Association of Museums, 1991), 23-30.

Donny R. George, *The Looting of the Iraq Museum, Baghdad*, Milbry Polk and Angela M. H Schuster, eds. (New York: Harry N. Abrams, 2005).

"One American committee. . . ." Joseph Veach Noble, "Report of the AAM Policy Committee," *Museum News*, May 1971, 22-23.

98 Allison Akbay "Collecting Cultural Property: Art Museums and Pre-Columbian Artwork" (unpublished master's project, John F. Kennedy University, 2003). Laura Green, Guatemala and the Museum of Fine Arts, Boston: Law, Ethics and Cultural Patrimony (unpublished paper that won the Marie Malaro Excellence in Research and Teaching Award at George Washington University, spring 2000). P. M. Messenger, *The Ethics of Collecting Cultural Property*, 2d ed. (Albuquerque: University of New Mexico Press, 1999).

Clemency Coggins, "Illicit Traffic of Pre-Columbian Antiquities," *Art Journal* 29, no. 1 (1969), 94-98.

Karl E. Meyer, *The Plundered Past* (New York: Atheneum Press, 1973). Curators of the University Museum of Pennsylvania, "The Philadelphia Declaration," *Antiquity* 44 (April 1970), 171.

99 Colin Renfrew, *Loot, Legitimacy and Ownership* (London: Duckworth, 2000), and Patrick J. O'Keefe, *Commentary on the UNESCO 1970 Convention on Illicit Traffic* (Leicester, U.K.: Institute of Art and Law, Ltd., 2000). Maria Papageorge Kouroupas and Ann J. Guthrie, "The Cultural Property Act: What It Means for Museums," *Museum News*, June 1985, 47. See also Linda F. Pinkerton, "Word to the Wise: Scrutinize Objects of Questionable Origin," *Museum News*, November/December 1989, 28-31.

100 G. Ellis Burcaw, "Active Collecting in History Museums," *Museum News*, March 1967, 21. See also Duncan Cameron, "The Museum: A Temple or the Forum," *Journal of World History*, no. 1 (1972). Thomas J. Schlereth, "Contemporary Collecting for Future Recollecting," *Museum Studies Journal* 1, no. 3 (spring 1984), 23-30.

"Old Masters [were] endangered species. . . ." John Walsh, then director of the Getty Museum, "The Museum's Collection," in Martin Feldstein, ed., *The Economics of Art Museums* (Chicago: University of Chicago Press, 1991), 24.

See *A Legacy of Leadership: Investing in America's Living Cultural Heritage since 1965* (Washington, D.C.: National Endowment for the Arts, September 2000), and Thomas W. Leavitt: "There's Hope for Montclair, NJ," *Museum News*, June 1972.

101 Thomas A. Livesay, "A Final Word," *History News* 51, no. 3 (summer 1996), 32.

In 1971 the Art Galleries at the University of California, Santa Barbara exhibited political posters, stating: "Let this [exhibition] be regarded as a signpost of our politically and culturally self-conscious times, rather than as a work of 'instant history.'" In 1972-73, curators at the Wichita Art Museum organized a traveling exhibition on "kitsch," featuring "commercial objects, generally shoddy, gawdy, and tawdry" such as plastic ferns, a night light in the shape of an astronaut, and a pink-plumed ballpoint pen. See Jan von Adlemann, "The Grotesque Around Us," *Museum News*, May 1973, 19; and a review of UC Santa Barbara's exhibit catalogue in *Museum News*, May 1971, 44.

104 Ellen Roney Hughes, "The Unstifled Muse," in Amy Henderson and Adrienne L. Kaeppler, eds., *Exhibiting Dilemmas: Issues of Representation at the Smithsonian* (Washington, D.C.: Smithsonian Institution Press, 1997), 156-157.

Robert McCormick Adams, quoted in Hughes, "The Unstifled Muse," 169.

Hughes, "The Unstifled Muse," 172.

Nancy Kolb, director, Please Touch Museum, quoted in "Collecting Thoughts," *Museum News*, September/October 1989, 56.

105 L. Thomas Frye, "Museum Collecting for the Twenty-First Century" in Lonn W. Taylor, ed., *A Common Agenda for History Museums* (Nashville: American Association of State and Local Histories, 1987), 9. See also Frye's "The Recent Past is Prologue," *Museum News*, November 1974, 24-27.

Scott Eberle and G. Rollie Adams, "Making Room for Big Bird," *History News*, autumn 1996, 23-24.

106 Lonnie G. Bunch, "Fighting the Good Fight: Museums in an Age of Uncertainty," *Museum News*, March/April 1995, 60.

John Kuo Wei Tchen, "Creating a Dialogic Museum," in Ivan Karp, Christine Mullen Kreamer and Steven D. Lavine, eds., *Museums and Communities: The Politics of Public Culture*, (Washington, D.C.: Smithsonian Institution Press, 1992), 289.

Walter Muir Whitehill, *Independent Historical Societies* (Boston: Harvard University Press, 1962), 404. Grace Cohen Grossman, *Jewish Museums of the World* (New York: Hugh Lauter Levin Associates, 2003), 30-32, 241-315. See also Rachel M. Howse, "A History of Jewish Archives 1947-Present," *Collections* 2, no. 1 (August 2005), 47-62.

Herlinda Zamora, "Identity & Community: A Look at Four Latino Museums," *Museum News*, May/June 2002, 37-41.

107 Robert Hemenway, *Zora Neale Hurston: A Literary Biography* (Urbana: University of Illinois Press, 1978).

William Yeingst and Lonnie G. Bunch, "Curating the Recent Past: The Woolworth Lunch Counter, Greensboro, North Carolina," in Henderson and Kaeppler, *Exhibiting Dilemmas*, 143-155. See also Peggy Thomson, *Museum People* (Englewood Cliffs, N.J.: Prentice-Hall, Inc., 1977), 206-208.

108 Christy Coleman Matthews, "A Colonial Williamsburg Revolution," *History News* 54, no. 2 (spring 1999), 6-11.

See Brian W. Thomas, "Power and Community: The Archaeology of Slavery at the Hermitage Plantation," *American Antiquity* 63, no. 4 (1998), 531-551.

109 See *History News*, spring 1999. Jennifer Eichstedt and Stephen Small, *Representations of Slavery: Race and Ideology in Southern Plantation Museums* (Washington, D.C.: Smithsonian Institution Press, 2002).

Charles Wright, an Alabama-born obstetrician who delivered more than 7,000 babies, is considered by many to be the father of the African-American museum movement.

Byron Rushing, "Afro-Americana: Defining it; Finding it; Collecting it," *Museum News*, January/February 1982, 33-40.

111 Jeffrey Gettleman, "Museum Revives MLK Assassination Questions," *San Francisco Chronicle*, Oct. 20, 2002, F3.

Rita Organ quoted in Marilyn Bauer and Janelle Gelfand, "Freedom Center Searches for Artifacts," *Cincinnati Enquirer*, June 16, 2002.

112 Martin Smith, quoted in Edward T. Linenthal, *Preserving Memory: The Struggle to Create America's Holocaust Museum* (New York: Viking, 1995),163.

Linenthal, *Preserving Memory*, 140-166. See also "Nazi Freight Car: U.S. Holocaust Memorial Museum," *Museum News*, November/December 1989, 42-43.

Emily Dyer, quoted in Linenthal, *Preserving Memory*, 157.

Edward T. Linenthal, "Oklahoma City, September 11, and the 'Lessons' of History," *History News*, winter 2002, 15.

113 Eric Lipton and James Glanz, "Artifacts of Anguish Saved for Posterity," *New York Times*, Jan. 27, 2002. See also Glenn Collins, "The Men Who Saved the Relics," *New York Times*, Nov. 25, 2003, n.p. "

W. J. Holland, quoted in David R. Waters, "W. J. Holland's Speech at the International Congress of Americanists, 13th Session, in 1902," *Annals of the Carnegie Museum* 71, no. 2, (May 28, 2002), 132.

Roger Echo Hawk, *Keepers of Culture: Repatriating Cultural Items under the Native American Graves Protection and Repatriation Act* (Denver: Denver Art Museum, 2002), 176.

114 For a more detailed analysis of NAGPRA see Echo-Hawk, *Keepers of Culture*, and Christina F. Kreps, *Liberating Culture: Cross-cultural Perspectives on Museums, Curation and Heritage Preservation* (London and New York: Routledge, 2003). James D. Nason, "Native American Intellectual Property Rights," in Bruce Ziff and Pratima V. Rao, eds., *Borrowed Power: Essays on Cultural Appropriation* (New Brunswick: Rutgers University Press, 1997), 240.

James Clifford, "Museums as Contact Zones," in *Routes: Travel and Translation in the Late Twentieth Century* (Cambridge Mass.: Harvard University Press, 1997), 188-199. Nason quoted in Dan Monroe, "Native American Repatriation: History, Requirements and Outlook," *Western Museums Conference Newsletter*, winter 1990/91, 4.

115 Personal interview, Robert Archibald of the Missouri Historical Society, Feb. 19, 2004. See also Robert Archibald, *A Place to Remember* (Walnut Creek, Calif: AltaMira Press, 1999), 56-58.

1988 AAM Annual Report, published in *Museum News*, January/February 1989, 8. Echo Hawk quoted in James D. Nason, "Beyond Repatriation: Cultural Policy and Practice for the Twenty-first Century," in Ziff and Rao, eds., *Borrowed Power*, 299.

"Siding with Native Americans. . . ." Dan Monroe, "Native American Repatriation," 4.

Memorandum dated Dec. 26, 1990, published in AAM 1991 Conference Sourcebook, 75.

116 Collections of the Sam Noble Museum discussed in personal correspondence with Peter Tirrell.

"By 2000 almost half of museums. . . ." Lazar, *Repatriating More Than You May Know*.

George P. Horse Capture, "Survival of Culture," *Museum News*, January/February 1991, 51.

117 Hector Feliciano, *The Lost Museum: The Nazi Conspiracy to Steal the World's Greatest Works of Art* (New York: Basic Books, 1997).

118 Nancy H. Yelde, Konstantin Akinsha and Amy L. Walsh, *The AAM Guide to Provenance Research* (Washington, D.C.: American Association of Museums, 2001), 68. Erik Ledbetter, "The Nazi-Era Provenance Internet Portal," *Museum News* May/June 2003, 29-33. AAM guidelines available from www.aam-us.org; Portal accessible at www.nepip.org.

Celestine Bohlen, "Major Museums Affirm Right to Keep Long-Held Antiquities," *New York Times*, Dec. 11, 2002. *Aviso* (American Association of Museums), March 2006.

119 Wilcomb E. Washburn, "Education and the New Elite: American Museums in the 1980s and 90s," *Museum News*, March/April 1996, 63.

Alma Wittlin, *Museums in Search of a Usable Future* (Cambridge, Mass.: MIT Press, 1970), 204.

James H. Duff, "Power of the Object," *Making a Difference: Tribute to the Katherine Coffey Award Recipients*, pamphlet published by the Mid-Atlantic Association of Museums, 1997, 39.

Elaine Heumann Gurian, "The Many Meanings of Objects in Museums," *Daedalus* 128, no. 3 (summer 1999), 165.

David Carr, *The Promise of Cultural Institutions* (Walnut Creek, Calif: AltaMira Press, 2003), 46.

124 William Henry Holmes, quoted in William Fitzhugh, "Ambassadors in Sealskins: Exhibiting Eskimos at the Smithsonian," in *Exhibiting Dilemmas: Issues of Representation at the Smithsonian*, Amy Henderson and Adrienne L. Kaeppler, eds. (Washington, D.C.: Smithsonian Institution Press, 1997), 210, 213-214. See also Curtis M. Hinsley, Jr., *Savages and Scientists: the Smithsonian Institution and the Development of American Anthropology, 1840-1910* (Washington, D.C.: Smithsonian Institution Press, 1981), 100-109.

"Hopi Snake Dance Group" discussed in James B. Richardson III, "The Section of Man," *Carnegie Magazine*, November 1980, 18-19.

125 Franz Boas, quoted in Ira Jacknis, "Franz Boas and Exhibits," in *Objects and Others: Essays on Museums and Material Culture*, George W. Stocking, Jr., ed. (Madison, Wis.: University of Wisconsin Press, 1985), 101.

J. D. Salinger, *Catcher in the Rye* (Boston: Little Brown and Company, 1951), 120-121.

For more information on habitat dioramas see Edward Alexander, "Carl Ethan Akeley," in *The Museum in America* (Walnut Creek, Calif: AltaMira Press, 1997), 33-49; Stephen T. Asma, *Stuffed Animals and Pickled Heads: The Culture and Evolution of Natural History Museums* (New York: Oxford University Press, 2001); Lara Bjork, Wildlife Dioramas and Natural History Museums in Theory and Practice (unpublished master's project, John F. Kennedy University, Berkeley, 2000); James L. Clark, *Good Hunting: Fifty Years of Collecting and Preparing Habitat Groups for the American Museum* (Norman, Okla.: University of Oklahoma Press, 1966); Donna Haraway, "Teddy Bear Patriarchy: Taxidermy in the Garden of Eden, 1908-1936," *Social Text* 11 (winter 1984-85); Karen Wonders, "Exhibiting Fauna—From Spectacle to Habitat Group," *Curator* 32, no. 2 (June 1989): 131-156, and "The Illusionary Art of Background Painting in Habitat Dioramas," *Curator* 33, no. 2 (June 1990), 90-116.

For more information on life groups, see Kevin Coffee, "The Restoration of the Haida Canoe Life Group," *Curator* 34, no. 1 (1991), 31-48; William Fitzhugh, "Ambassadors in Sealskins: Exhibiting Eskimos at the Smithsonian," in Henderson and Kaeppler, 206-245; Jacknis, "Franz Boas and Exhibits"; Barbara Kirschenblatt-Gimblett, *Destination Culture: Tourism, Museums and Heritage* (Berkeley, Calif.: University of California Press, 1998); and Richard Kurin, *Reflections of a Culture Broker* (Washington, D.C.: Smithsonian Institution Press, 1997), 84-93.

126 Period rooms discussed in Edward P. Alexander, *Museums in Motion* (Nashville: American Association for State and Local History, 1979), 185. See also James Deetz, "A Sense of Another World: History Museums and Cultural Change," *Museum News*, May/June 1980; Melissa Young Frye, "The Beginnings of the Period Rooms in American Museums: Charles P. Wilcomb's Colonial Kitchens, 1896, 1906, 1910," in *The Colonial Revival in America*, Alan Axelrod, ed. (New York: W. W. Norton & Company, 1985), 217-240; Edward N. Kaufman, "The Architectural Museum from World's Fair to Restoration Village," reprinted in *Museum Studies: An Anthology of Contexts*, Bettina Carbonell, ed. (Malden, Mass: Blackwell, 2004), 273-288.

Rodris Roth, "The New England, or 'Olden Tyme,' Kitchen Exhibit at Nineteenth-Century World's Fairs," in Axelrod, 159-183.

127 Karen Cushman, "Jane Addams and The Labor Museum at Hull House," *Museum Studies Journal*, spring 1983, 20-25.

James Deetz, quoted in Patricia West, "'The New Social History' and Historic House Museums: The Lindenwald Example," *Museum Studies Journal* 2, no. 3 (fall 1986), 23.

Linda Merrill, *The Peacock Room: A Cultural Biography* (Washington, D.C., and New Haven: Freer Gallery of Art, Smithsonian Institution and Yale University Press, 1998).

128 Gary Kulik, "Designing the Past," in *History Museums in the United States: A Critical Assessment*, Warren Leon and Roy Rosenzweig, eds. (Urbana and Chicago: University of Illinois Press, 1989), 12-17. Warren Leon and Margaret Platt, "Living History Museums," in Leon and Rosenzweig, 64-97. Amelia Peck, *Period Rooms in the Metropolitan Museum of Art* (New York: Abrams, 1996).

See Elizabeth Kennedy, Interpreting the Artist's Studio Memorial: An Exhibition Strategy of Museums of Western Art (unpublished doctoral dissertation, University of Pennsylvania, Philadelphia, 2003).

129 Waldemar Kaempffert, *From Cave-man to Engineer* (Chicago: Museum of Science and Industry, 1933), 13-15, 20-21. See also Jay Pridmore, *Inventive Genius: History of the Museum of Science and Industry* (Chicago: Museum of Science and Industry, 1996); and Herman Kogan, *A Continuing Marvel: The Story of the Museum of Science and Industry* (New York: Doubleday and Company, 1973).

Frank Jewett Mather quoted in Steven Conn, *Museums and American Intellectual Life, 1876-1926* (Chicago: University of Chicago Press, 1998), 228-229. Alexander Dorner, *The Way beyond "Art,"* (New York: New York University Press, 1958), 144-148.

America's literacy rates from National Center for Educational Statistics, www.nces.ed.gov.

130 See Jeannine Fiedler and Peter Feierabend, *Bauhaus* (Cologne: Konemann Verlagsgesellschaft, 1999).

Katherine S. Dreier and Marcel Duchamp, *Collection of the Societe Anonyme: Museum of Modern Art* (New Haven: Yale University Press, 1950), xvii; Robert L. Herbert, et. al., *The Societe Anonyme and the Dreier Bequest at Yale University: A Catalogue Raisonné* (New Haven: Yale University Press, 1984); Kathleen D. McCarthy, *Women's Culture: American Philanthropy and Art, 1830-1930* (Chicago: University of Chicago Press, 1991), 192-193; and Mary Anne Staniskewski, *The Power of Display: A History of Exhibition Installations at the Museum of Modern Art* (Cambridge, Mass., MIT Press, 1998), 317.

131 See Dietrich Holms, "The 1920s in Hanover," *The Art Journal*, spring 1963, 144; and Ernst Lueddeckens, "The Abstract Cabinet of El Lissitzky," *The Art Journal*, spring 1971, 265-266. Samuel Cauman, *The Living Museum: Experience of an Art Historian and Museum Director—Alexander Dorner* (New York: New York University Press, 1958), 88; and Curt P. Germundson, Alexander Dorner's Atmosphere Rooms: The Museum as Experience, unpublished paper presented at the College Art Association Conference, March 2004.

132 Eugene R. Gaddis, *Magician of the Modern: Chick Austin and the Transformation of the Arts in America* (New York: Alfred A. Knopf, 2000), 5.

Alfred Barr's thoughts on design discussed in Staniskewski, 61.

133 The Bauhaus credo discussed in J. E. Hamman, *Die Form*, 1930. See also Manlio Brusatin, *A History of Colors*, Robert H. Hopcke and Paul Schwarz, trans. (Boston: Shambhala Publications, 1991), 115-130. Brian O'Doherty, "Inside the White Cube," *Artforum*, November 1976, 42-43.

134 Victor J. Danilov, *Traveling Exhibitions* (Washington, D.C.: Association of Science and Technology Centers, 1978). Laurence Vail Coleman, *The Museum in America: A Critical Study* (Washington, D.C.: American Association of Museums, 1939), 208-209.

"Indian Art of the United States" discussed in Staniskewski, 87, 91-97.

135 Carlos Emmons Cummings, *East Is East and West Is West* (Buffalo, N.Y.: Buffalo Society of Natural Sciences, 1940), 114-115.

Sources on "Races of Mankind" include Tracy Lang Teslow, Representing Race to the Public: Physical Anthropology in Interwar American Natural History Museums (unpublished doctoral dissertation, University of Chicago, 2002); Willard L. Boyd, "Museums as Centers of Controversy," *Daedalus*, summer 1999, 213-214; and Marianne B. Kinkel, Circulating Race: Malvina Hoffman and the Field Museum's Races of Mankind Sculptures (unpublished doctoral dissertation, University of Texas at Austin, 2001); see pp. 140-146.

"Eastern Museums Circuit Saint Paul National Security Exhibit," *The Museum News*, Dec. 1 1941, 1.

136 "Airways to Peace" discussed in Staniskewski, 227-235.

"Dallas Armistice," *Time*, March 12, 1956, 70.

Eric Sandeen, *Picturing an Exhibition: The Family of Man and 1950s America* (Albuquerque: University of New Mexico Press, 1995), 39. "Aperture Sums Up Family," *New York Times*, July 24, 1955.

"Family of Man" toured the world through a program of United States Information Agency (USIA). Sources include *The Family of Man* exhibition catalogue (New York: Museum of Modern Art, 1955); John Anderson, "The Family of Man: Rudolph's Setting for a Photography Show," *Interiors*, April 1955, 114-117; Leon Anthony Arkus, "The Family of Man," *Carnegie Magazine*, November 1956, 297; Jacob Deschin, "Mankind in Pictures," *New York Times*, Sept. 21, 1952; Deschin, "Steichen Reports," *New York Times*, Dec. 14, 1952; Deschin, "Pictures Wanted," *New York Times*, Jan. 31, 1954; Deschin, "Panoramic Show Opens at Modern Museum, *New York Times*, Jan. 30, 1955; Deschin, "Family's Last Day," *New York Times*, May 8, 1955; Dorothy Grafly, "The Weathervane—Camera, Friend or Foe?" *American Artist*, May 1955, 32; Aline Saarinen, "The Camera Versus the Artist," *New York Times*, Feb. 6, 1955; Ben Shahn, "Art Versus the Camera," *New York Times*, Feb. 13, 1955; and Jonathan Weinberg, "The Family of Steiglitz and Steichen," *Art in America*, September 2001, n.p.

138 Terry Zeller, "From National Service to Social Protest: American Museums in the 1940s, '50s, '60s, and '70s," *Museum News*, March/April 1996, 52. Louis C. Jones, *The Farmers' Museum* (Cooperstown, N.Y.: New York State Historical Association, 1948).

139 "Restaurants, movie theaters. . . ." discussed in David Halberstam, *The Fifties* (New York: Villard Books, 1993), 185.

John Crosby, "What in the World," *New York Herald Tribune*, June 20, 1952, accessed on www.upenn.edu/Games/whatintheworldreview, June 2004. Rerun clips are also available on this website.

Robert Dierbeck, "Television and the Museum," *Curator* 1, no. 2, 34-44. See also Zeller, "From National Service to Social Protest," 54.

140 Dierbeck, 34. Ernest T. Luhde, "Television and the Museum," *The Museum News*, Feb. 1, 1951, 7.

"Recorded Gallery Tours Succeed at St. Paul," *The Museum News*, Feb. 15, 1942, 1. "Acoustiguide will never take the place of a well-trained docent," full-page ad on page 10 of *Museum News*, September 1963.

Bruno Gebhard, "Art and Science in a Health Museum," *Bulletin of the Medical Library Association* 33, no. 1 (January 1945), 39-49. See also "The Development of the Health Museum," *Museum News* 43, 6 (1965).

141 "Thank you for the Heart exhibit. . . ." from personal communication with Joel Bloom, former director, The Franklin Institute, and Ann Mintz.

Halberstam, x-xi. Lothar P. Witteborg, "Design Standard in Museum Exhibitions," *Curator* 1, no. 1 (January 1958), 29. Salinger, 120-121. W. Eugene Smith, *Popular Photography*, 1959, n.p.

America in the 1960s described in Halberstam, xi.

Alexander Girard quoted in Henry H. Glassie, *The Spirit of Folk Art: The Girard Collection* (New York: Henry N. Abrams, 1995), 17.

Allan Kaprow quoted in *Art in Theory, 1900-2000*, Charles Harrison and Paul Wood, eds. (Malden, Mass: Blackwell Publishing, 2003), 718. Robert Smithson, "Cultural Containment," reprinted in Harrison and Wood, 970-971.

142 Radical installations discussed in Brian O'Doherty, "The Gallery As Gesture," in *Thinking about Exhibitions*, Reesa Greenberg, et. al., eds. (London: Routledge, 1995), 334-340. Emily Wasserman, "Review," *Artforum*, September 1969, 56-62. Maurice Berger, *Fred Wilson: Objects and Installation* (Baltimore: Center for Art and Visual Culture, 2001), 22.

143 Bob Reardon and Jack Lambie, "Mathematics on Exhibition," *Museum News*, June 1961, 14-17. "The Work of Charles and Ray Eames: A Legacy of Invention," pamphlet from an exhibition about the Eameses organized by the Library of Congress. The exhibition traveled from 1999 to 2000. Jay Rounds, personal interview, March 2004.

145 Sources about the Exploratorium include copies of grants and news articles in the Exploratorium's archives and in-person interviews conducted by Jessica Strick in fall 2003 with Exploratorium staff members Ron Hipschman, Kathleen McLean, Peter Richards and Larry Shaw. The quotes are drawn from Frank Oppenheimer, "A Rationale for a Science Museum," *Curator*, November 1968, and *The Exploratorium, Special Issue*, March 1985 (dedicated to the memory of Frank Oppenheimer).

Elaine Heumann Gurian, "Noodling Around with Exhibition Opportunities," in *Exhibiting Cultures: The Poetics and Politics of Museum Display*, Ivan Karp and Steven Lavine, eds. (Washington, D.C.: Smithsonian Institution Press, 1991), 179.

146 Oppenheimer, "Exhibit Conception and Design," presented in Monterey, Mexico, at the International Commission on Science Museums, 1980.

147 Donald Garfield, "Interview with Michael Spock," *Museum News* 72, no. 6 (1993), 34-35, 58-60. Herminia Weishin Din, "A History of Children's Museums in the U.S., 1899-1997: Implications for Art Education and Museum Education in Art Museums," Ph.D. dissertation, Ohio State University, 1998. Vanessa Anne Van Orden, "Blazing New Trails: Community, Cultural and Age Issues in Children's Museums, 1968 to the Present" (undergraduate thesis, Wellesley College, 2000). Other sources include the author's conversations with Leslie Bedford, Elaine Heumann Gurian, Signe Hanson, Janet Kamien, Michael Sand, Dan Spock and Michael Spock over many years, as well her employment at BCM from 1986 to 1991.

148 Telephone interview with Michael Sand, Feb. 23, 2004.

Caryl Marsh, quoted in Wendy Pollock, "Discovery Rooms: An Alternative Experience of the Museum," *ASTC Dimensions*, November/December 1999, 9-11. See also Judith White, *Snakes, Snails and History Tails* (Washington, D.C.: Smithsonian Institution Office of Education, 1991).

Jeri Robinson and Patricia Quinn, *PLAYSPACE: Creating Family Spaces in Public Places* (Boston: Boston Children's Museum, 1984).

149 Garfield, "Interview with Michael Spock," 34-35.

For more on the Anacostia Museum, see "Drop-In Museums," *Museum News*, January 1967, 6; John R. Kinard and Esther Nighbert, "The Anacostia Neighborhood Museum," *Museum* 24, no. 2, 1972, 102-109; John R. Kinard, "The Neighborhood Museum as a Catalyst for Social Change," *Museum* 37, no. 4, 1985, 217-221; and Michele Gates Moresi, Exhibiting Race, Creating Nation: Representations of Black History and Culture at the Smithsonian Institution, 1895-1976 (unpublished Ph.D. dissertation, The George Washington University, 2003).

150 Thomas Hoving, *Making Mummies Dance* (New York: Simon & Schuster, 1993), 164-165.

Ellison was citing a sociological study by Nathan Glazer and Patrick Moynihan. Her footnote had been removed by the exhibition's organizer, Allon Schoener.

For more on the public reaction to "Harlem on My Mind," see Steven C. Dubin, *Displays of Power: Memory and Amnesia in the American Museum* (New York: New York University Press, 1999), 18-63; and Allon Schoener, ed., *Harlem on My Mind: Cultural Capital of Black America*, (New York: The New Press, 1995).

151 Joseph Veach Noble, "Drug Scene in New York," *Museum News* (November 1971), 10-15. See also Joseph Veach Noble, "Controversial Exhibitions and Censorship," *Curator* 38 no. 2, 1995, 75-77.

152 *Treasures of Tutankhamun*, exhibition catalogue (New York: Metropolitan Museum of Art, 1976); "Dummies for Mummies," *ARTnews*, November 1978; Sylvia Hochfield, "Egyptomania in New York," *ARTnews*, December 1978, 45-49; Hoving, 401-414.

153 Herbert Muschamp, "Crowds and Power," *The New Republic*, April 12, 1993, 38. Victoria Alexander, *Museums and Money: The Impact of Funding on Exhibitions, Scholarship and Management* (Bloomington: Indiana University, 1996), 47. Victor Danilov, "Corporate Sponsorship of Museum Exhibits," *Curator* 31, no. 3, 1988, 219.

"King Tut Returns," brochure from the Los Angeles County Museum of Art, December 2004.

154 ". . . aesthetic smorgasbords. . ." from Elaine Heumann Gurian, "Noodling Around with Exhibition Opportunities," in Karp and Lavine, 180.

A. Lewin, "Children's Museums: A Structure for Family Learning," *Hand to Hand* 3, 1989, 16. Association of Children's Museums, www.childrensmuseums.org, accessed October 2005.

The Exploratorium, *Looking at the Light*, exhibition catalogue (Washington, D.C.: Association of Science and Technology Centers, 1981).

Randi Korn, personal conversation.

155 Janet Kamien, "In the Eye of the Beholder," in *Transforming Practice: Selections from the Journal of Musems Education, 1992-1999*, Joanne S. Hirsch and Lois H. Silverman, eds. (Washington, D.C.: Museum Education Roundtable, 2000), 126-131.

Peter Sterling, "Peter Sterling Discusses Youth Museums as Agents of Change," *Hand to Hand* 1, no. 3 (1987), 4. Dana Sheridan, A Decade and a Half of Hand to Hand: The Emergent Identity of Children's Museums (unpublished paper, University of Virginia, 2002).

"Scholars urged natural history museums. . . ." Haraway, "Teddy Bear Patriarchy." In *Stuffed Animals and Pickled Heads* (p. 46) Stephen T. Asma writes that the grizzly bear diorama at the Field Museum "shows a mama bear snuggling her baby bear while papa protects them. . . . In reality of course, the female bear would have driven the father away in order to protect her cub from him." Boyd, "Museums as Centers of Controversy," 212.

Books that document the social critique of exhibitions include: Douglas Crimp, *On the Museum's Ruins* (Cambridge, Mass.: MIT Press, 1995); Dubin, *Displays of Power*; Karp and Lavine, eds., *Exhibiting Cultures*; Timothy Luke, *Shows of Force: Power, Politics, and Ideology in Art Exhibitions* (Durham, N.C.: Duke University Press, 1992); Sally Price, *Primitive Art in Civilized Places* (Chicago: University of Chicago Press, 1989); and Alan Wallach, *Exhibiting Contradiction: Essays on the Art Museum in the United States* (Amherst, Mass.: University of Massachusetts Press, 1998).

158 For more about scholars who influenced the changing approaches to exhibition design see Pierre Bourdieu, *Distinction: A Social Critique of the Judgement of Taste* (Cambridge: Harvard University Press, 1984); Jerome Bruner, *Actual Minds, Possible Worlds* (Cambridge, Mass: Harvard University Press, 1986); Mihaly Csikszentmihalyi, *Flow: The Psychology of Optimal Experience* (Perennial Books, 1991); John Falk and Lynn Dierking, *The Museum Experience* (Washington, D.C.; Whalesback Books, 1992); Howard Gardner, *Frames of Mind: The Theory of Multiple Intelligences* (New York: Basic Books, 1983); George Hein, *Learning in the Museum* (London: Routledge, 1998); Jessica Davis and Howard Gardner, "Open Windows, Open Doors, " in *The Educational Role of the Museum*, 2d ed., Eilean Hooper-Greenhill, ed. (London: Routledge, 1999), 99-104; Lois Silverman, "Visitor Meaning-Making in Museums for a New Age," *Curator* 38, no. 3 (1995), 161-70, and "Making Meaning Together: Lessons from the Field of American History," reprinted in Hirsch and Silverman, 230-238.

"Wolves and Humans" discussed by Lonnie Broden and Dick Leerhoff, telephone interview, March 2004, and Curt Hadland, e-mail exchanges, March and April 2004.

159 Aldona Jonaitis, "Chiefly Feasts: The Creation of an Exhibition," in *The Enduring Kwakiutl Potlach*, Aldona Jonaitis, ed. (Seattle: University of Washington, 1991), 21-23.

160 "Inviting environments" discussed in Lisa Roberts, *From Knowledge to Narrative: Educators and the Changing Museum* (Washington, D.C.: Smithsonian Institution Press, 1997), 71. See Margie Maynard, "Collecting Their Thoughts," *Museum News*, May/June 2004, 38-41; and Salwa Mikdadi Nashashibi, Visitor-written labels in U.S. Art Museums (unpublished master's project, John F. Kennedy University, Berkeley, 2002). Patterson Williams, quoted in Bonnie Pitman and Ellen Hirzy, *New Forums: Art Museums & Communities* (Washington, D.C.: American Association of Museums, 2004), 142.

For more on the Getty's Interactive Gallery, see Wade Richards and Margaret Menniger, "A Discovery Room for Adults," *Journal of Museum Education* 18, no. 1 (winter 1993), 6-11.

161 Digital technology in museums discussed in Marjorie Schwarzer, "Art & Gadgetry: The Future of the Museum Visit," *Museum News*, July/August 2001, 36-41, 68-69. See p. 73 for survey conducted by Mandy Smith.

Spencer R. Crew, *Field to Factory: Afro-American Migration 1915-1940* (Washington, D.C.: Department of Public Programs, National Museum of American History, Smithsonian Institution, 1987) and Spencer R. Crew and James E. Sims, "Locating Authenticity: Fragments of a Dialog," in Karp and Lavine, 159-175.

162 Selma Thomas, quoted in Ron Chew, "Collected Stories," *Museum News*, November/December 2002, 32.

Jeshahahu Weinberg, quoted in John Strand, "Jeshajahu Weinberg of the U.S. Holocaust Memorial Museum," *Museum News*, March/April 1993, 43.

163 Paul Martin, personal communication.

Barbara Franco, quoted in Ron Chew, "Collected Stories," *Museum News*, November/December 2002, 35.

Dan Spock, personal communication.

164 Joseph Veach Noble: "The Museum of Ideas," *Museum News*, October 1980, 21.

Challenges facing curators discussed in Julia M. Klein, "The Embattled Curator," *The American Prospect* 12, no. 14 (August 13, 2001), n.p.; John Killacky, lecture given at the Getty Center, Los Angeles, April 23, 2004, and subsequent personal communication with author; and Nancy Villa Bryk, "Reports of our Death Have Been Greatly Exaggerated: Reconsidering the Curator," *Museum News*, March/April 2001, 40.

See also Lisa Roberts, "Educators on Exhibit Teams: A New Role, A New Era," in Hirsch and Silverman, 89-97. Jay Rounds and Nancy McIlvaney, "Who's Using the Team Process? How's It Going?" *Exhibitionist*, spring 2000, 3-7.

165 Edward Rothstein, "Who Should Tell History: The Tribes or the Museums," *New York Times*, Dec. 21, 2004, n.p.

See Mary Panzer: "Panning the West as America: Or Why One Exhibition Did Not Strike Gold," *Radical History*, winter 1992, 105-113; "Showdown at The West as America Exhibition," *American Art*, summer 1991, 2-11; and Alice Thorson, "Myths Made Manifest," *New Art Examiner*, October 1991, 16-19.

166 Kathleen McLean, "The Museum as Muse: Artists Reflect," exhibition review, *Curator* 42, no. 3, 253-255.

See Lawrence Wechsler, *Mr. Wilson's Cabinet of Wonder* (New York: Pantheon Books, 1995) and Ralph Rugoff, "Beyond Belief: The Museum as Metaphor," in Robert Mangurian and Mary-Ann Ray, *Wrapper: 40 Possible City Surfaces for the Museum of Jurassic Technology* (San Francisco: William Stout Publishers, 1999), 99-103.

Fred Wilson, quoted in Marlene Chambers, "Critiquing Exhibition Criticism," *Museum News*, September/October 1999, 37. Berger, *Fred Wilson*. See also Lisa Corrin, "Mining the Museum," *Curator* 36, no. 4 (1993), 302-313; Judith E. Stein, "Sins of Omission," *Art in America*, October 1993, 110-115; and Fred Wilson and Lisa G. Corrin, *Mining the Museum* (New York: New Press, March 1994).

167 Neil Kotler, "Delivering Experience," *Museum News*, May/June 1999, 30-38, 58-61.

169 Kathleen McLean, *Planning for People in Museum Exhibitions* (Washington, D.C.: Association of Science and Technology Centers, 1993), 115.

Notes to pages 171-217

171 Terry Zeller, "Arthur C. Parker: A Pioneer in American Museums," *Curator* 30, no. 1 (March 1987).

Andrew Nelson, "Insider's Charleston," *National Geographic Traveler*, September 2005; www.nationalgeographic.com, accessed Oct. 13, 2005. Louise Anderson Allen, *A Bluestocking in Charleston: The Life and Career of Laura Bragg* (Columbia, S.C.: University of South Carolina Press, 2001); Linda Downs's review of *A Bluestocking in Charleston* in *Museum News*, May/June 2002, 28; and Stephanie E. Yuhl, *The Making of Historic Charleston: A Golden Haze of Memory* (Chapel Hill, N.C., and London: University of North Carolina Press, 2005).

172 "The public response . . ." in John Cotton Dana, "An Industrial Exhibit in a Municipal Museum," *The New Museum: Selected Writings by John Cotton Dana* (Washington, D.C.: American Association of Museums and the Newark Museum, 1999), 154.

173 Museums are "intensely human institutions . . ." in Lewis Wingfield Story, *The Denver Art Museum: The First Hundred Years* (Denver: Denver Art Museum, 1996), 75.

Richard Norton, "Training For Curators," letter to the editor, *The Nation*, Aug. 8, 1907, 119.

174 G. Brown Goode, *The Museums of the Future* (Washington, D.C.: Smithsonian, 1891), 445.

175 Thomas W. Leavitt, "The Beleaguered Director," in *Museums in Crisis* (New York: George Braziller, 1972), 94.

Zeller, "Arthur C. Parker," 41-62.

176 For more biographical information on Dana, see Edward Alexander, *Museum Masters: Their Museums and Their Influence* (Nashville: American Association of State and Local History, 1982), 379-407. Dana's comments in *The New Museum: Selected Writings by John Cotton Dana*: "How Museums and Schools May Aid Good Workmanship," 189. "Should Museums Be Useful," 144.

177 John Cotton Dana, *The New Museum* (Woodstock, Vt., Elm Street Press, 1917), 27.

The founding director of the San Francisco Museum of Modern Art was Grace McCann Morley. Morley was also active in the establishment of UNESCO and the International Committee of Museums (ICOM). The first director of the Whitney Museum of American Art was Julianne Force, a close friend of its founder Gertrude Vanderbilt Whitney. For more on Erna Gunther, see Lenore Zionitz, "Erna Gunther and Social Activism: Profits and Loss for a State Museum," *Curator* 29/4 (December 1986), 307-315.

178 Hilla Rebay von Ehrenwiesen discussed in Milton Lomask, *Seed Money: The Guggenheim Story* (New York: Farrar, Straus and Company, 1964).

For more on 1920s "friends" groups at the Cleveland Museum of Art and other museums see Judith Higgins Balfe and Thomas A. Cassilly, "Friends of Arts Institutions," in *Paying the Piper: Causes and Consequences of Art Patronage,* Judith Higgins Balfe, ed. (Urbana and Chicago: University of Illinois Press, 1993).

179 For a discussion of Sachs's work, see Janet Tassel, "Reverence for the Object," *Harvard Magazine*, September/October 2002, 48-58, 98; and Sally Anne Duncan, Paul J. Sachs and the Institutionalization of Museum Culture between the World Wars, doctoral dissertation, Tufts University, 2001. See also Kathryn Brush, "Marburg and Harvard: Purpose Built Architecture for Art History 1927," in *Art History and Its Institutions*, Elizabeth Mansfield, ed. (New York and London: Routledge, 2002); George M. Goodwin, "A New Jewish Elite: Curators, Directors, and Benefactors of American Art Museums," in *Modern Judaism* 18, nos. 2 and 5 (February and May, 1998), 51-60; and Sybil Gordon Kantor, *Alfred H. Barr, Jr. and the Intellectual Origins of the Museum of Modern Art* (Cambridge, Mass.: MIT Press, 2002), 52-77.

180 Regional organizations were founded in the Midwest (1927), New England (1928), the West (1935), the Mid-Atlantic states (1946), the Southeast (1951) and the Mountain Plains states (1953). Canadians founded their own support group—the Canadian Museums Association—in 1947.

AAM's 1928 *Bibliography of Museums and Museum Work* includes only one article (by John Cotton Dana) discussing the value of public service; most of the other articles focus on taxidermy.

Carnegie-funded museum pamphlets included T. R. Adam's *The Civic Value of Museums* (New York: American Association for Adult Education, 1937) and Paul Marshall Rea, *The Museum and the Community: A Study of Social Laws and Consequences* (Lancaster, Pa.: The Science Press, 1932). While Adam's pamphlet is primarily philosophical, Rea's is an intensive scientific study designed to determine the ideal number of visitors to a museum. Rea compared attendance and population data in the locales of 104 museums; his report was supported by 150 pages of elaborate logarithmic calculations done on slide rule. He concluded that larger museums (most notably the Metropolitan Museum of Art) were less efficient than smaller ones (most notably Rea's former charge, the Charleston Museum). He also accused museums of "insidious decadence" because they were guided by the ideas of donors and trustees, rather than public needs. Another influential report was *The Packard Report*, written by the chair of Dartmouth College's Department of Art and funded by the Rockefellers. The Packard Report was commissioned by the Museum of Modern Art and advocated for the founding of an education department that would be equal in influence to the museum's curatorial departments.

Edward Stevens Robinson, *The Behavior of the Museum Visitor* (Washington, D.C.: American Association of Museums, 1928).

181 In the 1930s, "Carnegie courses," designed for aspiring middle-class collectors, were offered at such places as the Cincinnati Art Museum and the San Francisco Museum of Modern Art.

See also "Keppel Report Points to Changes in Foundation Giving Since 1922," *The Museum News*, Jan. 1, 1942, 1; and Terry Zeller, "From National Service to Social Protest: American Museums in the 1940s, 50s, 60s and 70s," *Museum News*, March/April 1996, 48.

182 Henry L. Ward, quoted in Julie Christianson Stivers, *The Presence of the Past: The Public Museum of Grand Rapids at 150* (Grand Rapids, Mich.: The Public Museum of Grand Rapids, 2004), 19. Ward directed the Milwaukee Public Museum for 18 years, and moved to Grand Rapids in 1922.

"People were hungry . . ." from Howard Zinn, *A People's History of the United States* (New York: The New Press, 1997), 284.

Laurie E. Wertz, "Some Things Never Change," *Museum News*, February 1984, 26-27. Wertz reports on John Price Jones's study of funding at 14 museums from 1920 to 1938. Jones discovered that the museums received $22,664,534 in gifts during the 1920s and $24,781,201 in the 1930s.

183 Ned J. Burns, *Field Manual for Museums* (Washington, D.C.: National Park Service, 1941), 278.

Francis Henry Taylor quoted in "Reminiscences of Holger Cahill," Oral History Office, Columbia University, 1957, 339-340. Cited in Wendy Jeffers, "Holger Cahill and American Art," *Journal of the Archives of American Art* 31, no. 4 (1991) 8-9.

Zinn, 293.

". . . tools of the Communist party . . ." in Don Adams and Arlene Goldbard, "New Deal Cultural Programs: Experiments in Cultural Democracy," 1995 (accessed on www.wwcd.org).

184 "The government's approach . . ." from T. R. Adam, *The Civic Value of Museums* (New York: American Association for Adult Education, 1937), v-vi. Theodore L. Low, *The Museum as a Social Instrument* (New York: Metropolitan Museum of Art, 1942), 34.

185 "Museums of Honolulu Go Through Japanese Air Raids Unharmed," *The Museum News*, Jan. 15, 1942, 1 and 4. "Art Museum Directors Hold New York Meeting on War Emergency," *The Museum News*, Jan. 1, 1942, 1 and 4.

186 Zeller, "From National Service to Social Protest," 48.

In 1954, *Museum News* reported on a survey of 102 museums. City support had increased by two-thirds between 1939 and 1954 and had "probably" doubled between 1944 and 1954. In the fiscal year ending 1953, the surveyed museums had an aggregate operating income of $17 million; city support provided $8.4 million of that amount. See Wertz, "Some Things Never Change," 29.

Frank L. DuMond, quoted in Philip D. Spiess, "Toward a New Professionalism: American Museums in the 1920s and 1930s," *Museum News*, March/April 1996, 47. See also Stiver, *The Presence of the Past*.

Charles G. Wilder, "Exhibiting the Peaceful Atom," *Museum News*, November 1960, 28-33. In 1978, the Oak Ridge museum changed its name to the Museum of Science and Energy.

188 Beginning in 1946 and through the mid-1970s, there were several efforts to found a National Armed Forces Museum in Washington, D.C. See Joanne M. Gernstein London, A Modest Show of Arms: Exhibiting the Armed Forces and the Smithsonian Institution, 1945-76, unpublished doctoral dissertation, George Washington University, 2000.

". . . old boys' network" in Alan Shestack, "The Director: Scholar and Businessman, Educator and Lobbyist," *Museum News*, February 1984, 68. Thomas Hess, "Editorial," *Art News* 65, no. 7 (November 1966), 9.

The new emphasis on female volunteerism is reflected in museum annual reports of the 1950s. In the 1940s, for example, the Walker Art Center was most proud of its patriotic exhibitions such as "Halls of Montezuma." In its 1952 annual report, however, the museum noted that "the importance of the [Volunteer] Council to the Center should be perfectly obvious . . . its contribution to the Walker Art Center has been very great." Cited in John Ludwig, "The Role of the Performing Arts," *Museum News*, January 1967, 40.

189 Gregory Nosan, "Women in the Galleries: Prestige, Education, and Volunteerism at Mid-century," *Museum Education at The Art Institute of Chicago: Museum Studies* 29, no. 1 (2003), 40-71. Mary Naquin Sharp, phone interview, August 2003.

190 In 2003 McCarthy's life would become the subject of an exhibit in his hometown of Appleton, Wis.; the Outagamie County Historical Society's show was titled "Joseph McCarthy: A Modern Tragedy."

See "Dallas Armistice," *Time* LXVII, no. 11 (March 12, 1956), 70; and Francine Carrero, "Red, White and Blue Art," in *Jerry Bywaters: A Life in Art* (Austin, Tex.: University of Texas Press, 1994), 176-202. Jacqueline Allen of the Dallas Museum of Art helped with this research.

191 Milton Esterow, "Goodwin Slated to Get Arts Post," *New York Times*, Nov. 22, 1963, n.p.

192 Lyndon B. Johnson, quoted in Gary B. Nash, *American Odyssey: The United States in the Twentieth Century* (Glencoe, N.Y.: Macmillan/McGraw Hill, 1992), 601.

Victoria D. Alexander, *Museums and Money: The Impact of Funding on Exhibitions, Scholarship and Management* (Bloomington: Indiana University Press, 1996), xi.

NEA's Visual Arts program was run by Rene d'Harnoncourt, former curator at the Museum of Modern Art, with a committee of advisors who included Lloyd Goodrich of the Whitney Museum (an early proponent of federal museum funding), Martin Friedman of the Walker Art Center and Mitchell Wilder of the Amon Carter Museum.

193 George Weissman quoted in Sam Hunter, *Art in Business: The Philip Morris Story* (New York: Harry N. Abrams, Inc., 1979), 9.

The museum directors attending the Belmont conference were: W. D. Frankforter, Grand Rapids Public Museum; Louis C. Jones, New York State Historical Association; Sherman Lee, Cleveland Museum of Art; George E. Lindsay, California Academy of Sciences; Thomas M. Messer, Solomon R. Guggenheim Museum; Charles Parkhurst, Baltimore Museum of Art (and president of the American Association of Museums); H. J. Swinney, Adirondack Museum; Frank A. Taylor, United States National Museum (now National Museum of American History); Evan H. Turner, Philadelphia Museum of Art; Bradford Washburn, Museum of Science, Boston; and E. Leland Webber, Field Museum of Natural History.

Michael W. Robbins, ed., *America's Museums: The Belmont Report* (Washington, D.C.: American Association of Museums, 1969), v.

194 The first museums accredited by the American Association of Museums were the California Academy of Sciences, Natural History Museum of Los Angeles County, Fine Arts Center of Colorado Springs, Museum of Western Colorado, Winterthur Museum, Lock Haven Art Center, Children's Museum of Indianapolis, Mathers Museum of World Cultures, Museum of Science, Boston, Old Sturbridge Village, Spellman Museum of Stamps and Postal History, American Textile History Museum, Peabody Essex Museum, Public Museum of Grand Rapids, Science Museum of Minnesota, St. Joseph Museum, Pony Express Museum, Herbert F. Johnson Museum of Art at Cornell University, New York Botanical Garden, Solomon R. Guggenheim Museum, Portland Art Museum, Oreg., Columbia Museum of Art, Amon Carter Museum, McNay Art Museum, Burke Museum of Natural History and Culture, and Circus World Museum.

". . . upper-class values of trustees . . ." discussed in Grace Glueck, "Power and Aesthetics," *Art in America*, July 1971, 81.

Jay Pridmore, *Inventive Genius: The History of the Museum of Science and Industry* Chicago (Chicago: Museum of Science and Industry, 1996), 126.

The September 1970 edition of *Museum News* describes the disruption at the Waldorf Astoria as follows: "A casually clad individual walked to the speaker's podium and boldly announced that the 'official' theme of the 1970's convention was war, racism, sexism [a term so new at the time that AAM had to define it for its readers] and repression. As he left the stage a small group of protesters was gathering at the sides of the Ballroom and near the entrances. They wore stenciled signs which read 'Art Strike Against War, Racism, Sexism and Repression.' The business meeting was called to order . . . to permit Miss Nancy Hanks to deliver her keynote address. . . . After Miss Hanks' remarks . . . 30 of the demonstrators marched up to the stage and demanded . . . to have their speaker, Ralph Ortiz, director of El Museo del Barrio . . . present his remarks. He harshly accused museums of complicity in the atrocities of our day. . . . The loudspeaker system had been turned off, and apparently disabled. . . . For almost 20 minutes several small groups of artist-protesters argued with, berated and listened to AAM members. . . ."

See David Katzive, "Up Against the Waldorf-Astoria," *Museum News*, September 1970, 12-17. This issue of the magazine also documents reactions to these social protests: "an almost exactly even split between positive and negative responses."

195 John Hightower, "AAM General Session," *Museum News*, September 1970, 20.

Thomas Hess, "Editorial," *Art News* 65, no. 7 (November 1966), 27. See also Arthur Lubow, "The Curse of the Whitney," *New York Times Magazine*, April 11, 1999. For a discussion of how the situation had changed by the late 1990s, see Goodwin, "A New Jewish Elite."

196 Barry Schwartz, "Museums: Art for Who's Sake," *Ramparts* 9, no. 11 (1971), 38-49.

For more on women in the museum field, see Kendall Taylor, "Room at the Top," *Museum News*, June 1984, 31-37.; the entire issue of *Museum News*, February 1985, including Kendall Taylor, "Risking It: Women as Museum Leaders," (20-32); "Women in Museums: A Progress Report," *Museum News*, March/April 1997, 34-41; and Jane R. Glaser and Artemis A. Zenetou, eds., *Gender Perspectives: Essays on Women in Museums* (Washington, D.C.: Smithsonian Institution Press, 1994).

Glass ceiling discussed in "You've Come a Long Way Baby," *Museum News*, June 1972.

Susan Stitt, "The Search for Equality," *Museum News*, September/October 1975, 17-23. See also her comments in Glaser and Zenetou, *Gender Perspectives*, 149-152.

Eileen Dribin, "Museums Get a Taste of PASTA," *Museum News*, June 1972, 21-26.

Sophy Burnam, *The Art Crowd* (New York: David McKay, Inc. 1973), 221.

197 Azade Ardali, *Black and Hispanic Art Museums: A Vibrant Cultural Resource* (New York: Ford Foundation, 1989). In the introduction Mary Schmidt Campbell identifies two waves of black and Hispanic museums. The first, she claims, were tangible responses to the civil rights movement and include the DuSable Museum in Chicago (1961), the Studio Museum in Harlem (1967) and El Museo del Barrio in New York City (1969). Their success in garnering city and state support led to a second wave during the 1970s. Campbell foresaw that in the 21st century black and Hispanic museums would become more global in their approach, exhibiting and collecting the international influences on their cultures and communities.

Michael Whitney Straight, *Nancy Hanks: An Intimate Portrait* (Durham, N.C.: Duke University Press, 1988).

198 Mark Steyn, "The Imperfect Spy: Michael Straight (1916-2004)," *Atlantic Monthly*, March 2004, 46-47.

Sponsoring the Museum Services Act with Brademas were Sens. Claiborne Pell (R.I.) and Jacob Javits (N.Y.), and Reps. Frank Thompson (N.J.) and Dan Rostenkowski (Ill.), who was persuaded that museums had a positive economic impact on his Chicago district by Field Museum Director E. Leland Webber.

". . . a great release valve . . ." in Livingston L. Biddle, Jr., *Our Government and the Arts: A Perspective from the Inside* (New York: ACA Books, 1988), 296-297. Biddle, an aide to Sen. Pell, sat through nearly every minute of the hearings; he later succeeded Hanks as head of the NEA.

199 "Insuring Exhibits from Abroad," *Museum News*, May/June 1976, 25.

President Ford told this story to Timothy Chester, director of the Public Museum of Grand Rapids, in 1994. Personal communication, 2003.

For a perspective on IMS's founding, see Lee Kimche McGrath, "The ASTC Legacy and the Institute of Museum Services," *Curator* 38, no. 2 (July 1995), 79-86.

In an interview with the author on July 2, 2003, NSF Division Head George Tressel explained how he landed at the National Science Foundation: "In 1972, Guy Stever, former president of Carnegie Mellon University, took over the NSF. His first idea was to use government funds to conduct more in-depth research on why America was losing its edge and ordinary citizens shied away from science. I was working in Columbus, Ohio, at the time producing educational science films. When I heard Stever's 'ivory tower approach' to science education, I was shocked. I shot off a nasty letter to Washington that said something like '. . . you think understanding science means working in a lab and wearing a white coat. To the average person, science means understanding how their car runs. What makes you think this is going to change? Some damned study that says the same thing over and over again?' I was even more shocked at Stever's response: a one-way ticket to Washington, D.C., and a job at NSF with the mandate of developing real programs that excited a wide audience." See also George Tressel, "Thirty Years of 'Improvement' in Precollege Math and Science Education," *Journal of Science Education and Technology* 3, no. 2 (1994), 77-88.

200 "What Is the American Tradition in the Visual and Performing Arts?" *American Artist* 46, no. 474 (January 1982).

Nancy Hanks, "Foreword," in *Museums in Crisis*, Brian O'Doherty, ed. (New York: George Braziller, 1972), viii.

For more information on the development of museum studies programs, see William J. Tramposch, "A Companion to Change: The Seminar for Historical Administration, 1959-1984," *Museum Studies Journal*, fall 1984, 8-18; Philip D. Spiess II, "Museum Studies: Are They Doing Their Job?" *Museum News*, November/December 1996, 32-40; Candace Tangorra Matelic and Elizabeth Marie Brick, eds., *Cooperstown Conference on Professional Training, Conference Proceedings, November 16-19, 1989* (Nashville: American Association of State and Local History, 1990) and the April 1969 issue of *Museum News*.

Training programs include the American Legal Institution/American Bar Association's annual course on museum law (1973-present) and the Museum Management Institute, now the Getty Leadership Institute (1979-present). Influential publications of the era include Ellis Burcaw's *Introduction to Museum Work* (1975); *The Exploratorium Cookbooks* (1976), Helmut J. Naumer's *Of Mutual Respect and Other Things: An Essay on Museum Trusteeship* (1977), Barbara Newsom and Adele Silver's *The Art Museum as Educator* (1978) and Edward Alexander's classic text on museum history, *Museums in Motion* (1979).

Kenneth Starr, "A Perspective on Our Profession," *Museum News*, May/June 1980, 21-23. See also Raymond August, "So You Want to Start Your Own Profession! Fable, Fulfillment or Fallacy?" *Museum Studies Journal*, fall 1983, 16-24.

201 E. Leland Webber, "Government Relations and Legal Snares," *Museum News*, April 1983, 15.

Museum Ethics (Washington, D.C.: American Association of Museums, 1978). Funding for the publication was provided by the Rockefeller Brothers Fund.

202 Patricia Ullberg, "What Happened in Greenville: The Need for Museum Codes of Ethics," *Museum News*, November/December 1981, 26-29. I want to thank David Crosson for bringing this case to my attention. For more information on the evolution of AAM's ethical codes, see Robert R. Macdonald, "A Question of Ethics," *Curator* 37, no. 1 (1994), 6-9, and Alan J. Friedman, "Why Did the 1991 Code of Ethics Fail?" *Curator* 37, no. 1 (1994), 9-11; Hugh Genoways and Lynne Ireland, *Museum Administration: An Introduction* (Walnut Creek, Calif.: AltaMira Press, 2003), 223-240; and Hilde S. Hein, *The Museum in Transition: A Philosophical Perspective* (Washington, D.C.: Smithsonian Institution Press, 2000), 93-98.

Lee Rosenbaum, "The Scramble for Museum Sponsors: Is Curatorial Independence for Sale?" *Art in America*, January/February 1977, 10-14.

George Weissman's comments on "Two Hundred Years of American Indian Art," quoted in Hunter, *Art in Business*, 70.

203 Timothy W. Luke, "Hans Haacke: Unfinished Business," in *Shows of Force: Power, Politics and Ideology in Art Exhibitions* (Durham, N.C.: Duke University Press, 1992), 152-168.

Ronald Reagan, quoted in "Candidates' Views on Arts Spending," *State of the Arts* (Sacramento: California Arts Council, October 1980).

Museum advertisements discussed in Sondra J. Thorson, "The Changing Art of Museum Communication," *Museum News*, June 1986, 61-65.

Rep. Yates discussed in Ruth Dean, "Cultural Programs under Reagan: A Look at Midterm," *Museum News*, April 1983, 28-34.

204 Museums' contributions to local regions discussed in *National Endowment for the Arts, Economic Impact of Arts and Cultural Institutions* (New York: The Publishing Center for Cultural Resources, 1981). The study looked at six communities: Columbus, Ohio; Minneapolis/St. Paul; St. Louis; Salt Lake City; San Antonio; and Springfield, Ill..

NSF funds discussed in Tressel, "Thirty Years of 'Improvement' in Precollege Math and Science Education," 79-80.

205 Personal interview with George Tressel, July 2003.

Michael Useem, "Corporate Support for Culture and the Arts," in M.J. Wyszomirski and P. Chubb, eds., *The Cost of Culture* (New York: American Council for the Arts, 1989), 53.

"There's not much P.R. . . ." from Meta Overmeyer, Primerica Foundation, quoted in Lorraine Glennon, "Museum and the Corporation: New Realities," *Museum News*, January/February 1988, 39.

Joseph Veach Noble, "The Megashows Are Coming," *Curator* 30, no. 1, July 1987, 5-10.

206 Corporate sponsorships vs. blatant advertising discussed in Genoways and Ireland, *Museum Administration*, 131.

J. Carter Brown, "The Business of Creating a Partnership," *Museum News*, January/February 1988, 44.

American Family Association website, www.afa.net, accessed in January 2006.

"Cultural historians and artists. . . ." See James Deetz, "A Sense of Another World: History Museums and Cultural Change," *Museum News*, May/June 1980, and Lonnie G. Bunch, "Fighting the Good Fight," *Museum News* March/April 1995, 33.

Donald Wildmon, quoted in Joan Karen Selna, Cultural War: The Defeat of the Helms Amendment, unpublished master's thesis, San Jose State University, 1997, 36.

207 Richard Meyer, *Outlaw Representation: Censorship and Homosexuality in Twentieth-Century American Art* (London: Oxford University Press, 2002), 207. See also Nancy Einreinhofer, *The American Art Museum: Elitism and Democracy* (London: Leicester University Press, 1997), 74.

Kim Masters and Elizabeth Kastor, "NEA Advisors Kill 2 Grants, Defer 18: Action Called a Response to Endowment's Critics," *Washington Post*, May 14, 1990, B6. "A Summer of Discontent over Federal Arts Funding," *Museum News*, November/December 1989, 10-11. Pat Robertson, "To the Congress of the United States," *Washington Post* advertisement, June 20, 1990, A18. "George Bush on Record," *Museum News*, September/October 1992, 46.

Isabel Wilkerson, "Trouble Right Here in Cincinnati: Furor Over Mapplethorpe Exhibit," *New York Times*, May 29, 1990, A1. Dennis Barrie, "Fighting an Indictment: My Life with Robert Mapplethorpe," *Museum News*, July/August 1990, 63- 64.

208 Grace Glueck, "Publicity Is Enriching Mapplethorpe Estate," *New York Times*, April 16, 1990, C13.

The Newport Harbor Art Museum was no stranger to controversy. In 1988 the *Los Angeles Times* reported that a principal canceled a fourth-grade field trip to the museum because he thought an Eric Fischl painting of a nude teenage girl was too sexually graphic. See Allan Jalon, "Drawing the Line: Educators and Parents Worry Students May Learn the Wrong Lessons at Museums," *Los Angeles Times*, Feb. 14, 1988, 45A.

209 Lynne V. Cheney, *Telling the Truth* (New York: Simon and Schuster, 1995), 144-152.

The revisionist art historical approach used to develop "The West as America" was widely discussed in the 1990s. In addition to articles in the major newspapers, see Steven C. Dubin, *Displays of Power: Memory and Amnesia in the American Museum* (New York: New York University Press), 152-185; "Showdown at 'The West As America' Exhibition, *American Art*, summer 1991, 2-11; Paul Mattick, Jr., "At the Waterhole," *Arts Magazine*, October 1991, 20-23; Mary Panzer, "Panning 'The West As America': or, Why One Exhibition Did Not Strike Gold," *Radical History Review*, winter 1992, 105-122; B. Byron Price, "Field Notes: 'Cutting for Sign': Museums and Western Revisionism," *The Western Historical Quarterly* (May 1993), 230-234; Alice Thorson, "Myths Made Manifest," *New Art Examiner*, October 1991, 16-19; Alan Trachtenberg, "Contesting the West," *Art in America*, September 1991, 118-123, 152; and Alan Wallach, "The Battle over 'The West as America,'" in *Exhibiting Contradiction* (Amherst: University of Massachusetts Press, 1998), 105-117.

The controversy around the *Enola Gay* has been extensively documented and analyzed. This account is distilled from the following sources: Martin Harwit, *An Exhibit Denied: Lobbying the History of the Enola Gay* (New York: Springer-Verlag, 1996); the Air Force Association website: www.afa.org; Richard H. Kohn, "History and the Culture Wars: The Case of the Smithsonian Institution's Enola Gay Exhibition," *The Journal of American History*, December 1995; Wilcomb B. Washburn, "The Smithsonian and the Enola Gay," *The National Interest*, summer 1995; Philip Nobile, ed., *Judgement at the Smithsonian* (New York: Marlowe & Company, 1995); Steve Lubar, "Exhibiting Memories" in Amy Henderson and Adrienne Kaeppler, eds., *Exhibiting Dilemmas: Issues of Representation at the Smithsonian* (Washington, D.C.: Smithsonian Institution Press, 1997); and Thomas F. Gieryn, "Balancing Acts," in Sharon Macdonald, ed., *The Politics of Display: Museums, Science, Culture* (London and New York, Routledge, 1998), 197-228.

210 John T. Correll, "War Stories at the Air and Space Museum," *Air Force Magazine*, April 1994, 29.

211 IMLS grants to museums discussed in "True Needs, True Partners: Museums and Schools Transforming Education," Ellen Cochran Hirzy, ed. (Washington, D.C.: Institute of Museum Services, 1996).

212 Leslie Buhler, "The Business of Membership," *Museum News*, November/December, 1980, 42-49.

213 Led by Joel N. Bloom, director of Philadelphia's Franklin Institute, and Earl A. Powell III, director of the Los Angeles County Museum of Art, and incorporating the input of hundreds of museum professionals, *Museums for a New Century* documented the "expanding museum universe" and called on museums to play an increased educational role in their locales. Chaired by Bonnie Pitman, deputy director of what is now the Berkeley Art Museum, *Excellence and Equity: Education and the Public Dimension of Museums* went a step

further. As articulated by a taskforce of 25 museum leaders, it was a call to action, declaring that education and public service should be central to museums' missions and that museums should become more inclusive places that welcome diverse audiences.

M. Christine DeVita, "President's Essay," Wallace Foundation Annual Report 2000, 8.

In 1953, J. Paul Getty established a small museum in the Los Angeles area. When most of Getty's personal estate passed to a trust in 1982, its assets were so great that in addition to financing a new museum and center, the trust's board distributed tens of millions of dollars to such museums as the Southwest Museum (for an exhibition of Pueblo and Navajo textiles), the Skirball Museum (to bring an exhibition about Sigmund Freud to the West Coast) and the Center for the Study of Political Graphics (to catalogue 34,000 posters). Source: the J. Paul Getty Trust 1998-99 Annual Report.

For more on the Pew's initiative, see Bonnie Pitman and Ellen Hirzy, *New Forums: Art Museums & Communities* (Washington, D.C.: American Association of Museums, 2004).

The Wallace Foundation projects are documented in three reports: "Service to People: Challenges and Rewards" (2000), "Engaging the Entire Community: A New Role for Permanent Collections" (1999), and "Opening the Door to the Entire Community: How Museums Are Using Permanent Collections to Engage Audiences" (1998).

David Samuels, "The Failure of American Foundations: Philanthropical Correctness," *The New Republic*, Sept. 18 and 25, 1995.

". . . truly collaborating with audiences . . ." from Sarah Schulz, quoted in Pitman and Hirzy, *New Forums*, 142.

214 Courtney Spousta, Culture, Cocktails, Mingling, Meeting: The Phenomenon of Art after Hours Programming, unpublished master's project, John F. Kennedy University, Berkeley, Calif., 2000.

215 Thomas Krens, quoted in Tassel, "Reverence for the Object," 57.

Judith H. Dobrzynski, "'Sensation' Gone but Still Provocative," *New York Times*, Feb. 14, 2000, n.p.

216 Marjorie Schwarzer, "Turnover at the Top: Are Directors Burning Out?" *Museum News*, May/June 2002, 42-49, 67-69.

John Hopkins University study on museum finances discussed in "Listening Post Project Hears Coping Strategies," *Aviso*, March 2004, 2.

Robert R. Macdonald, "9/11: The World Transformed," *Museum News*, November/December 2001, 37.

ABOUT THE AUTHOR

245

Marjorie Schwarzer is professor and chair of the Department of Museum Studies at John F. Kennedy University, Berkeley, Calif. She was previously director of education at the Chicago Children's Museum and associate director of development at the Children's Museum in Boston. Schwarzer is the author of numerous articles on the museum field, including such topics as airport museums, architecture, visitor services, exhibitions and multiculturalism. She holds a B.A. in art history from Washington University in St. Louis and an M.B.A. from the University of California, Berkeley.

INDEX

Italic numbers indicate a caption.

Giuliani, Rudolph, 216

Goldberger, Paul, 46

Goode, George Brown, 174, 200

Goodrich, B. F., *35*

Goodwin, Phillip, 41–42

Grand Rapids Art Museum, Michigan *198*

grassroots museums, 105

Graves, Michael, *52, 53*

Great Depression, 14–15, 40, 182

green architecture, 64–65

Greenfield Village, Dearborn, Michigan, *38, 39, 39,* 40, 110–111, 164

Greenville County Museum of Art, South Carolina, 202

Grunfeld, Ernest Jr., 36

Guatemala, art thefts, 98

Guggenheim, Peggy, *76, 77*

Guggenheim, Solomon R., 43, 215

Guggenheim Museum, Bilbao, 59

Guggenheim Museum, Las Vegas, 62–63

Guggenheim Museum, New York, 41, 42–43, *42, 47, 57, 178, 215*

Guldbeck, Per, 138

Gunther, Erna, 177

Gurian, Elaine Heumann, 119, 145

▪ H ▪ ▪

Haacke, Hans, 203

habitat dioramas, 123–126

Hadland, Curt, 158

Haida, 125

Halberstam, David, 141

Halsey, R. T. H., 129

Hammond, Michael, 64

Hamp, Steven, 111

Hampton University Museum, Virginia, *9*

hands-on exhibitions, 148–149

Hanks, Nancy, 193, 197–198, *197,* 199, 200

happenings, 142

Haraway, Donna, 24

Harlem on My Mind, 150–151, *150*

Harris, Neil, 8–9

Harwit, Martin, 210

Hayden Planetarium, New York, 16, *16,* 185

Heard Museum, Phoenix, 57

Hearst, William Randolph, 73

Hebrew Union College, 106

Heinrich of Constance, *73*

Helms, Jesse, 206, 207, 208

Hendrickson, Sue, 85

Henry Ford Museum & Greenfield Village, Dearborn, Michigan, 39, *39,* 110–111, 164

Herbert F. Johnson Museum of Art, Cornell University, 61

Hermitage, Nashville, Tennessee, 108–109, *108*

Herzon and de Meuron, 61

Hess, Thomas B., 195–196

High Museum of Art, Atlanta, 52, 55, 62

Hightower, John, 195

Hillwood Museum and Gardens, Washington, D.C., *74, 76*

Hirschhorn Museum and Sculpture Garden, Washington, D.C., *46,* 47

Hispanics, 196

historical societies, 105

Historical Society of Pennsylvania, 196

history museums, 24, 126–129, 155, 161–164, 166–167

Hitchcock, Henry Russell, 41

Hodsoll, Frank, 204

Hofmann, Malvina, 135

Hogg, Ima, 79, *79*

Holl, Steven, 60, 61

Holland, W. J., 113

Holmes, William Henry, 124

holocaust, 111–112, 118

Honolulu Academy of Arts, 16

Hood, Marilyn, 54–55

Hopi, 124

Hornaday, William, *86,* 87

Horse Capture, George, 116

house museums, 126–129

house restorations, 126–129

Hoving, Thomas, 95–96, 150, 152–153, *153*

Roosevelt, Franklin Delano, 14–15, 76, 182

Roosevelt, Theodore, 88

Roots: The Saga of an American Family, 108, 110

Rose, Carolyn, 94

Rosenwald, Julius, 35, 129–130

Rosenwald, Lessing, 76–77

Rounds, Jay, 145

Rousseau, Henri-Julien-Félix, 95, *95*

Rowell, Alfred Lee, *188*

Rudolph, Paul, 137

Rugoff, Ralph, 166

Ruscha, Edward, 46, *46*

Rushing, Byron, 109–110

Russell, Charles M., 129

∎ S ∎ ∎

Saarinen, Eliel, 44

Saatchi, Charles, 215

Sachs, Paul, *92*, 93, 179

Safdie, Moshe, 62

Saint Louis Museum of Art, 189

Saint Paul Art Gallery, 140

salaries, 196

Salinger, J. D., 125, 141

Salisbury, Steven, 10

Salt Lake City Art Center, 148

Sam Noble Museum of Natural History, Norman, Oklahoma, 116

San Diego Museum of Art, 38

San Francisco earthquake, 69–70

San Francisco Museum of Art, 185

San Francisco Museum of Modern Art, 16, *56*, 57, 60, 91–92, 166

San Simeon, California, 73

Sand, Michael, 148

Sandburg, Carl, 137, *137*

Santa Barbara Museum of Natural History, 38, *38*

Sargent, John Singer, *10*

Schaming, Mark, *113*

Schinkel, Karl Friedrich, 30–31

Schoener, Allon, 150

scholarship, 24

Schomburg Arturo Alfonso, 107

Schwartz, Barry, 196

Schwarzer, Marjorie, 247

science education, 204–205

Science Museum of Minnesota, 15, *15*, 135–136, *156*, 158, 209

science museums, 18–19, 44–45, 51, 135, 139–140, 145–146, 154, 205

scientific method, 19

Scott, Dread, 209, *209*

Seattle Art Museum, 53, *53*, 117

security, 90

September 11, 112–113, *113*, *168*, 216

Serrano, Andres, 206

Sharp, Mary Naquin, 189

Shelburne Museum, Vermont, 80, *80*

Sheldon Memorial Art Gallery, University of Nebraska, 44

shops, 57, 214–215

Sickman, Laurence, 90

slave cabins, *108*

slavery, 108–109, 111

Smith, Martin, 111–112

Smith, Mrs. Edward B., 189

Smith, W. Eugene, 19

Smithsonian Institution, *11*, 12, 31, *31*, 124, 149, 174, 201, *208*, 209

Social Darwinism, 80

social history, 101, 160

social issues, 154–155

   drugs, 151–152

social reform, 172

Solar, Xul, *101*

sound, exhibitions and, 140

South Street Seaport Museum, New York, 26

Southeastern Center for Contemporary Art, Winston Salem, North Carolina, 206

Southwest Museum of the American Indian Collection, *87*

Soviet Union, 76

space race, 18–19, 45, 189